THE WILD AUSTRALIA SHOW

THE STORY OF AN ABORIGINAL PERFORMANCE TROUPE AND ITS AFTERLIVES

Aboriginal History Incorporated

Aboriginal History Inc. is a part of the Australian Centre for Indigenous History, Research School of Social Sciences, The Australian National University, and gratefully acknowledges the support of the School of History and the National Centre for Indigenous Studies, The Australian National University. Aboriginal History Inc. is administered by an Editorial Board which is responsible for all unsigned material. Views and opinions expressed by the author are not necessarily shared by Board members.

Contacting Aboriginal History

All correspondence should be addressed to the Editors, Aboriginal History Inc., ACIH, School of History, Research School of Social Sciences, ANU RSSS Building, The Australian National University, Canberra ACT 2600, or aboriginalhistoryinc@gmail.com.

WARNING: Readers are notified that this publication contains names and images of deceased persons.

THE WILD AUSTRALIA SHOW

THE STORY OF AN ABORIGINAL PERFORMANCE TROUPE AND ITS AFTERLIVES

PAUL MEMMOTT, MARIA NUGENT, MICHAEL AIRD, LINDY ALLEN, CHANTAL KNOWLES AND JONATHAN RICHARDS

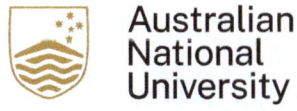

Australian
National
University

ANU PRESS

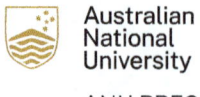 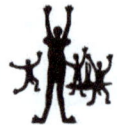

Published by ANU Press and Aboriginal History Inc.
The Australian National University
Canberra ACT 2600, Australia
Email: anupress@anu.edu.au

Available to download for free at press.anu.edu.au

ISBN (print): 9781760466930
ISBN (online): 9781760466947

WorldCat (print): 1514491551
WorldCat (online): 1514503146

DOI: 10.22459/WAS.2025

Cover design and layout by ANU Press. Cover image: Wild Australia Show performers from Northern Territory, Sydney, 1892. Source: Charles H. Kerry.

This book is published under the aegis of the Aboriginal History editorial board of ANU Press.

Contents

ACT III ENDURING

List of figures

Acknowledgements

This monograph was written as part of the Australian Research Council (ARC) Linkage Project [LP160100415] titled 'How Meston's "Wild Australia Show" shaped Australian Aboriginal History'. The six authors of this monograph acknowledge the other investigators on the research project —Dr Tim O'Rourke (University of Queensland) and Dr Richard Neville (State Library of New South Wales)—and the partner organisations—the Queensland Museum, Museums Victoria, and the State Library of New South Wales and their support staff. The contribution of all research assistants is acknowledged, especially Linda Thomson and Jessica Kane, as well as the staff of the Queensland State Archives.

We acknowledge and thank our First Nations advisers to this project, Alex Bond, Charles Passi, Milton Savage and Seriat Young, who assisted in the interpretation and understanding of the Wild Australia Show story from an Indigenous perspective and gave input on culturally sensitive issues and oral history. We also thank Joseph Geia and Jessica Lloyd for the background information on Gida's family connection to Genami and Kawara.

Lindy Allen wishes to thank Dr Charlotte Smith, formerly of Museums Victoria, who was originally a partner investigator on the project and undertook research on her specialist area of world expositions and exhibitions, but regretfully had to resign due to ill health; Michelle Stevenson, who assumed the vacant curatorial position (including curator of the Royal Exhibition Building) and supervised two undergraduate history students, Ellie Wallace and Bronwyn Akers, who undertook archival research at the State Library of Victoria and Public Record Office Victoria— mainly on the Australian Natives' Association (ANA), which, unfortunately, yielded few results (we subsequently learned that the ANA archive is held by Australian Unity), but their contributions and enthusiasm were much appreciated; and, finally, Mira Morris, who assisted in research on Kerry Studio postcards in Museums Victoria's collections and with research on the enlarged portrait by J. W. Lindt.

Maria Nugent thanks Saskia Roberts for research and editorial assistance. Thanks also to Laura Rademaker, Rani Kerin and Julia Hurst, Aboriginal History monograph series editors, who received the publication proposal with enthusiasm and expertly shepherded it from incomplete manuscript to publication with care, patience and good grace. Thanks, too, to the Aboriginal History Inc. Board, who make the Aboriginal History monograph series possible, and also to the staff at ANU Press, whose professionalism ensures high quality and open access. Maria also acknowledges and thanks her colleagues in the Australian Centre for Indigenous History at ANU, especially Dr Laurie Bamblett and Dr Robyn McKenzie, for providing a supportive, enjoyable and enriching research environment that is unerringly supportive of collaborative history projects and methodologies.

Abbreviations

ANA	Australian Natives' Association
ARC	Australian Research Council
BPA	Board for the Protection of Aborigines
NAA	National Archives of Australia
NSW APB	New South Wales Aborigines Protection Board
QBDM	Queensland Births, Deaths and Marriages
QSA	Queensland State Archives
SLNSW	State Library of New South Wales
SRNSW	State Records NSW

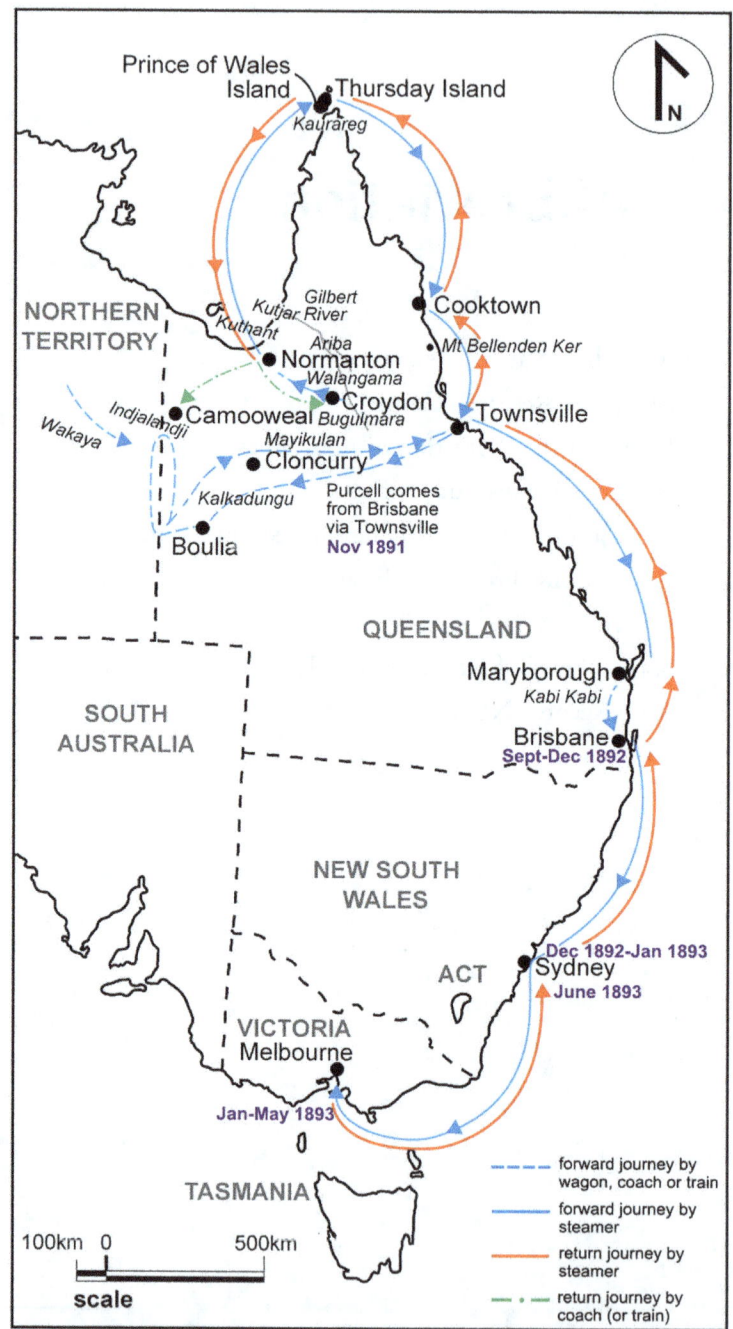

Figure 0.1: Map showing regions from which the Wild Australia Show troupe members came and its tour route, 1892–93

Source: Aboriginal Environments Research Collaborative, University of Queensland.

PRELUDE

1

Introducing the Wild Australia Show

Maria Nugent

On Saturday, 15 July 1893, under the heading 'Blacks Returning Home', the *Telegraph* (Brisbane) reported on 'the aborigines composing the Wild Australia troupe'.[1] The ship they were on, the steamer *Wodonga*, was passing through Brisbane before continuing northwards.[2] The entire troupe, bar one, was returning from a tour that had taken them through the eastern colonial capital cities—Brisbane, Sydney, Melbourne—and then back to Sydney. It had begun just seven months earlier in December 1892. The brief item in the Brisbane newspaper is informative, providing the return itineraries for the three distinct contingents that made up the short-lived troupe and the ill-fated Wild Australia Show.

Five troupe members—'three women and two men', the article explained—would disembark at Townsville. From there, they would then 'go out to Lake Nash, in the Georgina country'.[3] This group of Wakaya had been the first to be recruited into the troupe (Chapter 3). They had been away from home the longest and had the furthest to travel home once they got ashore.

---

1   Readers are advised that some quotations contain terms and phrases that are no longer in common use, and that are likely to be considered racist and to cause offence. That is not our intention. These terms and phrases are retained within quotations from archival material for the purpose of demonstrating historical ideas and attitudes only. 'Blacks Returning Home', *Telegraph* (Brisbane), 15 July 1893, 6.
2   During their layover in Brisbane, the troupe members stayed at the Immigration Barracks at Kangaroo Point.
3   'Blacks Returning Home', 6.

The next stop was Thursday Island, 'where two men, one woman, and a boy land', the article continued.[4] This was the small cohort led by 'King Gida' (Chapter 5); it had included another young man, but he remained temporarily and mysteriously behind in Sydney when the SS *Wodonga* put out to sea (Chapter 10).

'The balance of the aborigines', the report noted, 'go to Normanton and Croydon'.[5] They numbered 17, mostly young men and a few women, who had been recruited into the troupe from camps around those north Queensland frontier towns in the Gulf of Carpentaria (Chapter 4).

Readers of the *Telegraph* were assured two things about the returning performers: that the 'whole party are in good health', and at each disembarkation point, local police would be waiting to 'take charge' of them.[6]

The return journey of the troupe members from their three-city schedule represents one kind of ending to the Wild Australia Show. It marks the point when the 27 troupe members, who had been brought together from three distinct regions in northern Queensland (as the return itinerary indicates) to perform, were returned home. Having lived, travelled and performed with each other, often under challenging conditions, over a period of about seven months, the adventure was now over—and somewhat earlier than expected. Disbanded and returned to the places where they had been recruited and 'signed on', never again would they perform as the Wild Australia Show.

If participation in the tour is for the majority of the troupe members the time when they were written into history, the return home marks the moment when they (again) drop out (see Chapter 11). They exit stage left, and their disembarkation from the SS *Wodonga* is mostly the end of what is recorded of them and what we have been able to learn of their lives.[7] This is a phenomenon that is as perplexing as it is frustrating and disappointing.

---

4   Ibid.
5   Ibid.
6   Ibid.
7   But, see: P. Memmott, 'Gida (c. 1849–1899)', *Australian Dictionary of Biography*, National Centre of Biography, The Australian National University, published online 2022, adb.anu.edu.au/biography/gida-31121/text38497; P. Memmott, 'Kudajarnd (c. 1845–c. 1905)', *Australian Dictionary of Biography*, National Centre of Biography, The Australian National University, published online 2022, adb.anu.edu.au/biography/kudajarnd-31444/text38897; P. Memmott, 'Yamurra (c. 1863–?)', *Australian Dictionary of Biography*, National Centre of Biography, The Australian National University, published online 2022, adb.anu.edu.au/biography/yamurra-31141/text38528. See also: P. Memmott, J. Richards, J. Kane, 'A Man of the "Wild" Queensland Frontier: King Gida of the Kaurareg', *Memoirs of the Queensland Museum—Culture* 12 (June 2021): 27–71, doi.org/10.17082/j.2205-3239.12.1.2021.2021-03.

Our initial expectation that there would be family memory and history to tap into gradually proved unfounded, although interest in, and curiosity about, the troupe members in their places of origin was palpable when we shared what we knew through a travelling banner exhibition (see Chapter 11 for further detail). Why hadn't their experiences as travelling performers who visited the southern cities left an enduring impression among the kin and communities to which they belonged and returned? Why weren't memories and knowledge about them passed down from generation to generation? These are questions that have hovered as we have worked together as an interdisciplinary team to reconstruct the story of the Wild Australia Show, and strove to tell its story, as far as possible, through the eyes of the performers themselves.

If the perspectives of most of the troupe members can be hard to come by and remain somewhat elusive, the same is not true for the enterprise that was the Wild Australia Show. Fuelled by publicity, boosterism and self-promotion, not to mention scandal and notoriety, the Show generated a quite capacious textual and visual archive that allows aspects of it to be known in considerable detail. Given the big personalities of the two 'showmen'— or speculators—behind the enterprise (see Chapter 2), and their tendency to stage their disputes with each other in public (see Chapter 10), it can be quite a task to keep them in the background so that the performers can step into the limelight. Our efforts to diminish the space occupied by the settler showmen is, we suspect, one shared with the troupe members too. We get occasional, but revealing, glimpses of a dynamic struggle between performers and 'managers', and between 'managers' and other stakeholders (like financial backers or colonial government agents), particularly when the textual archive is read 'against and along the grain', and the visual archive is viewed 'beyond the frame'. In the story we tell, we seek as much as possible to tease out the subtle shifting politics of relationship, power and authority as we ask questions about who was really running the Show (see chapters in Act II especially).

After the Show's only tour was suddenly over, the troupe members returned home, the business affairs wound up and the partners pursued other schemes, but the Wild Australia Show went on to have a long afterlife, or series of afterlives (see Chapter 11). This book, and the project from which it emerges,[8] might be said to constitute one of those *afterlives*—even as it also examines the ways that the Wild Australia Show, and its surviving 'traces', have endured. While usually unacknowledged at the time, different versions and derivations of the Show were staged by other Aboriginal performers throughout the twentieth century (Chapter 11). Fashioned along the lines of the hugely popular 'Wild West Shows', the original Wild Australia Show in turn influenced other troupes closer to home and became a rough template for them.

But it is the persistent afterlives of the many photographs of the Wild Australia Show troupe members, whether as a whole, in small groups or individually, that especially interests us (Chapter 11), not least because the photographs have been so vital to reconstructing and making public the forgotten story of the Wild Australia Show.[9] These photographs expose, in different ways than the textual archive, one of our key themes: how to see the personhood and identity of the performers, which appear to us as flashes or glimpses before they become obscured and erased again. The irony here is that it is this very same archive, which had previously been circulated in ways that increasingly came to deny the performers their personal histories and identities, and disconnect them from their history as performers, that has been the means by which the lives and experiences of the Wild Australia Show performers have (belatedly) come back into view (Chapter 11). They have, in turn, become resources for other efforts to re-story the Wild Australia Show and other Aboriginal and Torres Strait Islander performers.

A history told in three acts

This book, then, tells the story of the Wild Australia Show from its inception in the minds of its architects to its various afterlives. It begins with a prelude consisting of two chapters designed to set the scene. This chapter (Chapter 1) introduces the Wild Australia Show; Chapter 2 presents the two colonial men who dreamt up the scheme and who wore many hats as its architects, fundraisers, publicists, producers and tour managers. At the start of the 1890s, the controversial and irrepressible Archibald Meston and the

---

8   Australian Research Council Linkage Project [LP160100415], 'How Meston's "Wild Australia Show" Shaped Aboriginal History'. Project partners: University of Queensland, The Australian National University, Museums Victoria, Queensland Museum and State Library of NSW, 2016–20.
9   For more detail, see: M. Aird and P. Memmott, 'Photographic Identification of the Troupe Members of the Wild Australia Show', *Memoirs of the Queensland Museum—Culture*, 12 (June 2021): 7–26, doi.org/ 10.17082/j.2205-3239.12.1.2021.2021-02.

resourceful—if somewhat credulous and lesser known—Brabazon Purcell entered into what appears to have been a hastily hatched partnership to create the Wild Australia Show. Intriguing individuals in their own right, Meston and Purcell nevertheless belong to a recognisable class of colonial men who sought to monetise frontier experience, to exploit Indigenous people for financial gain and to profit from styling themselves as experts on Aboriginal culture and practices (Chapter 2).

Seemingly devised in 1891, their scheme to form a travelling troupe of Indigenous performers from the far northern reaches of Queensland was fuelled by continuing global interest in exhibiting 'exotic' cultures to metropolitan audiences. This was the era of international exhibitions, fairs and expositions, and of popular entertainments known as 'human zoos' and 'native villages'.[10] When it was announced that a 'world's fair' would be held in Chicago in 1893 as a commemoration of the four-hundredth year since Columbus's arrival in the Americas, many hopped onto the bandwagon, Meston and Purcell among them.[11]

In Australia, Meston and Purcell's contemporaries and competitors were men such as Robert A. Cunningham and Harry Stockdale, both of whom had more experience in 'show business' and were better connected. They enjoyed considerably more success than the hapless pair behind the Wild Australia Show. By the 1890s, Cunningham had already toured a group of Queensland Aboriginal people through North America and Europe, a history painstakingly documented by Roslyn Poignant and more recently fictionalised by Katherine Johnson.[12] Notoriously, Cunningham had taken a group from Fraser Island (K'gari), and the tour was marked by tragedy,

---

10   For more on this, see: P. Blanchard et al., eds, *Human Zoos: Science and Spectacle in the Age of Colonial Empires* (Liverpool: Liverpool University Press, 2008); G. Boetsch et al., eds, *Human Zoos: The Invention of the Savage* (Paris: Musee du quai Branly, 2011); S. Qureshi, *Peoples on Parade: Exhibitions, Empire, and Anthropology in Nineteenth-Century* (Chicago: University of Chicago Press, 2011), doi.org/10.7208/chicago/9780226700984.001.0001.

11   For more on this, see: P. Raibmon, 'Theatres of Contact: The Kwakwaka'wakw Meet Colonialism in British Columbia and at the Chicago World's Fair', *Canadian Historical Review* 81, no. 2 (June 2000): 157–90, doi.org/10.3138/CHR.81.2.157; G. Scott, 'Village Performance: Villages at the Chicago World's Columbian Exposition 1893' (PhD thesis, New York University, 1991); D. Beck, *Unfair Labor? American Indians and the 1893 World's Columbian Exposition in Chicago* (Lincoln: University of Nebraska Press, 2019), doi.org/10.2307/j.ctvggx4fm; R. LaPier and D. Beck, 'The World Comes to Chicago (The 1893 World's Columbian Exposition)', in *City Indian: Native American Activism in Chicago, 1893-1934* (Lincoln: University of Nebraska Press, 2015), 17–33, doi.org/10.2307/j.ctt1d98ch6; R. Rydell, *All the World's a Fair: Visions of Empire at American International Expositions, 1876–1916* (Chicago: University of Chicago Press, 1987).

12   R. Poignant, *Professional Savages: Captive Lives and Western Spectacle* (New Haven: Yale University Press, 2004); K. Johnson, *Paris Savages* (Sydney: Ventura Press, 2019).

death and violence. This did not appear to dissuade him from repeating the exercise when the 1893 Chicago Exposition plans were announced.[13] By the middle of 1893, it was reported in the Queensland Parliament that:

> Eight aboriginal blacks were taken from Queensland in August [1892] last by Mr. Cunningham, with the knowledge and consent of the then Chief Secretary, who secured a bond for their safe return within three years.[14]

Harry Stockdale's exploits have not attracted as much historical interest as Cunningham's. In the Australian colonial press, he was typically described as an explorer, hunter and horseman who travelled extensively through the Northern Territory and had amassed large numbers of Aboriginal artefacts (although many were destroyed by fire before they could be sold by auction).[15] By the 1880s, he was also touring and exhibiting Aboriginal people. In preparation for the Australian colonies' participation in the Chicago World's Fair, Stockdale's services were called upon by the colonial committee coordinating Australian contributions.[16]

Given their previous experience, both Cunningham and Stockdale were in a good position to capitalise on the opportunity Chicago presented. Meston and Purcell, by contrast, appear far more opportunistic. Swept up in the excitement, the inexperienced Meston and Purcell seem to have quite recklessly decided to enter the fray and styled themselves as 'showmen' with a view to take a troupe on a world tour. Without much thought or planning, they began to recruit for a troupe of Queensland Aboriginal people, and this is where we choose to begin in earnest our version of the story of the Wild Australia Show, since it is through the processes—and politics—of 'recruitment' that we first meet the men, women and one child who would eventually make up the troupe. And it is important for the

---

13   For information about Cunningham's Aboriginal troupe, see: 'Theatrical Gossip', *Melbourne Punch*, 23 August 1888, 10. See also: Police magistrate, Townsville, to colonial secretary, 16 June 1892, asking: 'If RA Cunningham will be permitted to take away Aboriginals in his travelling show', QSA ITM6935, 1892/7334, Register of Letters Received, January 1892 – December 1892, COL/B32; 'At Poverty Point, *Bulletin* (Sydney), 10 September 1892, 7; 'Australian Blacks to Chicago', *Bulletin*, 22 October 1892, 6.
14   Queensland, *Parliamentary Debates*, 'Removal of Queensland Aborigines', *Legislative Assembly*, 4 July 1893, 144 (Horace Tozer, colonial secretary).
15   P. Egan, 'Specimens Lost to the Australian Museum', Australian Museum, 14 March 2011, australian. museum/blog-archive/museullaneous/specimens-lost-to-the-australian-museum/.
16   For information about Stockdale, see: 'Coogee Palace Aquarium', *Daily Telegraph*, 9 March 1889, 2; 'The Aquaria', *Australian Star*, 11 March 1889, 8; 'The Chicago Exhibition', *Daily Telegraph*, 9 January 1892, 4.

story we tell to meet those men and women on their own Country before they become known through the frame of touring troupe members, as the transformations they undergo begin there and then.

As soon as the fledgling plan and partnership were struck, Purcell set out for far western Queensland to recruit the troupe and to collect artefacts, the latter with the intention to profit from their exhibition and sale (Chapter 3). Despite being a rash and ill-conceived venture, over the course of a year to 18 months, the partners did somehow manage to assemble a group of 27 Aboriginal and Torres Strait Islander people, who entered—willingly or perhaps otherwise—into performing and touring. As we reveal across the four chapters that make up Act I, all written by Paul Memmott, that achievement was as much, if not more, due to the willingness of performers to 'sign on', for both push and pull reasons, than to the partners' prowess and acumen. What we seek to show by focusing each chapter on the regions and contexts from which members of the troupe were drawn is that motivations for joining were not uniform. The Wild Australia Show was made up of more than one cultural and linguistic group, each with their own particular dances, material culture, body markings and performance repertoires.[17] Indeed, such diversity was a feature that was routinely highlighted in the publicity for Wild Australia. It was a key selling point.

Unlike some other acts at the time and since, the Wild Australia Show was not presented as pan-Aboriginal. Rather, the imputed commonality among the troupe members that was marketed—and manufactured and exaggerated— was their supposed 'wildness', or relative lack of exposure to white people. This was the trope on which the Show, as conceived by Meston especially, largely relied. As theatre historian Jane Goodall notes of exhibition cultures and practices in this late nineteenth-century period, just the right amount of 'wildness' to make stage shows appear authentic was required.[18] And there is ample evidence across the expansive Wild Australia Show archive to demonstrate what a fiction this claim was. The reconstruction of the recruitment drives spelt out in 'Act I: Recruiting' shows just how far white settlers had encroached on Aboriginal people and their estates. Similarly,

---

17   For contrasting examples, see: A. Haebich, *Dancing in Shadows: Histories of Nyungar Performance* (Perth: UWA Press, 2018), which traces histories of performance within a large regional cultural area and group, and as a means for resistance and survival; A. Harris, *Representing Australian Aboriginal Music and Dance, 1930–1970* (London: Bloomsbury, 2020), doi.org/10.5040/9781501362965, which examines a broad range of Aboriginal public performance across Australia with a focus on the mid-twentieth century.
18   J. Goodall, *Performance and Evolution in the Age of Darwin: Out of the Natural Order* (London: Routledge, 2002), 85, doi.org/10.4324/9780203471494.

Meston's carping criticism of Robert A. Cunningham for exhibiting what the former described (disparagingly) as 'civilized' Aboriginal people—'ordinary tame town blacks who spoke English fluently'[19]—can be read as a rhetorical device used to shore up the claim that his own troupe was, by contrast, composed of truly 'wild' Aboriginal people—and thus of greater interest to audiences wanting to experience the unfamiliar (or 'Other').

Once the 27 people who would come to make up the troupe are introduced in Act I, the book's second part (Chapters 7–10) considers the ways in which the Wild Australia Show took shape and developed as its repertoire was created, choreographed, rehearsed, performed and toured. Like the shifting relations within the company, this too is a dynamic process that changes, sometimes only subtly, from venue to venue, from city to city, from daytime to night-time, and over time, as the tour proceeds, nerves fray, conflicts erupt, homesickness descends and fatigue sets in.

In keeping with our close attention to place and context as influencing behaviour, emotion and experience, in 'Act II: Touring', a chapter is devoted to each place where the troupe played. We begin in Brisbane (Chapter 7), then go to Sydney (Chapter 8), then onto Melbourne (Chapter 9), before returning to Sydney (Chapter 10) and then home. In each chapter, we analyse the troupe's program and the various shows given, teasing out the ways in which the performers pushed the boundaries of the repertoire and turned the stages and other arenas where they appeared into cultural—or intercultural—spaces. This all happened against a fluctuating backdrop of financial mismanagement, fickle audiences, inclement weather, mixed reviews, government interference or indifference, and economic downturn as the 1890s depression began to bite. As the obstacles and challenges multiplied once the tour proper was underway, it is hard not to view the Wild Australia Show through a prism of failure and disappointment. But that sells it well short. The pleasures and joys of performing and travelling for the troupe members are also part of the story.

By the tour's end, though, the acrimony that had festered between the business partners and backers, and derailed their original plans for a world tour, became insurmountable. Things were in tatters. The business partners' pettiness touched everyone in their orbit. As soon as the Show was over, they, predictably, took each other to court. This kept the Wild Australia Show in the public eye for longer, but for all the wrong reasons. Little came

---

19 'Meston on Cunningham', *Telegraph* (Brisbane), 28 November 1892, 4.

of it, except that it generated, as court cases typically do, a detailed retelling and a record of the debacle that might otherwise not have existed. The breakdown of the business partnership behind the Wild Australia Show has gifted to the present a rich seam of archival material for reconstructing—and for reinterpreting—its story.

And yet, as replete as those court records are, the key methodological problem we have already highlighted remains. No matter the insults they flung and the accusations they made, Meston's and Purcell's testimonies in court provide only a narrow and opaque window onto the lives, experiences and feelings of the troupe members they had sought to exploit for financial gain and personal glory. And whom, in so many other ways, they had essentially, and spectacularly, failed. In the book's final chapter, we wonder whether this is a contributing factor to the troupe members not having left a visible imprint in family and community memory. Since they did not return as the celebrated world travellers they had been promised to become, but instead came home (under police escort) as the poorly treated participants in yet another failed settler dream and scheme, might it be the case that they wanted quickly to forget the whole shebang? Or, more prosaically, was it simply not the most important nor memorable thing they did in their lives—a mere blip rather than an apex?

Most efforts to plumb the experiences of Indigenous performers labouring under colonial conditions grapple with the challenge of how to work productively with an archive that is both patchy and lumpy—an archive that does not faithfully document the perspectives in which we are most interested but records to excess issues and concerns that we do not necessarily share. We have sought to overcome the lacunae in both the settler–colonial sources and in Aboriginal family and community memory by pursuing approaches to writing histories of public performance and popular culture that seek to bring hidden perspectives to the fore. In doing so, we have been able to draw on the experiments, approaches and insights of others who are similarly involved in producing 'performer-centred' accounts of colonial exhibition culture and that reveal Indigenous performers' agency—and autonomy—even under profoundly constrained conditions.

In recent scholarship on cultural performance, live exhibitions and world's fairs during the late nineteenth and early twentieth centuries, the question of what 'performing' and 'being exhibited' meant to Indigenous performers themselves has come, quite urgently, to the fore.[20] This is a theme that cultural historian Ilaria Vanni pursues in her insightful account of two young Aboriginal men, Stan Loycurrie and Jack Noorywauka, from central Australia who travelled in 1929 to perform as part of an art exhibition at a metropolitan museum. Querying the dominant framing of Aboriginal performers through the trope of 'captivity', which assumes both a high degree of coercion to participate and strict limits upon permissible expressive performance, Vanni offers instead a counter-narrative that emphasises the men's active and deliberate engagement in the work of performance and exhibition, and the ways in which they negotiated the choices, compromises and mobilities it required. By focusing attention on more private documents, such as personal letters, diary entries and other 'snippets', where cracks in the public façade are more likely to appear, Vanni picks away at casual assumptions about coercion, exploitation and racism that can work to obscure other interpretative possibilities. Most revealing is the ways in which she reconstructs from the surviving records a locally grounded, culturally informed and Aboriginal-controlled decision-making process that sees these two young men 'chosen' by their kin and 'communities', rather than selected and persuaded by brokers like a local missionary, to make the trip to Melbourne to show their culture to the world.[21]

The prospect that the Wild Australia Show troupe members were equally— or similarly—agentive as Vanni has shown for Loycurrie and Noorywauka has not typically been entertained by the few historians who have considered the matter. Historian Richard Broome, for instance, has made a hugely valuable contribution to the field by demonstrating that performing and exhibiting was a form of labour in the settler economy, which many Aboriginal people willingly sought since they could have some control over how they would expend their time, skills, knowledge and earnings.[22] But Broome explicitly excludes the Wild Australia Show troupe members from such a cohort of Aboriginal workers. Rather, he argues that 'given [Archibald Meston's] authoritarian, paternalist personality, the Aboriginal men in his show were

20   Raimbon, 'Theatres of Contact', 161.

21   I. Vanni, 'The Archive and the Contact Zones: The Story of Stan Loycurrie and Jack Noorywauka, Performers at the 1929 *Australian Aboriginal Art* Exhibition, Melbourne', *Journal of Australian Studies* 38, no. 3 (2014): 314–30, doi.org/10.1080/14443058.2014.921231.

22   R. Broome, 'Theatres of Power: Tent Boxing Circa 1910–1970', *Aboriginal History* 20 (1996): 1–23, doi.org/10.22459/AH.20.2011.01; R. Broome, 'Enduring Moments in Aboriginal Dominance: Aboriginal Performers, Boxers and Runners', *Labour History*, no. 69 (Aboriginal Workers) (1995): 171–87, www.jstor.org/stable/27516397; R. Broome, 'Aboriginal Workers on South-Eastern Frontiers', *Australian Historical Studies* 26, no. 103 (1994): 202–20, doi.org/10.1080/10314619408595960.

unlikely to have had much control over the proceedings'.[23] We beg to differ, since the evidence for Meston's imputed authority over the Wild Australia Show troupe is faint. Indeed, often, the reverse situation is apparent.

The image that Broome paints of Meston wielding an iron fist over Aboriginal people belongs more squarely to a post–Wild Australia Show period, when, as southern protector of Aborigines in Queensland from 1898 to 1904, he became increasingly arbitrary and paternalistic in the ways he sought to control Aboriginal people's lives. It is in *that* role that Meston is lodged in the collective memory of Aboriginal people in Queensland today. Our analysis of the Wild Australia Show, however, suggests that he was more likely to be at the mercy of the men (and women) he had brought together to tour as Wild Australia, and we would go further to suggest that this might have contributed to why he was quick to abandon the Show at the first opportunity (see Chapter 9). While we acknowledge Meston's desire to laud power over the troupe, it is quite clear that it was only rarely realised (see chapters in 'Act II: Touring' in particular). On more than one occasion, he found himself both sidelined and outshone by the performers.

Nor do we adopt an approach that casts all 27 troupe members in the exact same light—or as equally vulnerable to exploitation, for instance. When we look across the entire archive pertaining to the Wild Australia Show, and across the whole span of time from 'recruitment' (and earlier) to 'return' home (and beyond), a more nuanced and dynamic picture of power, authority and hierarchy, both within and without the troupe, emerges. On the one hand, the Wild Australia Show archive points to various efforts by the Show's managers and other agents, including police and police magistrates, to coerce and control the troupe, with varying degrees of effectiveness and success. On the other hand, it reveals (in less direct ways) that there was a clear internal leadership—or hierarchy—within the troupe. Men like Kudajarnd and Gida, who are introduced in Chapters 3 and 4, respectively, were already leaders of their families and groups when they joined, and they remained responsible for their small 'contingents' within the group. Yamurra (introduced in Chapter 6), who appears to have been invited by Meston to accompany the troupe as an intermediary or broker,[24] embodied a different authority due to his wider experience with whitefellas and his ability to speak English. He was also already a public performer,

---

23   Broome, 'Enduring Moments in Aboriginal Dominance', 173.
24   See: S. Konishi, M. Nugent and T. Shellam, eds, *Indigenous Intermediaries: New Perspectives on Exploration Archives* (Canberra: ANU Press, 2015), doi.org/10.22459/II.09.2015.

having performed with and for Meston on earlier occasions. What we have not given sufficient attention to is the gendered nature of authority and power within the troupe, especially the treatment of its five female members, and the ways in which the enterprise depended upon their (largely hidden) labour (e.g. as companions), knowledge and skills both within performances and in the day-to-day existence of the troupe on tour.

Finally, we are interested in pursuing questions about the performers' motivations, even in the knowledge that they cannot be satisfactorily answered. In grappling with this, one approach has been to devote the first third of the book (Chapters 3–7) to understanding the troupe members within the ancestral Country and cultures, and the historical and material conditions from which they came when they joined the Wild Australia Show. We consider what they, or their immediate ancestors, might have lived through and how these direct and/or inherited experiences might have shaped their choices. To do this, we build on the intimate knowledge about the regions from where the troupe members hail, including Paul Memmott's sustained work with the Wakaya in the border regions and with groups in the Gulf. Drawing on hard-won familiarity with northern and western Queensland gained over decades of collaborative research with Aboriginal people, as well as a rich vein of historical, anthropological, geographical and linguistic research, for those chapters Paul Memmott has created fictionalised vignettes that imagine what an encounter with Purcell during his recruitment drives might have looked like through the eyes of some of those who joined him. To distinguish them from the text proper, we have highlighted these imagined scenarios by using a shaded box to remind readers they are creative re-enactments of unrecorded events rather than 'factual' or 'empirical' descriptions. Even so, they are not pure imagination since they are grounded in reliable information about the people, cultures and places involved.

By taking a long run up to the commencement of the Wild Australia Show tour, we likewise seek to disrupt an approach that is only interested in Aboriginal performers where and when they step upon the public stage of performance and, by implication, of history. That there are few to no records of most of the individual troupe members *before* they join the tour (and indeed after they leave it) is not sufficient reason to ignore completely other parts of their lives. If the promise or ambition to write a 'performer-centred' history is to be fulfilled, then it is vital to understand who the performers were (and how they might have seen themselves), and where and what they came from, before their lives took a turn and they found themselves being written and photographed 'into existence'. They were, at the very least, already performers, skilled in the dances and ceremonies of their culture. But they were also survivors of an often brutal frontier—which was not yet over in some of the places from where the troupe members came.

Critically important for this task of introducing the performers in the round requires, as we have intimated, bringing diverse and interdisciplinary perspectives (from fields such as anthropology, linguistics, cultural geography and visual culture) to bear on our interpretation of ahistorical archives and other traces. Vital, too, is guidance from cultural advisers. We have benefited in immeasurable ways from the input of Charles Passi, Milton Savage and Alex Bond, whose perspectives have guided our approach to, and interpretations of, what is in the historical records as well as linking us up with individuals to whose histories this relates.

More broadly, we have been inspired by contemporary Indigenous performance and, particularly, in recent restagings of past performances, such as those staged by Jackie Sheppard at the Yirramboi First National Arts Festival in 2017, or in the ensemble piece *Natives Go Wild!* developed by Rhoda Roberts, which had a short season at the Sydney Opera House in 2019 (see Chapter 11).[25] Contemporary creative engagements with past performance open up new horizons of interpretation and ways of seeing.

In crucial ways, this circles back to the final part of the book, 'Act III: Enduring', in which we trace the ripples of the Wild Australia Show once the tour proper was over. In a chapter called 'Afterlives', the last in the book, we consider what happens once the Show is over. We look for references to and memories of the troupe members; we look askance at Meston's dogged pursuit of, and involvement in, Aboriginal performance and exhibition. But it is the enduring currency and circulation of the large number of photographs created during the Wild Australia Show, most of them by three major photographers or studios of the late nineteenth century, that most captures our imagination. Engaging with this photographic archive, our analysis has been enabled and guided by Michael Aird's unsurpassed knowledge of the images of the Wild Australia Show. He has not only been able to reconstruct the original photographic archive that was produced at

---

25   T. Yunkaporta, 'Wild Australia: Reliving the Shocking Story of Indigenous Slave-Performers', *Guardian*, 6 May 2017, www.theguardian.com/artanddesign/2017/may/06/wild-australia-reliving-the-shocking-story-of-indigenous-slave-performers; L. Behrendt, 'Natives Go Wild Review—First Nations Circus Is a Potent Mix of Defiance and Triumph', *Guardian*, 23 October 2019, www.theguardian.com/stage/2019/oct/23/natives-go-wild-review-first-nations-circus-is-a-potent-mix-of-defiance-and-triumph.

the time but also to follow the contours of its circulation ever since. His approach to interpreting images of Aboriginal people—as evidence of, and witnesses to, their personhood and agency—aligns with our broader quest to reinstate the Aboriginal performers as the stars of the show. That way of viewing the images has allowed us to *see* things that might have otherwise been overlooked.

There is no doubt that the Wild Australia Show photographs were highly mobile and circulated far and wide beyond the bounds of the Show itself. They became detached from the troupe and increasingly circulated as 'arguments', to use Jane Lydon's term, about race: about where Aboriginal and Torres Strait Islanders putatively 'belonged', both within a hierarchy of cultures of the world *and* in time—past, present and future.[26] Marketed and sold domestically and internationally (as postcards, calling cards and other small formats), the photographs worked to depersonalise—or dehumanise— the performers, stripping them of their names, cultural identities and biographies as they were increasingly rendered as generic types, figures or symbols. In a process that uncannily parallels the ways in which public and intimate knowledge of the individual performers dissipates once they are returned to their Country, the circulation of photographs of them likewise works to hide or erase the 'living' person in the image. In the final chapter of the book, we revisit some recent exhibitions about the Wild Australia Show that have begun to reverse that process, using the original photographs to re-story the Show and to restore the humanity and individuality of its little- known performers.

In keeping with our interest in collective enterprises, and the ways in which they are always more than a sum of their parts, we have pursued a communal and collaborative approach to preparing this work. This includes pursuing a mode of authorship that does not assume a common voice, but embraces a diversity of perspectives. The preferred writing styles of individual authors, often tailored to certain topics, are a hallmark of the assembled text. The authors bring particular kinds of expertise to the task. Through their extensive experience in native title, Paul Memmott and Michael Aird are adept at using linguistic, geographical and anthropological approaches and knowledge. Michael is also a leading expert in visual and photographic analysis; an interest also shared by Chantal Knowles and

---

26   J. Lydon, *Eye Contact: Photographing Indigenous Australians* (Durham: Duke University Press, 2006), doi.org/10.2307/j.ctv125jfqq; J. Lydon, *Flash of Recognition: Photography and the Emergence of Indigenous Rights* (Kensington: NewSouth, 2012).

Lindy Allen, who are experienced museum professionals and curators, and so bring their expertise in working with, and interpreting, material culture and museum collections. Jonathan Richards is an archival historian who has devoted his time to documenting Queensland's Native Police, and so it is not surprising that there is a fair amount of attention to their operations in the places and periods covered in this book. He also has a particular interest in Archibald Meston's many interests and enterprises, and has provided the biographical detail on him and his business partner, Purcell. Maria Nugent is a social and cultural historian who uses cross-cultural approaches to read and interpret historical records in an effort to tease out 'marginal' and 'hidden' histories. She is also knowledgeable about Aboriginal people in Sydney through her work with the La Perouse Aboriginal community. Due to our various locations and site-specific knowledge—Paul, Michael, Jonathan and Chantal in Queensland, Lindy in Victoria and Maria in New South Wales—we divided authorship of chapters accordingly.

The project to prepare a comprehensive account of the Wild Australia Show troupe was initially spearheaded by Michael Aird and Paul Memmott. From their mutual interest, a broader project (of which this book is just one product) grew, and over a number of years and through different approaches, the largely negative representations of the Wild Australia Show have been reversed and knowledge about the troupe has steadily accumulated, spawning other projects to rewrite histories of Aboriginal performers and performances in biographically and contextually rich ways. Where historical traces and records had worked to create distancing and objectifying, we sought to introduce proximity and intimacy; where there had been depersonalising representations, we sought to highlight humanity through biographical detail; and where there had been denigration and diminution, we countered with recognition, acknowledgement and celebration. By all these means, as well as by removing obstacles and obfuscations that have kept the performers' lives, oeuvres and experiences out of sight, we seek to return them to their rightful place—centre stage.

2

Introducing Archibald Meston and Brabazon Purcell

Jonathan Richards

Archibald Meston and Brabazon Purcell had previously used their families and friends to earn a living and they adapted and manipulated these same networks to organise and deliver the Wild Australia Show. Their precise aims and hopes remain a mystery: Meston always claimed he was motivated for 'the benefit of the aboriginals'[1] but Purcell never left any clues at all.

Meston's previous experiences in business and politics had been abject failures, but he was determined to make a name for himself in Queensland's colonial economy. Purcell, who had been a cattle drover and horse dealer, probably had much more experience with Aboriginal people than Meston, but he was also unable to earn a living as a businessman. Their partnership began when they both participated in an Aborigines Protection Society 1891 event in Brisbane, but we can only speculate as to what they hoped they could realistically achieve when they set off on their 'world tour' with a troupe of 'wild' Aboriginal and Torres Strait Islander people.

---

1   Readers are advised that some quotations contain terms and phrases that are no longer in common use, and that are likely to be considered racist and to cause offence. That is not our intention. These terms and phrases are retained within quotations from archival material for the purpose of demonstrating historical ideas and attitudes only.

Meston in South Queensland

Archibald Meston was a man who took advantage of circumstances and situations for his own benefit, and this included briefly joining organisations to advance his own interests. However, his movements prior to the 'Wild Australia' episode are often difficult to trace because his specific recall of dates, events and individuals tended to change in his later years. He apparently had, particularly in his earlier years, the ability to secure financial loans and positions of influence through his friends and family connections.

Much of his writing was based on personal experience, especially exploration, and as literary historian Cheryl Taylor has noted, 'the hundreds of poems, stories and articles' that Meston published between 1870 and his death in 1924 were his 'chief means of raising his profile'.[2] His first poem, 'The Ocean', published in April 1870 (when he was 19), was followed by others written when visiting his sister's family at Nerang Creek.[3] Meston's 'A Storm at Night: Seen from the Top of the MacPherson Range', evidently inspired by his travels, first appeared in 1871 and was repeated in 1876 in an early issue of the *Ipswich Observer*.[4] His education included a wide reading of classical literature, from which florid quotes embellished his published work.

He first visited Queensland in late 1870 at the age of 18 (two years after he finished school), travelling from his family home near Grafton in northern New South Wales to Brisbane on a coastal schooner.[5] Meston later claimed that he was warmly welcomed:

> One day I was introduced to Arthur Macalister, the Premier in two Ministries, and as I was a nephew of Robert Meston, who was a great friend of Macalister, he invited me to a run down the bay with a Parliamentary party on the following day.[6]

---

2   C. Taylor, 'Constructing Aboriginality: Archibald Meston's Literary Journalism, 1870–1924', *Journal of the Association for the Study of Australian Literature* 2 (2003), 121.

3   A. Meston, 'Original Poetry. The Ocean', *Clarence and Richmond Examiner*, 19 April 1870, 4; A. Meston, 'The Drowned One. A Tale of the Covenanters', *Queenslander*, 24 December 1870, 8; A. Meston, 'Soliliquy on a Child', *Queenslander*, 21 January 1871, 6.

4   A. Meston, 'A Storm at Night: Seen from the Top of the MacPherson Range', *Evening News*, 24 October 1871, 3; 'Original Poetry. A Storm at Night', *Ipswich Observer*, 12 January 1876, 4.

5   'Departures', *Clarence River Examiner*, 20 September 1870, 2; A. Meston, 'Nerang Memories', *Queenslander*, 7 August 1920, 42. The schooner made one voyage from Grafton to Brisbane in September 1870.

6   A. Meston, 'Early Brisbane: 53 Years Ago—Some Personal Recollections', *Brisbane Courier*, 7 July 1923, 19.

He later provided more detail on this first visit to Brisbane and also wrote of a walking tour, in the same period, from Benowa (the sugar plantation owned by his brother-in-law, Robert Muir) at Nerang (south of Brisbane), through the MacPherson Range back to Grafton.[7] This overland journey, from Nerang Creek to the Richmond River via the Coomera and Logan rivers, provided material for multiple articles in his later years.[8]

Meston and his wife Frances, with their baby daughter Toressa, moved from Grafton to Brisbane just before August 1874 when his election as the founding secretary of the Queensland Caledonian Benefit Society was announced.[9] He was employed as the manager of Dr Waugh's Pearlwell Sugar Plantation on the Brisbane River (near Oxley Creek) by late 1874 when their second child, Harold, was born.[10] He became the editor of the *Ipswich Observer* in 1876, and some of his first editorial pieces on snakes and his childhood on the Clarence appeared soon after. He also began writing (under the name of 'Ramrod') for the *Queenslander* about this time.[11]

Meston gave his first political speech in July 1876 at Ipswich, and was elected as the member of the Legislative Assembly for Rosewood in 1878.[12] In 1879, he borrowed £250 from newspaper owner John Isambert to purchase a half share in Scott Smith's coal mine at Walloon, west of Ipswich. However, the business venture was a complete disaster:

> During the whole year of operations the expenses were heavy, and heavy losses were made on nearly all the coal sent to a Brisbane market, the only coal showing any profit being that sold to the gasworks and the railway department.[13]

---

7   A. Meston, 'Lost Tribes at Moreton Bay', *Brisbane Courier*, 19 June 1923, 8; A. Meston, 'Lost Tribes of Moreton Bay', *Brisbane Courier*, 14 July 1923, 18; 28 July 1923; 19 and 25 August 1923, 19; A. Meston, 'Old Moreton Bay Tribes', *Brisbane Courier*, 20 October 1923, 18; 10 November 1923, 19; 1 December 1923, 19; A. Meston, 'The Moreton Bay Tribes', *Brisbane Courier*, 5 January 1924, 18; A. Meston, 'Southport in 1869!', *Boomerang*, 26 April 1890, 14.

8   A. Meston, 'A Bush Memory', *Bulletin*, 24 May 1923, 48; A. Meston, 'Australian Christmases, Both Merry and Solemn', *World's News*, 22 December 1923, 11; A. Meston, 'South Coast Memories: The Old, Wild Days', *Brisbane Courier*, 17 March 1924, 10.

9   'Sanny Himsel', *Queenslander*, 8 August 1874, 9; 'Queensland Caledonian Benefit Society', *Telegraph* (Brisbane), 11 August 1874, 2.

10   'Station, Farm, and Garden', *Queenslander*, 19 September 1874, 5; Queensland Birth Certificate 1874/B/17961; A. Meston, 'First Queensland Sugar', *Brisbane Courier*, 13 June 1916, 6.

11   [A. Meston], 'Smiles' by 'Ramrod', *Ipswich Observer*, 15 January 1876; [A. Meston], 'A Day's Shooting' by 'Ramrod', *Queenslander*, 5 February 1876, 15.

12   'Ipswich', *Brisbane Courier*, 18 July 1876, 2.

13   Insolvency documents including list of creditors, Insolvency File: MESTON, Archibald, QSA ITM1058056, 1881/1023.

The losses incurred by Smith and Meston meant that he soon returned to writing:

> During the year I was a partner in the coal mine I remained out of employment as a journalist to look after the business of the mine and hoping every month would show an improvement. Before dissolving the partnership I had to accept the position of editor of the *Daily Observer* to obtain an income to keep my family.[14]

Paid journalism proved to be the most important income throughout Meston's life.

He acquired the nickname 'The Sacred Ibis' in 1879 after mentioning embalming, the pyramids and other Egyptian stories in a parliamentary speech.[15] In April 1881, using the pen-name 'Maroogaline', he contributed his first lengthy column ('Notes from Bananaland') to the *Bulletin* in Sydney; many more contributions to the *Bulletin*, and to other newspapers and magazines in eastern parts of Australia, followed.[16]

Meston in north Queensland

Forced into insolvency in 1881, Meston's seat in Parliament was forfeited and he moved north where he became (briefly) the editor of the *Townsville Herald*.[17] According to one newspaper, his bankruptcy and consequent ejection from Parliament were personal failures: 'Meston seems to have fallen under the displeasure of his old political associates, and to have been cast out of the great Liberal fold.'[18]

---

14   Insolvency documents including list of creditors, Insolvency File: MESTON, Archibald, QSA ITM1058056, 1881/1023.
15   'Political Froth by an Abstainer', *Queenslander*, 9 August 1879, 168.
16   'Notes from Bananaland' by 'Maroogaline', *Bulletin*, 23 April 1881, 5; A. Meston, 'Old Moreton Bay Tribes. Their Languages', *Brisbane Courier*, 20 October 1923, 18: 'Having told them the name given to me by the Yoocumburra was "Maroogaline", from marroo the hand, and galine strong, they promptly named me "Keeningdutta" from their keening the hand, and datta strong, strong handed.'
17   'Members Adjudged Insolvent' *Queensland Parliamentary Debates* 37 (1882): 1–2.
18   'Current News', *Queenslander*, 5 November 1881, 581.

In August 1881, Meston travelled to Townsville and north along the coast.[19] Decades afterwards, he wrote that he went to the Johnstone River and Dunk Island in 1881, claiming that he was 'looking for sugar land'.[20] He first visited Cairns at the end of the same year, announcing in early 1882 his intention of managing a sugar plantation at the Barron River, north of the town. Popular topics of conversation in north Queensland at the time were sugar cultivation, the building of railways to the hinterland and the 'depredations' of 'the blacks'. Meston and his pen actively participated in all three discussions.

Meston duly submitted a lease application for Selection 139 on the Barron River.[21] This 160-acre block, located on the southern bank of the river, close to Freshwater Creek, would cost him £4 per annum.[22] Nearby, Selection 137 was 'taken up' in the name of his mother-in-law, Hannah Shaw, and his new business partner, Horace Brinsmead, successfully applied for Selection 138.[23] According to Meston's eldest daughter (Toressa), the proximity of thick scrub near the house meant 'we were not allowed to move outside without Father and his gun'.[24]

The thick coastal rainforest was soon cleared by Chinese tenant farmers. Like many European settlers in northern Australia, Meston was not averse to using Chinese labour to clear the land while simultaneously complaining about the increasing Chinese presence in Australia. Meston's selection on the Barron River was described by one visitor:

> Mr Meston … had leased a deal of his land to Chinese on clearing leases, and had about 70 acres cleared for absolutely nothing. The lessees, too, supply him with as much and as many vegetables as he requires.[25]

19   A. Meston, 'The Cave Skeleton', *North Queensland Register*, 20 December 1893, 25; A. Meston, 'Bits of History. Grave and Gay Pictures from the Past', *Daily Mail*, 21 September 1923, 8.

20   'Northern Sanatorium', Correspondences with attachments in Home Secretary's Office, QSA ITM2375529, 1901/12785; 'The Fitzgeralds', *Daily Mail*, 18 January 1919, 9; A. Meston, 'Australian Islands and Their History', *World's News*, 20 January 1923, 7–8; 'Early Exploration in North Queensland. Dalrymple's Travels in the 70's between Cardwell and Cooktown', *Cairns Post*, 8 December 1923, 11.

21   Selection File: Meston, Archibald, QSA ITM37870.

22   Ibid.

23   Selection File: Shaw, Hannah, QSA ITM37868; A. Meston to W. C. Hume, undersecretary for lands, Selection File: Brinsmead, Horace George, QSA ITM37869, 1882/10380.

24   Toressa Meston, 'The Homes I Lived in before My Marriage', Cairns Historical Society, 89/220/437.

25   'A Visit to Cairns by a Southerner', *Queensland Times*, 7 October 1884, 3.

Meston's business associate, Horace Brinsmead, a salesman for the family business (Brinsmead Pianos of London), was an English boxing champion, and Meston probably met him through his own keen interest in the sport. In early 1882, Meston stated that the latest sugar mill, 'which will arrive in time for the 1883 crop', had been ordered in Glasgow for Brinsmead and Co.[26] Two years later, peripatetic journalist 'The Vagabond', who visited Meston in 1883, said the mill 'to be made in London' would be 'erected in time for the season of 1885'.[27]

In 1892, another partner in the Freshwater Creek enterprise, Sydney insurance agent Charles Royle, stated:

> I met Mr A. Meston in Brisbane, and he told me these lands were about to be thrown open, and that so well did he think of the speculation that he was prepared to give up his seat in Parliament and proceed at once to Cairns, take up the land, and grow sugar.[28]

Royle also claimed that the 'contract for a complete sugar plant' was made by him, not Meston.

Meston had one more task to complete before he permanently moved to the north. In late 1882, he briefly returned to northern New South Wales, delivering lectures on 'Sugar growing and sugar land in Queensland' and 'Queensland life and scenery, soil and climate'. As a former resident of the Clarence River district, he exploited his family's network of contacts in the settler communities as he boosted the potential of northern parts of Queensland. He was also paid £100 by the Queensland Government to 'investigate the sugar industry in the Clarence & Richmond districts'.[29]

Meston spoke about 'the aboriginals of the north' in his lectures, describing them as 'a fine race of men standing over six feet high, with good chest development, and fine limbs, realising the ancient Greek ideas of the beauty of the human form'.[30] These appear to have been the first public lectures that Meston gave on 'the Aboriginal natives', a tentative foray into 'expertise', although he probably knew very little about the north at that stage. He had

26   [Untitled], *Brisbane Courier*, 20 February 1882, 3.
27   'In Northern Queensland. The Sugar Industry' by 'The Vagabond', *Argus*, 8 March 1884, 4.
28   'The Black Labour Question', *Brisbane Courier*, 3 February 1892, 7.
29   Executive Council Minutes, 22 August 1882, Colonial Secretary's Office—Executive Council Minutes, QSA ITM844876, 1882/47.
30   'Odd Notes', by 'A. Bohemian', *Week*, 21 October 1882, 13.

only personally 'seen' local people during his brief first sojourn in the Cairns and Townsville districts, and there is no evidence of any interaction from this period.

In November 1882, Meston travelled to Sydney, persuading at least three individuals to engage him as their land selection agent in Cairns.[31] Two more would-be canefarmers signed up in Brisbane and Cairns.[32] By December, Meston was back in Cairns welcoming Premier Thomas McIlwraith to town.[33] Soon after, he spent 10 days exploring south of Cairns, reporting the discovery of 'an extensive area of sugar land' that, he said, was 'swarming with blacks'.[34] Meston said the party had been attacked twice, apparently his first reference to a violent clash with Indigenous people.

Elected to the Cairns Divisional Board in February 1883, Meston wasted little time, quickly becoming chairman.[35] He badgered authorities in Brisbane for more money to improve roads and for better policing in the north. In June, he criticised prospector and explorer Christie Palmerston, accusing him of exaggerating the roughness of the terrain and using 'blacks' tracks' to investigate possible railway routes to the hinterland.[36]

He already fancied himself as a 'collector' of exotic artefacts. Meston wrote to the *Brisbane Courier* about wooden rainforest swords, stating that he 'found' them on the Russell River, south of Cairns, while exploring for sugar country.[37] This appears to have been Meston's first attempt at collecting ethnological objects. One sword was given to the *Courier* editor and other weapons were apparently donated to the Queensland Museum.

The Cairns Divisional Board, under Meston's chairmanship, announced that a loan of £1,000 would be sought to build a road from Cairns south to the Johnstone River.[38] At the end of 1883, Meston penned a fierce anti-Chinese article, warning Queenslanders they were 'a serious danger to the

---

31   Application from C. J. Royle to lease Selection 332, Selection File: Royle, Charles John, QSA ITM37993, 1883/994; Application from E. C. Batt to lease Selection 333, Selection File: Batt, Edmund Compton, QSA ITM37994, 1883/994; Application from T. C. Jamison, Sydney, to lease Selection 343, Selection File: Jamison, Thomas Carnes, QSA ITM38004.

32   Selection File: MacNaughtan, Samuel, QSA ITM37983; Selection File: Cohen, John Jacob, QSA ITM37985.

33   'The Premier in the North', *Queenslander*, 2 December 1882, 787.

34   'Queensland News', *Brisbane Courier*, 13 December 1882, 5.

35   'Meston, the "Sacred Ibis", is now Chairman of the Cairns (North Queensland) Divisional Board', in 'Personal Items', *Bulletin*, 10 March 1883, 5.

36   A. Meston, 'Johnstone River Deputation', *Brisbane Courier*, 2 June 1883, 5.

37   A. Meston, 'Native Wooden Swords', *Brisbane Courier*, 7 June 1883, 3.

38   A. Meston, 'Cairns Divisional Board', *Queensland Government Gazette* 33 (1883): 1603.

colony'.[39] However, he praised the Chinese several months later for their diet and avoidance of alcohol, qualifying his remarks: 'The vitality of the European is higher and his endurance greater than that of any black or yellow race as a decided rule.'[40]

Meston resigned from the Cairns Divisional Board in June 1884, about the same time that sugar prices fell by one-third.[41] The *Queenslander* reported that:

> there has been great dissatisfaction during the last six months with the Cairns Divisional Board ... Mr. A. Meston has been acting as chairman during the last eighteen months, and it is alleged he has been sitting illegally.[42]

According to the local paper, Meston:

> has good abilities which, properly exercised, would benefit the community, but, owing to his persistent neglect of the duties devolving upon the position he occupied on the board, there is a widespread feeling of mistrust towards him.[43]

Frances and the children left Cairns for Brisbane, followed four weeks later by Meston.[44]

Soon afterwards, the local paper described Meston's recent performance as a 'puppet-show', reflecting, they said, 'the overwhelming self-glorification which permeates his every action'.[45] In late 1884, neighbours successfully challenged Meston's attempted purchase of the only landing reserve on the Barron, a dispute that he described as 'purely the outcome of personal ill-feeling'.[46] Meston ultimately failed to gain any friends or allies in the Cairns district.

---

39   A. Meston, 'Labour for the Plantation', *Brisbane Courier*, 3 December 1883, 3.
40   'The North Queensland Climate', *Brisbane Courier*, 17 March 1884, 5.
41   Telegram, F. T. Wimble to colonial secretary, Correspondence—Divisional Boards, Cairns Divisional Board, QSA ITM108551, 1884/2114; Cairns Divisional Board to Works Department, Correspondence—Divisional Boards, Cairns Divisional Board, QSA ITM108551, 1884/2234; P. Griggs, 'Sugar Plantations in Queensland, 1864–1912: Origins, Characteristics, Distribution, and Decline', *Agricultural History* 74, no. 3 (2000): 637, doi.org/10.1215/00021482-74.3.609. He rejoined the Board in 1887.
42   'Country News', *Queenslander*, 5 July 1884, 7.
43   'Cairns Divisional Board', *Cairns Post*, 17 July 1884, 2. One could compile a thesis on Meston's sojourn in Cairns.
44   'Shipping', *Cairns Post*, 17 July 1884, 2; 'Shipping', *Brisbane Courier*, 22 August 1884, 4.
45   'Local Items', *Cairns Post*, 11 September 1884, 2.
46   Selection File: Meston, Archibald, QSA ITM37870, 1884/21842; 'Cairns Divisional Board', *Cairns Post*, 13 November 1884, 2; 'Cairns Divisional Board', *Cairns Post*, 11 December 1884, 2.

The downturn in the sugar industry changed Meston's plans. He returned to Brisbane where he involved himself with a campaign to overturn the death sentence of two white men found guilty of murdering Pacific Islanders onboard the *Hopeful*:

> He made further remarks about the shooting of blacks by the native police, and produced a rifle with 29 nicks on it which he said represented so many blacks killed. If they protected the South Sea Islanders why not first protect their own native population.[47]

No evidence of the rifle's provenance was given. A few days later he called for a commission of inquiry into the Native Police, describing the force as 'an entirely unwarranted waste of public money'.[48] He also claimed that pioneer settlers in the north could 'take care of themselves', even if they had 'occasionally to shoot blacks from necessity', but 'we have less consideration for our own blacks than for the South Sea cannibals. Every month in North Queensland there are cases of kidnapping worse than those of the *Hopeful*'.[49] As a result of the public protests, the death sentences of the *Hopeful* perpetrators were commuted to life imprisonment.

At the same time, Meston offered his opinion on the murder of selector Donald McAuley at the nearby Mulgrave River, saying:

> Those who know the blacks will realise the truth of my assertion that the safety of pioneer settlers can only be fully secured by absolutely prohibiting the blacks from coming in sight of the place, and shooting them if they persist in it.[50]

'The Mulgrave blacks will pay dearly for that murder, even more dearly than they paid for the recent murder on the Russell', he said. Meston's attitudes towards Aboriginal people were still, at that time, not so enlightened.

Some six months later, in early 1885, he returned to Cairns, becoming the editor of the *Cairns Chronicle*, a pro-McIlwraith paper. Soon after, he wrote his first article about the Barron Falls, proclaiming that 'in the years that are coming these falls will be to Australia what Niagara is to America'. However, adding details of his own visit, he noted: 'we had to maintain a fire all night, each of us keeping three hours watch to guard against a surprise by

---

47 'The Condemned Men. Open Air Meeting', *Telegraph* (Brisbane), 22 December 1884, 4–5.
48 A. Meston 'Commissions of Inquiry. To the Editor of the Brisbane Courier', *Brisbane Courier*, 27 December 1884, 3.
49 Ibid.
50 A. Meston, 'The Mulgrave Murder', *Brisbane Courier*, 31 December 1884, 5.

the blacks'.[51] Residents of Cairns, confident the hinterland railway would start from their town, twice elected Meston to deputations that travelled to Brisbane during this time.[52]

In September 1885, Hannah Shaw (Meston's mother-in-law) was granted freehold title of Selection 137 on Freshwater Creek.[53] Although no proof has been found, Hannah's purchase of land at a time when she did not appear to have any income suggests that she was a 'dummy' selector for Royle and and his partner Samuel Griffiths, who owned the block in mid-1887.[54] Two days after the successful purchase of Hannah's selection, Meston completed and signed his will, leaving his entire property, money and life insurance to his wife, Frances.[55] The close timing of these two events is currently unexplained but intriguing!

Meston then announced that he would stand for Parliament as a candidate for the Mulgrave electorate, but soon withdrew 'owing to the pressure of private business'.[56] Meston's insolvency, which began in 1881, was finally annulled in November 1885. He wrote to parliamentarian Thomas McIlwraith offering his unwavering support, describing Samuel Griffith as 'my most unscrupulous enemy'.[57] Surviving letters and records show that Meston's political loyalties changed according to his personal circumstances.

In January 1886, selector Charles Townsend was found murdered near the Russell River, and an inquest was held at Cairns.[58] Meston, interested himself in the case, dismissed the judge's findings and called for further investigations, stating: 'No Northern man who knows anything about the blacks, especially in that district, would voluntarily stay a single night in the place where Townsend was killed.'[59] Police Magistrate H. M. Chester, asked to report by the Crown Law Office, stated: 'the agitation by the *Cairns Chronicle*, and Mr. A. Meston, is owing to professional rancour against a rival journalist.'[60]

---

51 Disputes between Meston and others over the comparison between the Barron and Niagara Falls continued until the editor of the *Queenslander* ordered the subject closed in March 1886; A. Meston, 'The Barron Falls in Flood Time', *Queenslander*, 20 February 1886, 292.

52 [Untitled], *Brisbane Courier*, 25 January 1886, 4; 'Roundabout', *Queensland Figaro & Punch*, 30 January 1886, 191.

53 Application to purchase Selection 137, Selection File: Shaw, Hannah, QSA ITM37868, 1885/23676.

54 'Freshwater Creek Estate. Its Soil, Timbers and Fruit-Trees', *Cairns Post*, 26 October 1887, 3.

55 Will Files—Brisbane, Meston, Archibald, QSA ITM904506.

56 'Local Items', *Cairns Post*, 1 October 1885, 2; 'Local Items', *Cairns Post*, 5 November 1885, 2.

57 A. Meston to T. McIlwraith, Sir Thomas McIlwraith Papers, John Oxley Library, OM64-19/83.

58 Inquiry regarding C. H. Townsend, Inwards Correspondence, Colonial Secretary's Office, QSA ITM847202, 1886/5092.

59 A. Meston, 'Fate of Townsend. To the Editor of the Brisbane Courier', *Brisbane Courier*, 24 February 1886, 2.

60 H. M. Chester, police magistrate, Cairns, to Crown Law Office, Colonial Secretary's Office, Inwards correspondence, QSA ITM847202, 1886/216.

The dissolution of Meston's business partnership with Horace Brinsmead, C. J. Royle and P. P. Samuel was announced in June 1886.[61] Brinsmead's insolvency of almost £12,000 was announced in mid-1887. He blamed Meston for his financial embarrassment, stating that 'the cause of the insolvency' was his liability for his 'late partner's creditors and heavy loss sustained through my late partner's insolvency and his failure to carry out his obligations to one'.[62] Brinsmead, a financially broken man whose name was bestowed on a Cairns suburb, later returned to England.[63]

In 1889, Meston testified at the Cairns hearings for the Royal Commission into the Sugar Industry, stating: 'I arrived here in the end of 1881, representing myself and three capitalists who were desirous of becoming possessed of land on which they could form a sugar plantation.'[64] However, a change of government meant the end of cheap coloured labour ('it would be utterly impossible to go into the production of sugar with white labour'), so they cancelled the order for a mill and abandoned their sugar-growing plans. In 1888, Meston said that he advocated 'an Australia … free from the degradation of cheap labour'.[65]

Alternative ventures

Meston's dream of becoming a sugar baron had turned sour and he needed a new vocation. During the late 1880s, he became an enthusiastic property speculator, especially once the Barron River route (close to his selection) was chosen for the hinterland railway from Cairns. In March 1886, he wrote about 'the white tents of the railway surveyors who are camped on the old rafting-ground'.[66] In February 1887, he sent an 'urgent' request for the title to his land, because:

> the railway has brought out a lot of people who want to build shops & houses, etc., on acres & half acres & some of them came to me as I have the only cleared land available in this locality and want to lease a few acres.[67]

61   'Agricultural Operations in the Cairns District', *Queenslander*, 26 June 1886, 32.
62   Audit Insolvency Files, BRINSMEAD, Horace George, QSA ITM1054625.
63   'Suicide of Mr. G. H. Brinsmead', *London Times*, 23 July 1908, 14.
64   'Report of the Royal Commission Appointed to Inquire into the General Condition of the Sugar Industry in Queensland', *Queensland Parliamentary Votes and Proceedings* 4 (1889): 61.
65   'Personal Items', *Bulletin*, 2 June 1888, 9.
66   A. Meston, 'New Year's Eve on the Barron', *Brisbane Courier*, 10 March 1886, 2.
67   Selection File: Meston, Archibald, QSA ITM37870.

Meston, recently re-elected to the Cairns Divisional Board, began advertising blocks for lease at his 'Cambanora Estate'.[68] A sportsground on his land was in use by mid-1887. The railway contractor paid Meston £500 for permitting a branch line to traverse his block, then purchased all the timber from his selections 'on both sides of the Barron River', and leased a site for a sawmill.[69] Meston had purchased four blocks of land on the northern bank of the Barron from Simeon Lord in mid-1887.[70]

In May 1887, police reported that Meston, in his capacity as a justice of the peace, had issued warrants for the arrest of persons 'sly grog selling at the Barron River'. They added:

> A hotel has been lately opened on Mr Meston's land near his own house, which is the cause of his action in issuing a warrant and in fact he sat on the Bench as a Licensing Justice when the license for the above house was granted.[71]

Meston's offer to lease buildings and a paddock to the police was approved in July.[72] The Kamerunga police station existed for three years, from 1888 to late 1891.

Relations with his new tenants were not always harmonious. Meston charged two of his tenants (who had previously tried to open an inn on his land) with libel in June 1887.[73] Behind in the rent, they erected a sign stating:

> Warning. To A Meston. If you do not keep away from my house during the absence of my husband, trying to commit indecent or felonious assaults on me, you will get a bullet into your worthless carcass, if you escape the ropes of the gallows, which you deserved long ago.[74]

The charge against the wife was quickly dismissed, and her husband's case was later quietly dropped by the attorney-general.[75]

---

68 'Cambanora Estate', *Cairns Post*, 18 May 1887, 3.

69 'Local Items', *Cairns Post*, 27 August 1887, 2.

70 A. Meston, Brisbane, to Lands Department, Selection File: Meston, Archibald, QSA ITM37870, 1889/14506.

71 Senior Sergeant Halloran, Cairns, to Inspector Morisset, Port Douglas, Police stations—Homestead, Koorboora, Kallanda, Kamerunga, QSA ITM290299, 1887/3768.

72 Telegram, Inspector Morisett, Cairns, to commissioner, Police stations—Homestead, Koorboora, Kallanda, Kamerunga, QSA ITM290299, 1887/5131.

73 'Licensing Court', *Cairns Post*, 7 October 1886, 2; 'Police Court', *Cairns Post*, 18 June 1887, 2.

74 Miscellaneous (unnumbered) criminal files—Supreme Court, Northern District, Townsville, QSA ITM270933; 'Queensland News, Cairns', *Brisbane Courier*, 30 June 1887, 2.

75 'Local Items', *Cairns Post*, 24 August 1887, 2.

A provisional school for the newly proclaimed township of Kamerunga, adjacent to Meston's land, was approved in August 1887, and in April 1888, Meston chaired a meeting to push for the upgrade of the provisional school to a permanent one.[76] With no other site available, the hall that he built on his land in late 1887 was rented to the school committee for £60 per year.[77] Meston was still demanding and receiving rent for this building in 1894.[78]

In late June 1887, Meston announced in the Cairns paper that 'all his household furniture and effects' (including firearms) would be auctioned in July.[79] The reasons for this clearance are unknown, but Meston was dealing with the fallout from his abortive Russell River settlement scheme. In 1880, he had told a group of men in northern New South Wales that he could 'persuade the Queensland Government' to allow them to select land, boasting in Parliament of his attempts, saying 'he could bring up a hundred small capitalists to take up land for sugar-growing' if the terms of the Land Act were 'liberal enough'.[80]

By 1882, those who had agreed to invest in land began abandoning their selections. 'I selected on the Russell River through my agent Mr. A. Meston', said one, 'under the impression that … it would be held to be in compliance with the residence clause'.[81] Another wrote that he had learned of 'a misapprehension of the Queensland land laws'.[82] A third was called upon to 'show cause' against forfeiture on the grounds of 'not being a resident of Queensland' in August 1886.[83]

A fourth New South Wales farmer protested in July 1887: 'Mr. A. Meston as agent for the Queensland government, on visiting here advised me with others to take up Sugar Land on the Russell River.'[84] Asked 'what reason he had for supposing Mr. A. Meston was an accredited agent for the Queensland Government to induce residents of New South Wales to take up land in Queensland', he replied: 'from what was said and what I heard I certainly

---

76   Kamerunga to Department of Public Instruction, School Correspondence Files for State Schools, QSA ITM15038, 1888/3143.

77   J. Whitaker, Kamerunga to Department of Public Instruction, School Correspondence Files for State Schools, QSA ITM15038, 1889/3365.

78   'Kamerunga State School', School Correspondence Files for State Schools, QSA ITM15038.

79   'Cambanora Sale', Cairns Post, 29 June 1887, 3 and 9 July 1887, 3.

80   'Legislative Assembly, Supply', Queensland Parliamentary Debates, 1880, 654–5.

81   Selection File: Batt, Edmund Compton, QSA ITM37994, 1883/1516.

82   Ibid.

83   R. T. Hartley, [Notice by Land Commissioner's Office], Cairns Post, 12 August 1886, 1.

84   A. Meston, 'Cambanora', to Lands Department, Selection File: Jamison, Thomas Carnes, QSA ITM38004, 1887/17558.

believed he was a paid agent of the Queensland Government'.[85] Nothing was ever publicly said, but there was clearly a financial risk to Meston if any of the would-be sugar growers decided to pursue legal action against him. Meston might be capable of persuading others to join his schemes, but even he knew that he could not successfully defend charges of fraud or false pretence.

Mountain climbing, mission pursuits and other ventures

The property venture had not worked out as well as he probably hoped, and some other income was needed urgently. Business and politics had also not been great successes. Meston sustained two major conspicuous obsessions throughout his life: one was game shooting and the other was climbing Mount Bellenden Ker, south of Cairns. Whereas game hunting only brought in money from a few published articles, articles and talks on mountain climbing proved more lucrative.[86] Meston wrote at least 20 lengthy descriptive articles about Bellenden Ker between 1889 and 1923, and in 1924 he was paid £2/2/- for each article.[87]

In February 1889, Sergeant Edmund Whelan of the Native Police, Harry Barnard and Meston climbed the mountain, and he began writing the first of many articles about the ascent. Later, he also gave public lectures on Bellenden Ker. He returned to the massif in mid-1889, accompanied by botanist F. M. Bailey, museum collector Kendall Broadbent, his teenage son Harold Meston, a Yorkshireman named Walter Beman and three Melanesian carriers.[88] Whelan and four troopers joined them.

Although his mountain climbing stories and lectures had provided some temporary income, he desperately needed a more reliable revenue stream. Meston had been reading newspaper stories for the last few years about Aboriginal performers visiting Sydney and other places, and evidently decided that his next endeavour would be one that involved showmanship

---

85   T. C. Jamieson, Rocky Mouth, to Lands Department, Selection File: Jamison, Thomas Carnes, QSA ITM38004, 1887/20013.

86   Meston mentioned firearms, and the shooting of birds and other wildlife in more than 70 articles and letters.

87   L. A. Meston to public curator regarding A. Meston estate, Will Files—Brisbane, Meston, Archibald, QSA ITM904506/9.

88   A. Meston, 'Bellenden-ker Scientific Expedition', *Brisbane Courier*, 7 October 1889, 5.

and his newly acquired 'expertise' in Indigenous culture and weaponry. Meston returned to Brisbane, joined the Aborigines Protection Society and visited the Bribie Island Mission. He immediately offered to give a public lecture in Brisbane on behalf of the society.

Anglican missionary John Gribble spoke in Brisbane about his endeavours in the Cairns district, stating that he received the impression that Samuel Griffith and Colonial Secretary Horace Tozer 'were deeply interested in the welfare of the aboriginal tribes'.[89] He initially praised Meston:

> to whom I had been strongly recommended in New South Wales as an authority in all matters pertaining to the blacks and the Bellenden Ker region … [He] did me no small service in introducing me to the different departments of the Government, as well as running over the charts with me and indicating routes and positions.[90]

However, relations between Gribble and Meston were to sour much later after control of the Fraser Island Aboriginal Reserve was transferred from Southern Protector of Aborigines Meston to the Anglican Board of Missions in 1899.[91]

In September 1891, Meston publicly challenged Tozer to provide transport and accommodation so that Aboriginal children from the Bribie Island Mission might visit Brisbane to perform a public concert.[92] Although initially reluctant, Tozer finally agreed to support the excursion. The performance and Meston's lectures were a great success. A photograph was taken of the Bribie Island party with members of the Aborigines Protection Society— including Meston and his soon-to-be business associate Brabazon Purcell (see Figure 2.1).[93] Not long afterwards, Meston was reported to be 'collecting a company of wild singers and making preparations to tour England and America'.[94]

---

89 'Missionary Pioneering in Northern Queensland', *Brisbane Courier*, 7 September 1891, 7; 'The Sketcher. Missionary Pioneering in Northern Queensland', *Queenslander*, 12 September 1891, 511.
90 Ibid.
91 A. Meston to home secretary, Mission Schools, Correspondence re Aboriginal Schools and Missions, QSA ITM997082, 1900/2378; 'Aborigines', *Telegraph* (Brisbane), 15 March 1900, 4.
92 A. Meston, 'Letters to Editor. Mr. Tozer's Promises', *Brisbane Courier*, 18 September 1891, 6.
93 Photograph, Stan Colliver Collection, Queensland Museum, EH1148.
94 'At Poverty Point', *Bulletin*, 24 October 1891, 9.

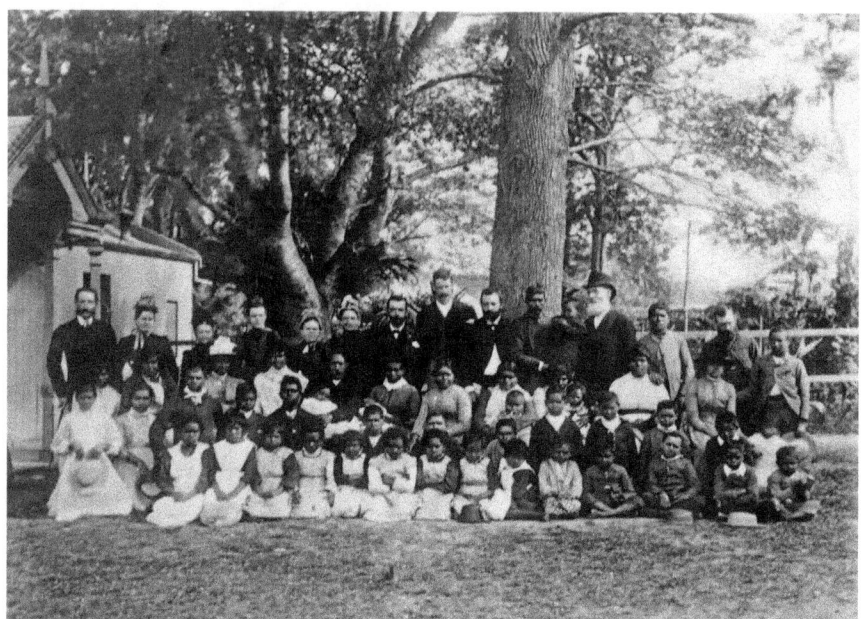

Figure 2.1: Residents of the Bribie Island Mission with Archibald Meston, Brabazon Purcell and others, Botanic Gardens, Brisbane, 12 October 1891
Source: Colliver Collection, Queensland Museum.

Meston made one last trip north in December 1891, accompanying two Italian scientists collecting museum specimens on Bellenden Ker (see Chapter 7). However, the Italians found climbing in the heat of the tropics onerous, so Meston proceeded alone, unsuccessfully attempting to capture an Aboriginal woman in the process.[95] He did not reveal what he planned to do with the woman if he had succeeded.

Eventually, Meston relocated to Brisbane, evidently supporting himself and the family by the proceeds of his writing. In 1891 alone, he produced more than 20 articles and published letters. Topics included gold mining, a review of Lumholtz's *Among Cannibals*, 'Lost Leichhardt', 'Dr Lauterer's Lecture', 'The Correct Pronunciation of Wallangarra', 'Aboriginal Names', 'Historical Facts', 'Literary Frauds', 'Ray Fishes', 'Hospital Reminiscences', 'The Lyre Bird', 'Mr Tozer's Promises', 'Bribie Island', 'Names of Steamers', 'The Race of Jindoobarrie' (a poem), 'The Late Joseph Fleming', 'First Brisbane River Steamer', and regular features in the *Boomerang* ('Field Shooting in

---

95   A. Meston, 'Bellenden Ker Revisited II', *Queenslander*, 5 March 1892, 462.

Queensland') and the *Bulletin*.[96] His first book, *Queensland Railway and Tourists' Guide*, was published for the Queensland Government in 1890, and he also delivered several lectures on 'The Manners and Customs of the Blacks' that year.

In mid-1891, the Columbian World's Fair and Exposition to be held in Chicago in 1893 was announced. News of Meston's intention to take a party of Aboriginal performers there first appeared in southern papers during late 1891 (see Chapter 7).[97] Apparently, his recent lectures in Brisbane were 'such a genuine success' that he 'decided to gather a troupe of wild blacks and take them to the World's Fair at Chicago'. As one newspaper reported:

> Mr Meston will take the aborigines (about 30 or 35) via New Zealand to San Francisco, and will probably show in the southern colonies en route, and on his return we shall see him in Tasmania.[98]

Meston was obviously convinced that he would make a good return on his investment.

The Wild Australia Show was Meston's biggest financial gamble. We know from his (second) insolvency file and other records from whom he borrowed money to finance it. His biggest debtors were the Queensland National Bank Ltd (£907), Public Service Commissioner Thomas Mylne (£500), solicitor Harold Lilley and businessman Thomas Cowlishaw (£105), his brother-in-law William Miller (£100), his sister Helen Cameron (£100),

---

96 A. Meston, [Untitled], *Queenslander*, 3 January 1891, 27; Ramrod [A. Meston], 'Field Shooting in Queensland', *Boomerang*, 7 February 1891, 21; A. Meston, 'Lost Leichhardt', *Evening Observer*, 21 March 1891; A. Meston, 'Letters to Editor. Dr. Lauterer's Lecture', *Brisbane Courier*, 23 March 1891, 7; A. Meston, [Untitled], *Brisbane Courier*, 30 March 1891, 4; A. Meston, [Untitled], *Brisbane Courier*, 10 April 1891, 4; A. Meston, 'Historical Facts. To the Editor of the Chronicle', *Toowoomba Chronicle*, 9 May 1891, 3; 'Lost Leichhardt', *Brisbane Courier*, 18 June 1891, 6; A. Meston, [Untitled], *Brisbane Courier*, 23 June 1891, 4; A. Meston, [Untitled], *Brisbane Courier*, 30 July 1891, 5; A. Meston, 'Hospital Reminiscences', *Telegraph* (Brisbane), 10 August 1891, 4; A. Meston, [Untitled], *Brisbane Courier*, 3 September 1891, 5; A. Meston, 'Letters to Editor. Mr. Tozer's Promises', *Brisbane Courier*, 18 September 1891, 6; A. Meston, 'Bribie Island', *Brisbane Courier*, 21 September 1891, 3; A. Meston, [Untitled], *Brisbane Courier*, 25 September 1891, 5; A. Meston, 'Bribie Island', *Queenslander*, 26 September 1891, 607; A. Meston, 'The Late Joseph Fleming', *Brisbane Courier*, 28 September 1891, 6; A. Meston, 'First Brisbane River Steamer', *Telegraph* (Brisbane), 26 October 1891, 2.
97 'At Poverty Point', *Bulletin*, 24 October 1891, 9; 'A Wild North Show', *Launceston Examiner*, 14 December 1891, 3; 'A Wild North Show', *Hobart Mercury*, 19 December 1891, 3; 'Amusements', *Tasmanian*, 19 December 1891, 17.
98 'A Wild North Show', *Launceston Examiner*, 14 December 1891, 3.

Finny Isles & Co. (£86/19/2), the Australasian United Steam Navigation Company (£81), Brabazon Purcell (£111) and others. By 1896, his debts totalled over £2,000.[99] He had no assets.

Brabazon Purcell

The creators of the 'Wild Australia Show', Archibald Meston and Brabazon Purcell, a journalist/showman and a stock agent, were an unlikely combination, but both evidently saw the Show's potential to earn them money as being well worth their joint efforts. Neither seemed to have considered the potential pitfalls and problems that the venture might encounter, and both appeared fairly oblivious to the needs and experiences of the Indigenous performers. Although Meston advertised the Show as an opportunity for city dwellers to learn about Aboriginal culture and heritage, we could easily believe that his primary motivation was just to make money.

Purcell's reasons for becoming involved, apart from financial gain, are less clear. We know much less about his life before 'Wild Australia' than Meston's. He usually signed his name as 'Brab.' and he had spent the previous two or three decades in rural Australia, mostly droving cattle and selling horses. Purcell gave details of his life during a number of public lectures and others contributed more. He stated in 1894 that he had 'some thirty years experience in the back country'—that is, from the age of about 9 or 10.[100]

During the 1880s, when Meston was busy dreaming of becoming a sugar baron in north Queensland, 'Brab.' Purcell was mostly droving cattle from New South Wales and Queensland stations to southern markets. Purcell seems to have been at ease with Aboriginal people, perhaps as a result of his upbringing or of his experiences in rural districts. He was to later organise food and shelter for the Wild Australia Show performers in both Melbourne and Sydney (see Chapters 9 and 10). He stayed with the Aboriginal performers in Melbourne after Meston deserted them and eventually organised their repatriation to Queensland.

---

99   List of creditors for insolvency of A. Meston, Audit Liquidation Files, MESTON, Archibald, QSA ITM1615768, 1897/6716.
100   B. H. Purcell, 'The Tax on Stallions. To the Editor of the Brisbane Courier', *Brisbane Courier*, 17 September 1894, 6.

The few details that we have found answer some questions but raise even more. The son of Brabazon and Henrietta Amanda (née Brown) Purcell, Brabazon Harry Purcell was born in St Kilda, Melbourne, on 21 May 1856.[101] Purcell junior was the eldest of several boys (Brabazon, possibly Arthur and Lambert) and two girls (Eleanor and Henrietta). Sent to work after his father's untimely death in 1865, nine-year-old Brabazon soon became the family's breadwinner.[102]

Purcell gained employment through his family connections and probably worked for his uncle, stock and station agent George Dougharty, at some early stage of his life. He claimed in 1893 that his late father was a 'personal friend' of explorer Robert Burke.[103] In 1851, Dougharty 'left Australia for the United States with the late Mr. Brabazon Purcell, who afterwards became his brother in-law'.[104] Dougharty managed and later sold a string of large pastoral stations for Benjamin Boyd in the early 1850s, including Ulupna (also called Strathmerton) on the south side of the Murray River.[105]

One 1892 correspondent, J. Rogers, stated that Purcell's 'vast experience' with 'the aboriginals of nearly all the Australian provinces' began when he was young:

> Years ago, on the Murray river, he could strip a bark canoe, spear fish, stalk game, throw the boomerang (left handed), dance and sing corroborees, and track with the best of the blacks, by whom he was dubbed Waawi ('brother'), and who are said to have put the tribal scars on Purcell as a sign of brotherhood.[106]

Dougharty and Purcell's father had been partners in the 'Horse and Carriage Repository' at Lonsdale Street, Melbourne, after their return from California.[107] Dougharty, described as 'the leading stock and station agent in Melbourne', would have been a valuable connection for Purcell up to his (Dougharty's) death in 1889.[108] Brabazon Purcell senior also worked

---

101 QBDM, Death Certificate 1904/C1094.
102 'Family Notices', *Argus*, 12 June 1865, 4.
103 [Untitled], *Table Talk*, 22 November 1889, 3.
104 Ibid. Dougharty was the brother-in-law of Henrietta Purcell.
105 The station was sold in 1856 just before Brabazon Purcell junior was born.
106 'At Poverty Point', *Bulletin*, 5 November 1892, 8.
107 'The Biographer. An Australian Pioneer', *Australasian*, 23 November 1889, 34.
108 'Old Sydney' by 'Old Chum', *Truth*, 15 June 1924, 16.

as a property agent and speculator, selling land at St Kilda. Horses were a constant feature of Purcell's life, in contrast with Meston, who only seems to have ridden horses when he was young.[109]

Purcell had spent much more time in the 'outside' districts than Meston had and seemed to have a broad network of friends and colleagues from St Kilda to Charters Towers, and inland to central Australia. He spoke of his 'old friend the manager Mr John Buckley' at Noranside Station on the Burke River, and of his 'friend M. Costello' (presumably John Costello's son Michael) at Lake Nash in 1892.[110] His 1893 piece 'Only a Pair of Boots', written after the Wild Australia Show debacle, mentioned 'Carter, McLean, Robertson, and others on the Edwards, Murrumbidgee, Lachlan, and Darling Rivers', suggesting that he also spent some time in southwest New South Wales.[111]

It would be useful to know more about Purcell's family history and business career. He said that he went to the Paroo River in western Queensland in 1876, and to the Darling River in 1879.[112] One 1896 letter mentioned a conversation with drover George Johnston in 1876.[113] In 1893, Purcell wrote that the late G. W. Johnston, presumably the same person, was his cousin, and 'exhibited pituri in Melbourne' during the late 1860s, a subject of interest in the later Wild Australia Show (see Chapter 7).[114]

His 1892 paper about 'pitchery' prompted criticism from one Georgina River resident: 'Mr. Purcell's twenty-five years' bush experience proves beyond doubt that he did not happen to have gained that experience in that particular bush where the pitchery grows.' But he was defended by another: 'Mr. Peberdy is entirely wrong when he asserts that Mr. Purcell has had no experience in the pitchery country, as I know otherwise.'[115]

109 Meston said he first visited the Bunya Mountains in 1892, 'myself on foot and the other eight on horseback', see: 'The Bunya Mountains: A Beautiful Region', *Daily Mail*, 2 September 1905, 1.
110 B. H. Purcell, Brisbane, to colonial secretary, Colonial Secretary's Office, Inwards Correspondence, QSA ITM847448, 1892/13729.
111 B. H. Purcell, 'Only a Pair of Boots', *Queenslander*, 23 December 1893, 1222.
112 'Our Australian Blacks', *Australian Star*, 25 March 1893, 7.
113 B. H. Purcell, 'Mr. George Phillip's Interview. To the Editor', *Queenslander*, 29 February 1896, 421.
114 'Our Australian Blacks', *Australian Star*, 25 March 1893, 7.
115 'Meetings. Royal Society of New South Wales', *Sydney Morning Herald*, 20 January 1893, 6; C. E. Peberdy, 'Letters to the Editor. Pitchery', *Queenslander*, 18 February 1893, 298; 'Our Australian Blacks', *Australian Star*, 25 March 1893, 7; 'Letters to the Editor. More Pitchery' by 'Ameroo', *Queenslander*, 22 April 1893, 730.

In 1893, Purcell claimed that he was initiated by the 'Kargooluahs' at 'Gooladdie' station in the Warrego district during this period.[116] Nowadays, Cooladdi—described as 'Australia's smallest town'—is a pastoral property and a township, between Charleville and Quilpie, not far from Yarron Vale (today's 'Yarronvale'), once part owned by Dougharty, where his brother Lambert Purcell worked during the 1880s. This is Bidjara Country, and Yarron Vale was an important drovers' crossing point over the Paroo River. Two 1881 public notices for Yarron Vale are signed 'B.H. and R.H. Purcell, Manager'.[117] Perhaps Brabazon also briefly worked there.

Purcell said he had 'experience' with Aboriginal people in Victoria, New South Wales, the Northern Territory, South Australia and Queensland.[118] In 1893, he told the members of the Royal Geographical Society in Melbourne that the 'tribal mark' that he received 'through undergoing the bora' was 'generally recognised by the natives, and had been the means of saving his life on many occasions'.[119] However, one letter that he wrote in 1895 stated that he had 'often tried to use' Aboriginal people for prospecting 'in the North' without success.[120] Another of his letters was overtly racist: 'Who will deny the fact that a white man always stands the hot climate better than the original inhabitants of the soil?'[121]

Shipping news and unclaimed mail notices record his movements from northern sheep and cattle stations in Queensland to Sydney and other towns, often returning by steamer. Dougharty sold cattle for 'Purcell and Muirhead' in 1879 and 1880; grazier John Muirhead lived at Elgin Downs, near Clermont in Central Queensland.[122] 'Mr Purcell, on behalf of Messrs John Geo Dougherty & Co, took delivery of 748 head mixed cattle at Wilcannia' in late 1880.[123]

---

116 'Our Australian Blacks', *Australian Star*, 25 March 1893, 7.
117 'Notice', *Western Star*, 27 July 1881, 3; 'Notice', *Western Star*, 17 August 1881, 3.
118 T. Bridge, Cardwell, to colonial secretary, Colonial Secretary's Office, Inwards Correspondence, QSA ITM847483, 1893/12670; J. Coghlan, Glenormiston, to Colonial Secretary, Colonial Secretary's Office, Inwards Correspondence, QSA ITM847483, 1893/12837.
119 'Royal Geographical Society', *Argus*, 6 February 1893, 3.
120 'Correspondence', *South Australian Register*, 28 May 1895, 4.
121 'The White Bull', *Australasian*, 27 July 1895, 6.
122 'Live Stock Market', *Age*, 24 December 1879, 4; 'Pastoral News, Stock Movements and Markets', *Maitland Mercury*, 2 December 1880; 'The Sketcher: A Ramble in the West', *Queenslander*, 8 July 1882, 44.
123 'Pastoral News, Stock Movements and Markets', *Maitland Mercury*, 2 December 1880, 2.

A drover named 'B. N. Purcell' took a mob of cattle from Queensland to Melbourne in late 1882, and a letter for 'H. B. Purcell' went unclaimed at Eulo, near Cunnamulla, in mid-1883.[124] Unclaimed letters for 'B. H. Purcell' and 'R. H. Purcell' were recorded at Thargomindah and Yarrow Vale in 1884.[125] An unclaimed letter for 'B. H. Purcell (drover in charge of cattle) via Thargomindah and Windorah' was listed in late 1885.[126] Another droving trip by 'B. H. Purcell' was recorded in 1886, as were two unclaimed letters for 'Brab. H Purcell, Dotswood' (near Charters Towers).[127] More unclaimed letters for 'P. H. and B. H. Purcell' were held at Murwah near Charleville and at Towerhill near Muttaburra in late 1887 and early 1888.[128]

In mid-1888, when Meston was planning the next stage in his political and entrepreneurial career, Purcell, evidently living in Brisbane, became an active member and honorary judge of the Queensland National Association and the Queensland Turf Club. He moved a rule change at the Queensland Turf Club and joined Smith and Greenwood's company of 'Auctioneers, Stock, Station and General Agents' in the city.[129]

In mid-1889, when Meston was busy climbing Bellenden Ker, Purcell advertised that he was now in business by himself and would pay cash for 'any number of kangaroo, wallaby, opossum and bear skins' at his Brisbane office.[130] At the beginning of 1890, Purcell was exporting ponies to Batavia in the Dutch East Indies and importing prize-winning pigs from New Zealand.[131] More horses were sent to Batavia in late 1890.[132]

---

124 'Intercolonial Pastoral News', *Queenslander*, 18 November 1882, 721; 'List of Unclaimed Letters for the Month of July, 1883', *Queensland Government Gazette* 33 (1883): 471.
125 'List of Unclaimed Letters for the Month of February, 1884', *Queensland Government Gazette* 34 (1884): 810.
126 'List of Unclaimed Letters for the Month of October, 1885', *Queensland Government Gazette* 37 (1885): 1832.
127 'Tambo', *Morning Bulletin*, 30 September 1886, 6; 'Queensland News: Cunnamulla, October 28', *Brisbane Courier*, 29 October 1886, 5; 'List of Unclaimed Letters for the Month of December, 1886', *Queensland Government Gazette* 40 (1887): 307.
128 'List of Unclaimed Letters for the Month of September, 1887', *Queensland Government Gazette* 42 (1887): 638; 'List of Unclaimed Letters for the Month of February, 1888', *Queensland Government Gazette* 43 (1888): 1050.
129 'Meetings', *Telegraph* (Brisbane), 17 May 1888, 1; 'Public Notices', *Brisbane Courier*, 5 June 1888, 8.
130 'Advertising', *Queenslander*, 20 July 1889, 99.
131 [Untitled], *Brisbane Courier*, 25 December 1889, 4; 'Current News', *Queenslander*, 5 April 1890, 629; 'Advertising, *Supplement to Warwick Examiner*, 16 January 1892, 1.
132 'Horseracing', *Week*, 13 December 1890, 21.

In February 1891, when Meston was preparing his *Railway Guide* for publication,[133] Purcell was in Rockhampton, probably watching the 'Wirth Bros. Wild West Show', featuring 'Red and Dusky Warriors, Genuine American Indians, All the Greatest Tribes Represented' and 'Thrilling Incidents of Indian and Cowboy Exploits'.[134] In June 1891, while Meston was writing articles and letters, Purcell was waiting in Brisbane for 33 horses to arrive from a property near Grafton.[135]

However, problems with the ponies previously sent to Batavia emerged in late 1891, resulting in a falling out between Purcell and several other stock agents, and the threat of legal action. One disgruntled buyer served Purcell with a writ, to which he replied: 'I am not worth a cent having had many business reverses.'[136] Purcell was declared insolvent in late 1892, owing substantial amounts of money to other parties, including coffee-grower and horse-buyer Charles Hall at Java, businessmen Wyndham & Cardell at Tamworth, and explosives company Rackarock & Co. in Sydney.[137]

At some point, probably in the latter half of 1891, Meston and Purcell made a business deal together. Both had experienced financial downturns and evidently saw the venture as a good way to make some quick money. Gathering, moving and displaying Aboriginal people probably seemed—to them—a splendid way to combine their skills. When Meston, the Aboriginal children from Bribie Island Mission and the members of the Aborigines Protection Society had their photograph taken in the Brisbane Botanic Gardens, Purcell was there assisting.[138] Although Meston's motivations are relatively clear, Purcell's reason for joining the Aborigines Protection Society was never recorded.

They travelled together to Townsville on the SS *Wodonga* in December (see Chapter 3).[139] Their agreement, 'a deed of partnership prepared by A. J. Thynne', was apparently signed in late 1891.[140] Although Meston and Purcell may have met by chance, the hunger of both men for quick

---

133 The first reviews of Meston's *Railway Guide* appeared in April 1891. See: *Telegraph*, 16 April 1891, 2; *Brisbane Courier*, 17 April 1891, 6. See also: 'Men We Mark No 5' (cartoon), showing Archibald Meston 'Railway Guide, Philosopher and Friend of the Blackfellow', satire of the *Queenslander's* 'Men of Mark' series, in the *Boomerang*, 23 May 1891, 10.
134 'Advertising', *Morning Bulletin*, 21 February 1891, 1.
135 Insolvency File, PURCELL, Brabazon Harry, QSA ITM1060489.
136 Ibid.
137 Ibid.
138 'Bribie Island Aboriginals', *Telegraph* (Brisbane), 12 October 1891, 2.
139 'Shipping News. Arrivals', *Northern Mining Register*, 9 December 1891, 14.
140 Insolvency File, PURCELL, Brabazon Harry, QSA ITM1060489.

financial gain (and their shared ignorance of the pitfalls, costs, risks and adverse ethical impacts associated with any touring entertainment venture) meant they had no difficulties in persuading each other that 'Wild Australia' would definitely succeed.

In December 1891, Meston announced his intention to visit 'Europe, and America, on a lecturing tour with his troupe of picked aboriginals'. Purcell, now described as 'his partner', was west of Boulia 'among the Kalkadoon tribes, five or six of whom he will bring down to the coast. He is also making a complete ethnological collection from the blacks of the far west' (see Chapter 3).[141] Purcell's first recruiting expedition took him into familiar territory, giving him the opportunity to visit old friends while Meston organised the Sydney shows.

Meston and Purcell, motivated by financial interests, clearly believed that they could make money from this scheme. Meston repeatedly said the troupe 'cost him a lot': 'I am powerless to do anything having expended all I had and even left my family short of funds.'[142] He went on: 'The total cost of collecting the blacks, and weapons, and purchasing scenery and outfit was borne by me alone, and represents an expenditure of over £1000.'[143] In April 1893, he wrote to amateur ethnologist A. W. Howitt about Purcell: 'had I never seen him I would have been at least a couple of thousand pounds better and been saved a heap of misery'.[144] The tour coincided with an economic depression, which was a contributing factor in its failure, but Meston continually blamed Purcell, describing him as 'an unfortunate choice of partner with whom it was impossible for me to continue'.[145]

After the troupe returned to Queensland in the middle of 1893 (see Chapter 10), Purcell resumed his previous life, working with horses and cattle, and writing occasional letters to the newspapers.[146] He wrote

141 'Meston's Party', *Cairns Post*, 30 December 1891, 2. The Boulia district was not the territory of the Kalkadoon people.
142 B. H. Purcell to A. Meston, Colonial Secretary's Office, Inwards Correspondence, QSA ITM847483, 1893/12837.
143 'Sundry Shows', *Bulletin*, 25 March 1893, 6.
144 Howitt Papers, Museums Victoria, MV/XM259. In 1895, Meston said the troupe cost him '£1200 and two years of valuable time'. See: 'The Case of the Aborigines', *Queenslander*, 14 September 1895, 503.
145 A. Meston to colonial secretary, 12 June 1893, Colonial Secretary's Office, Inwards Correspondence, QSA ITM847483, 1893/6869.
146 'Tax on Stallions', *Brisbane Courier*, 17 September 1894, 6; 'The Horse Industry', *Queenslander*, 20 July 1895, 128; 'On Spaying Mares', *Australasian*, 29 February 1896, 7.

about stock diseases and offered his experiences of possible cures.[147] Perhaps as a result of his experiences with the Wild Australia troupe, he also gained the confidence to write about frontier violence.

In his short story 'Only a Pair of Boots', a character named George Johnstone moved further west after he found the Darling River 'becoming too civilised' and dealt with an attack by Aboriginal men on an isolated station and the subsequent reprisals.[148] It would be illuminating to know how much of the story was based on Purcell's own experiences and if he had ever participated in violent punitive expeditions. Brabazon Purcell died after a stroke at Toowoomba Hospital in March 1904.[149] He was 47 years old.

Conclusion

As this chapter has shown, Meston and Purcell used their networks and supporters to organise and deliver the Wild Australia Show. Their aims and hopes were mixed. In 1895, Meston declared:

> My primary object was to raise a fund with which to inaugurate
> a scheme for the benefit of the aboriginals, to show what could be
> done and leave the Government to extend and continue.

However, this may have been a justification for the fiasco dreamed up after the event.[150] Purcell never ventured his reasons.

The analysis of Meston's life course in the Cairns region leaves no doubt about his negative values and hostilities concerning Aboriginal people, but he achieved a complete reversal of this position in 1891 when he joined the Aborigines Protection Society. Why did the leopard change its spots? Was it purely self-interest or genuine curiosity and concern? Purcell, on the other hand, had been employed as a bushman and bush traveller and had built a knowledge of the inland frontier territories in the 1870s and 1880s; as such, he was familiar with the 'good' and the 'bad' among both Aboriginal people and the European settlers in the backblocks.

---

147 'Inoculation for Pleuro-Pneumonia', *Brisbane Courier*, 22 January 1894, 3; 'The Tick Pest', *Brisbane Courier*, 30 March 1898, 7; 'The Tick Question', *Brisbane Courier*, 10 June 1898, 7.
148 'Only a Pair of Boots', *Queenslander*, 23 December 1893, 1222.
149 QBDM, Death Certificate, 1904/C1094.
150 'The Case of the Aborigines', *Queenslander*, 14 September 1895, 503.

Meston's experiences in business and politics had been failures, but his determination to carve his own niche in the colonial economy was almost unstoppable. Purcell's background as a cattle drover and horse dealer suggests that he had much more experience with Aboriginal people than Meston had, but he was equally incompetent in business. Their 'accidental' and 'ill-fated' partnership obviously came about after they each had joined the Aborigines Protection Society and participated in the 1891 excursion from Bribie Island to Brisbane. From that seemingly incidental event, the idea for what would become the 'Wild Australia Show' was seeded.

ACT I
RECRUITING

3

In the borderlands

Paul Memmott

The recruitment of the Wild Australia Show performers commenced in late November 1891 and was undertaken in a series of steps stretching over almost a year. By October 1892, the troupe destined to tour was assembled in Brisbane to begin their training and rehearsal for Meston's Wild Australia Show (see Chapter 7). The itineraries taken by Brabazon Purcell and, to a lesser extent, Meston for reconnaissance and recruitment can be roughly pieced together by drawing on newspaper accounts and some correspondence, complemented by later evidence given at a court case that reprised details of the disastrous enterprise (see Chapter 10).

Recruitment journeys were taken by ship, on horseback and wagon, and by train. And they involved various local agents who facilitated the business partners' efforts to secure performers for their anticipated and announced world tour. By retracing the journeys taken to recruit performers, describing the country and regions traversed, and the camps, stations and settlements visited in the process, it is possible to glean the contexts experienced by the troupe members at the time they either volunteered or were commandeered to join the scheme. Frustratingly, Purcell's accounts of his encounters and interactions with potential and future troupe members, and his methods for convincing them to 'sign on', are fragmentary at best, but nevertheless they suggest something about how the troupe ultimately came together. And this has bearing, we believe, on the ways in which the Wild Australia Show troupe would come to function as a fairly cohesive group while on tour.

Beyond briefly introducing all the troupe members, our aim across this chapter and the following three is to situate the performers in their ancestral Countries at the time they joined the troupe. We are interested in understanding the conditions, both past and present, that they and their kin faced when the prospect of travelling the world was presented to them. We begin in northwest Queensland, on the border with the Northern Territory of South Australia, since this was the first region Purcell visited looking for potential recruits. In subsequent chapters we follow him to the Gulf of Carpentaria (Chapter 4) and into the Torres Strait (Chapter 5). We also travel into Kabi Kabi Country around the Mary River north of Brisbane (Chapter 6), but without Purcell, since this is where the last troupe member, a man known as Bob (or Yamurra), hailed from. He joined the troupe, we surmise, at Archibald Meston's invitation.

In each region, we pay attention to local circumstances because our conviction is that such a focus can take us closer to understanding—or at the very least to speculating plausibly—about the possible motivations for young and not-so-young men and women to throw in their lot in with Mr 'Brab' Purcell. Or if throwing their lot in suggests a high degree of individual freedom that they probably did not enjoy on the rough and violent pastoral frontier that was north and northwest Queensland in the late nineteenth century, then we may learn something of the nature of their vulnerability in being swept up in the speculators' plan. Some were volunteers; others, loyal partners who were prepared to accompany their mates. Still others were innocent bystanders—or simply short on other options. Their varied circumstances remind us to be sensitive to a plurality of local historical and cultural contexts when writing histories of Indigenous performers and performances working and touring under colonial conditions.

From Brisbane bound for North Queensland

As Chapter 2 explained, Brabazon Harry Purcell was a junior partner in Meston's Wild Australia Show project. He had been promised a third share of the profits. While Meston sought financial backers, Purcell's primary role at the outset was to collect artefacts and recruit performers from the frontiers of outback Queensland. The business agreement the two men struck included that Meston would pay all of Purcell's travel expenses. Once the plan was hatched, Purcell set out almost immediately to try to locate people willing to join a troupe for a world tour. Recalling the circumstances several years later, he explained that:

On November 16th 1891 Mr A. Meston agreed with me to select
and get together a troupe of aboriginals for a tour round the world
…With that intention I started from Brisbane with him on the
28th November 1891 for Cloncurry and the west.[1]

When Purcell struck out, it seems that Meston was probably already
booked to leave Brisbane bound for Cairns on that same day.[2] He had
plans to revisit Mount Bellenden Ker with two Italian men, Giovanni
Podenzana and Ruggiero Schiffini, whom the newspapers described as
scientists and collectors. Signor Pondezana is known for his extensive
ethnographic collection acquired in Australia and Japan, and now
housed in the G. Podenzana Civic Ethnographic Museum (Museo Civico
Etnografico G. Podenzana) in La Spezia. That trio disembarked at Cairns
on 3 December 1891, and five days later they had ventured forth with
a couple of 'Kanaks' to climb the peak. They were away for about a week,
mainly collecting 'rare birds' and 'new fruits'.[3] Limited evidence hints that
there was an understanding that Meston would conscript some performers
and collect artefacts from the rainforest region, but this does not appear to
have happened.

Meston and the two Italians remained in the northern rainforest region for
all of December 1891 and January 1892. On 19 December, according to
one report, they went shooting for two days on the Lower Barron River.
Their itinerary then included the Barrier Reef Islands by boat from Cairns,
followed by a week on the Russell River, before going to the upper Barron
River and the Chillagoe Caves. If Meston had intended to conscript troupe
members from the rainforest peoples, he failed to deliver, but he most
likely augmented the supply of artefacts for the tour since we know he was
assisting the Italians to procure artefacts and a number of rainforest shields
were among the stage props used by performers once they began performing
the Wild Australia Show.

Purcell might well have been a late addition to the SS *Wodonga*'s passenger
list, simply tagging along with Meston once they had agreed to pursue
their scheme. While the arrival of Meston and the Italian sojourners in

---

1   Readers are advised that some quotations contain terms and phrases that are no longer in common
use, and that are likely to be considered racist and to cause offence. That is not our intention. These
terms and phrases are retained within quotations from archival material for the purpose of demonstrating
historical ideas and attitudes only. B. H. Purcell to colonial secretary, 21 July 1893, Colonial Secretary's
Office, Inwards Correspondence, QSA ITM847483, 1893/8474.

2   Meston is listed separately (with the two Italians) from Purcell in printed passenger lists.

3   'Shipping', *Australasian*, 29 August 1891, 1; 'Meston's Party', *Cairns Post*, 30 December 1891, 2.

Cairns was daily anticipated by the local press and then enthusiastically announced once they arrived,[4] Purcell's movements received no coverage. As the 'explorers' established a base in Cairns, Purcell seems to have travelled west from Townsville by train to Hughenden, the terminus at the time, and then caught the coach service on to Cloncurry and thence to Boulia (before returning via the same route). Starting out at Cloncurry in early December, he went from pastoral run to pastoral run in a north–south traverse along the Georgina River close to the Queensland – South Australia (now Northern Territory) border. This region of the western Queensland frontier had only been permanently settled since the 1870s.[5] To the west there were no settlers until the Overland Telegraph Line, some 500–600 kilometres away, was well established. Traditionally oriented Aboriginal people were still moving between their tribal lands in the deserts lying to the west and the semi-sedentary camps on the border region pastoral stations.

An account of Purcell's whereabouts on Christmas Day 1891, and in the early new year, came to light some 11 months later upon the publication of a detailed account he wrote about the implementation of bore technology on far western Queensland stations. The article reveals that he spent Christmas Day with the manager of Goodwood Station and his wife. That station was situated close to Boulia but within an aggregate of leases forming a much larger property (Goodwood, Warenda, Fort William). After Christmas, Purcell accompanied the manager, W. Cush, on a tour of all the newly sunk bores, recording in the process an account of their depths, strata, flows and casing technologies. Purcell also reported on successful new bores on Sandringham, Roxborough and Carandotta stations, although it is unclear if he actually visited all these places. In producing this report, one of his few published works,[6] he seems to have been distracted from the Wild Australia Show undertaking. But it could have been a useful way of being guided around the local region and learning of the various Aboriginal pastoral station camps.

---

4   'General News', *Cairns Post*, Wednesday 18 November 1891, 2, reports that Meston and two Italians were heading to Cairns on 'Saturday next'. 'Shipping. Departures', *Brisbane Courier*, Monday 30 November 1891, 3, has B. H. Purcell listed on the same ship with A. Meston and two Italians on 28 November, bound for Cooktown via ports. Meston and the two Italians disembarked from SS *Wodonga* in Cairns on Thursday 3 December; it is, however, likely that Purcell had left the ship earlier, perhaps at Townsville or Rockhampton. Once in Cairns, Meston and the two Italian travellers departed for Bellenden Ker on 8 December 1891.

5   H. Fysh, *Taming the North* (Sydney: Angus and Robertson, 1950). See also: article on Warenda Station by H. G. Lamond in *Walkabout* 21, no. 2 (1955): 38, 41, 42.

6   B. H. Purcell, 'Artesian Water in the Far West. Irrigation in the Interior', *Queenslander*, 26 November 1892, 1052.

A brief press report on Purcell's progress, published on 3 February 1892, locates him on the Georgina River, and tells of a recruited troupe member who was seven feet (210 cm) tall 'of magnificent physique, handsome, but melancholy cast of countenance, and is the boss fighter of his tribe—the well-known Calcadoons [Kalkadoon/Kalkadungu]'.[7] The man's height was a topic to tantalise readers:

> With regard to the native giant, which Mr Purcell was reported to have discovered, and who was stated to be over seven feet high, he informs us that, although himself above the ordinary height, he had to throw back his head to see the eyes of the enormous aboriginal.

By June, the 'giant' had been excluded from the enterprise:

> Unfortunately, owing to the state of the native's health, Mr Purcell found that it would be impossible to take him away, and he was reluctantly compelled to leave him behind.[8]

Another report on early progress to recruit performers comes from press accounts of a telegram that Meston received from Purcell in early April 1892. By that time, Purcell had 'been five months travelling over the far Northwest, collecting ethnological specimens and obtaining accurate information concerning the habits and customs of the wild and comparatively unknown tribes'. It continued:

> He has just returned to Urandangie from a long journey into the Northern Territory of South Australia. Besides weapons and all available articles of interest Mr. Purcell has secured some fine specimens of wild blacks, including the famous Calcadoonas, the tribe of all others most interesting to science.[9]

These two reports are clearly based on Purcell's telegrams from Urandangie. They are typical of much of the journalistic commentary that sought to sensationalise the Wild Australia Show venture by dwelling on a human of large proportions and a preoccupation with the Kalkadungu, who had gained a fierce fighting reputation through their guerrilla warfare against settlers between 1878 and 1885. The reports also confirm that Meston stipulated only very fit people be conscripted, people who embodied the physically demanding hunter-gatherer lifestyle that the Wild Australia Show was designed to exhibit.

---

7   'Local and General', *Northern Mining Register* (Charters Towers), 3 February 1892, 5.
8   'A Trip to the Far West', *Northern Mining Register*, 8 June 1892, 35.
9   'Current News. By Telegraph and Otherwise', *Queenslander*, 9 April 1892, 710.

Purcell's travel itinerary can then be traced for a few days through the diary of John Costello of Lake Nash Station. The Lake Nash cattle station was situated on the border between Queensland and the Northern Territory of South Australia, some 450 kilometres along a rough road north of Boulia. Costello was a pastoralist who established new stations on the expanding pastoral frontier during the mid-nineteenth century, initially in the Cooper Creek – Diamantina River region in the mid-1860s and 1870s, and thence in the southwest Gulf of Carpentaria in the mid-1880s. He purchased Lake Nash in 1879, placing a manager there and sometimes spending time there himself.[10] In 1891, he moved his family from 'The Valley of the Springs' on the Limmin River near Borroloola to Lake Nash, which was on the telegraph line from Camooweal to Urandangie (the terminus). They remained there for several years.[11]

Costello's references in his daily diary to Purcell are brief but illuminating, suggesting that the latter was at that time more intent on collecting 'curios' than recruiting performers:

5/4/1892:

Went down to Urandangie this morning had lunch and got the mail. Got back to Headingly in the evening. Saw Purcell—Meston's partner who is gathering curios.

10/4/1892:

Meston's partner—Purcell—arrived here today. He is gathering blacks' curios for an aboriginal exhibition, which they are going to take around the world.

11/4/1892:

Purcell trading with the blacks for curios. His show should be a success in America & England.

14/4/1892:

Purcell—Meston's partner went away today—he obtained a few curios from the blacks they will start the show in August.[12]

10   'Intercolonial', *Week*, 2 August 1879, 6.

11   M. M. J. Costello, *Life of John Costello* (Sydney: Dymock's Book Arcade, 1930); C. Lynch, 'Mr and Mrs John Costello', in *North Queensland Pioneers*, comp. J. Black (Charters Towers: North Queensland Newspapers for Country Women's Association, 1932).

12   Item 11, John Costello diary, in McClure Family Papers, mainly of George C. A. M'Clure, 1823–1828, 1856–1910, MLMSS 465, SLNSW.

A more detailed report published in the *Northern Mining Register* suggests the same, noting that 'Mr Purcell, after leaving Cloncurry, in December last, made his way to Buckingham Downs and then to Warenda Station. At the latter place, he obtained a few native weapons'. Later, in relation to his time in 'Pituri country', it notes: 'While in this part of the country, Mr Purcell succeeded in gathering together a considerable portion of his collection, in addition to various weapons obtained at Idamere and Kahlo [Carlo].' The collection was described as 'really magnificent and varied', consisting of spears, boomerangs, fighting sticks, shields, stone axes, stone knives and sandals from the 'Workii' (Wakaya) and 'Ullawarrie' (pres. Alyawarr) and ritual objects made of shells, bone pointers in a hollow pelican bone sheath, string bags and fabric, belts of human hair, possum fur tassels, stone adze and kangaroo-skin waterbag. There is also mention of lizards, reptiles, birds, bird feathers, herbs, plants and grasses, as well as many more items anticipated to arrive from many other corners of the Northern Territory.[13] One of the enduring mysteries of the Wild Australia Show is what happened to the collections that Purcell assembled during his first reconnaissance trip.

The report in the *Northern Mining Register*, which covers the period from November 1891 to June 1892, continued by listing other stations and places that Purcell visited, although it must have puzzled some local readers who were familiar with the region since the route seems to zig zag. It takes him from Herbert Downs up the Georgina River to Idamere (now Glenormiston) before heading further west from Kahlo (Carlo) into Wakaya Country. After leaving Lake Nash, Purcell reportedly headed along the Field and Hay rivers.

This, and other sources, suggests that Purcell made forays in three directions: one traverse started from Boulia and was to the west to Glenormiston Station (then named 'Idamere') and further west to the Toko Waterhole in the Toko Range, thence across the border to the vicinity of the headwaters of a small creek (Linda Creek) that floods out into the Simpson Desert. The second traverse was to the south of Glenormiston to Carlo Station and the headwaters of the Mulligan Creek where the habitats of the pituri plant (*Duboisia hopwoodii*) occur. The third and by far the longest traverse was up the mid-reaches of the Georgina River to Urandangie, Lake Nash and thence to the upper branches of either the Ranken or Georgina rivers. What is interesting in the account are the observations on the environmental

---

13   'A Trip to the Far West'.

conditions he witnessed: the dry conditions 'as very little rain had fallen' in the first and second regions compared with the better seasonal conditions he saw during his third traverse, which he described as 'splendid'.[14]

During his travels, Purcell was learning about local environments, particularly the regions where pituri grows. The pastoralists presumably assisted him to gain specialist knowledge of the Aboriginal 'pituri culture', some of which he conveyed to the press by telegram from Boulia (or perhaps Cloncurry). He would later capitalise on his firsthand experience of the primary pituri-growing habitat when the Wild Australia Show tour started by giving lectures on this topic (see Chapter 7). He found that the pituri habitat was largely restricted to a relatively small region, where it grew in small clumps on the crests of the parallel sand ridges. In describing it, he provided a number of Aboriginal placenames in this district and was able to explain how pituri was prepared for consumption, including the other additives applied when chewing it for medicinal use or sustenance during travel or simply for pleasure:

> The narcotic was used by the Urania tribes, whose centre was Toko, and by the Momamworas, and the Urrunderas. The Workis were responsible for sending the pitchery up the Rankin and James Rivers, and had special messengers for barter, who secured all they could. It was also sent to the Seymour and O'Shaughnessey Rivers.[15]

These groups have been identified more accurately by anthropologists and linguists as the Yuranya or Antekerrepenh (Purcell's 'Urania') in the Toko region, who were close trading partners with the Arrernte to the west (Purcell's 'Urunderas') and the Alyawarr to the northwest (Purcell's 'Ullawarrie'). The Wakaya (his 'Workis') were a northern trading group who travelled down the Georgina from its headwaters. Purcell was soon to encounter one of its leaders, who would be the first to commit to the Wild Australia Show venture. The detailed report in the *Northern Mining Register* explains how his recruitment drive was progressing once he had encountered the Wakaya:

---

14   Ibid.
15   'Meetings. Royal Society of New South Wales', *Sydney Morning Herald*, 20 January 1893, 6.

> The natives Mr Purcell has been gathering together, are now in a camp near the border. He will probably, however, only pick six from the number, four boys and two gins. They will belong to the Workii and the Calcadoon tribes. The boys are all Mickas [high-level initiated men], healthy and of fine physique.[16]

As in much of Purcell's writing, geographic accuracy is often suspect and wanting. Purcell refers to the 'Ullawarrie tribe who frequent the McDonald [Macdonnell] ranges' but he was never any closer than 250 kilometres to these ranges, and it is more likely that these people were Alyawarr[17] from the Sandover River and Davenport Ranges, southwestern neighbours of the Wakaya. Both of these groups were known to come into the perennial Georgina River waterholes for trade and ceremony, including Lake Nash, which lay in Bularnu Country.[18]

In Purcell's official account of his trip provided later in correspondence to the Queensland colonial secretary, he wrote of his western traverse over the border upon leaving Boulia:

> then left for the Georgina River secured 4 men 2 women of the Arania tribe Linda Creek Northern Territory, S.A. [South Australia]. One man was a noted murderer and I was specially requested to remove him. He showed hostility to the driver of my van [wagonette][19] but after securing [him] to another [man, they] escaped that same evening. I took the others along and found that the men and women remaining were related so allowed them to depart.[20]

The then manager of Idamere was Jeremiah Coghlan, who was later to strongly criticise Purcell over this incident, accusing him of 'using force in securing the blacks' and said that he used handcuffs and leg-irons.[21]

---

16   'A Trip to the Far West'.

17   Also written as Alyawarra, Alyawarre and Illauira in the ethnographic literature. The Macdonald Ranges are to the west of the Simpson Desert in the vicinity of the Alice Springs Telegraph Station.

18   W. Roth, *Ethnological Studies among the North-West-Central Queensland Aborigines* (Brisbane: Government Printer, 1897), 134–5; P. Memmott, M. Langton and J. Stead, *Wakaya/Alyawarra Claim Book, Including Anthropologist's Report, History of Cultural Change* (Alice Springs: Central Land Council, 1988).

19   Square brackets in quoted correspondence indicates uncertainty about making the correct transcription of words given the difficulties of reading handwritten correspondence.

20   B. H. Purcell to colonial secretary, 21 July 1893, informing him of his association with A. Meston concerning Aborigines in north, west and south Queensland, Colonial Secretary's Office, Inwards Correspondences, QSA ITM847483, 1893/8474.

21   J. Coghlan, Glennormiston, to McDonald, police magistrate, Boulia, Colonial Secretary's Office, Inwards Correspondences, QSA ITM847483, 1892/9589.

(Coghlan was also to become an important collector of artefacts for the Queensland Museum.) In his defence against Coghlan's charges, Purcell was to write:

> I returned to Northern Territory where I found others willing to come away and after taking them before Michael Costello Esq. J.P., S.A. [John Costello's son] who explained to them what they were wanted for I brought them into Cloncurry and eventually to Brisbane delivering to Mr Meston together with a large number of curios weapons.[22]

It is informative that Purcell thought it appropriate to go before a justice of the peace when he 'secured' a second contingent of performers after he had let the first go. As he wrote in July 1893, some 20 months after he entered into partnership with Meston to form the Wild Australia Show venture:

> after some months and before collecting any aboriginals I wired Meston to get 'Government permission' for removal of any blacks in this colony to the coast. He replied on the 7th June 1892 to Boulia 'Colonial Secretary says no permission required except leave colony take your time no hurry best wishes A. Meston, Brisbane'.[23]

Purcell's actions at the time, and the subsequent criticisms of him, reveal the ways in which kidnapping, enslaving and other forms of forced removal were features of the Queensland frontier in this period, and, moreover, that there were divided views about the ways in which Aboriginal 'workers' should be treated. Over the next few years, in the lead-up to the passing of the *Aboriginals Protection and Restriction of the Sale of Opium Act 1897*, there was vigorous debate on the rights and wrongs of Aboriginal people being used as slave labour on pastoral properties, as amply reported by various newspaper correspondents.

Aside from this larger issue of the particular methods that Purcell used to convince Aboriginal people in this northwest region to join him, and whether he had any authority at all for what he was engaged in, more mundanely, it indicates that he spent at least seven months trying to fulfil Meston's remit. During that half year, he travelled, reconnoitred, observed, acquired artefacts and encountered many people, before finally transporting the first contingent of troupe members—five in number—back to the coast.

---

22   B. H. Purcell to colonial secretary, 21 July 1893, Colonial Secretary's Office, Inwards Correspondence, QSA ITM847483, 1893/8474.
23   Ibid.

This was not, however, the end of his time in this region. In early July 1892, Purcell returned to Lake Nash and his visit there was again recorded in John Costello's diary entries, although the exact purpose of his visit in relation to conscripting the Wakaya group is unclear. Had he returned to retrieve the collection he had assembled? Was he hoping to recruit more performers? Or both? With his usual brevity, Costello noted:

3/7/1892:
Purcell arrived today with wagonette getting his collection together.

6/7/1892:
Purcell went away today, but did not succeed in getting any blacks. He went up the river and will probably be back in a few days.[24]

How was Purcell travelling and living during his lengthy period in the colonial borderlands? We have little reported information on this, although Paul Memmott's many decades working in the same region helps to inform our interpretation. What we do know is that Purcell had a history of travelling in the backblocks of New South Wales and Queensland, as covered in Chapter 2, as a drover and a stock agent. Through this experience, he understood the mores of the colonial bushman and of the Aboriginal pastoral worker. Indeed, his social capital in the homesteads and small town frontier establishments would have been his knowledge of horses and cattle, stock movements and sale prices, and his repertoire of personal experiences and adventures. This would have elicited hospitality from some station owners to reside overnight and dine with them at their homesteads, as he did with Mr Cush of Goodwood. But there would have been others who took a dislike to him because of the nature of his mission, and Mr Coghlan of Glenormiston appears to fall into this category. John Costello's attitude towards him is harder to detect from his brief and neutral records.

Racism and hatred of Aboriginal people were rife, dividing pastoralists between good and bad in the eyes of both Aboriginal survivors and pastoral communities. When Purcell was doing his rounds, it was only seven years since the Kalkadungu guerrilla war (1878–85) in and around the Northwest Highlands. It was eventually quelled by the Native Police under the leadership of Inspector Urquhart with support from a posse of pastoralists, led by the Scottish pastoralist Alexander Kennedy, who was intent on

24   Item 11, John Costello diary, in McClure Family Papers, mainly of George C. A. M'Clure, 1823–1828, 1856–1910, MLMSS 465, SLNSW.

taking numerous leases over the Kalkadungu's mountainous territories.[25] At the end of this warfare, there were very few Aboriginal people living in the bush: it was simply too dangerous with patrols of Native Police pursuing campaigns of violent dispersal. Local tribespeoples who had not fled vast distances had to resign themselves to a life in sedentarised pastoral camps as slave labour, working as stockmen, fence builders, bore pumpers, axemen, station butchers, domestics and cooks. In return they received basic rations of tea, sugar, flour and tobacco, simple clothes and the offal and discarded parts of cattle after butchering for the white pastoral workers, and secured station protection from assaults and harassment, including from the Native Police.

It was to the various pastoral camps that Purcell would have gone in a bid to barter for artefacts for the tour. For this purpose, he would have purchased a basic set of gifts and trading commodities from the Cloncurry and Boulia stores, choosing relatively lightweight things such as pipes, tobacco, penknives, tomahawks, cheap jewellery, bright cloths and useful leather items. It is likely that he stockpiled bundles of artefacts at several stations and towns, and returned towards the end of his mission (i.e. July 1892) with a hired wagon to transport both people and traded goods. While travelling between stations on horseback, and probably with an additional packhorse, he would have drawn on his acquired bush skills, sleeping out in the open in a swag, shooting game for meat and cooking on an open fire. He would have come to distinguish the subjugated Aboriginal camp people of western Queensland from the still traditionally living desert Aboriginal people coming from over the South Australian border and travelling back and forth across the frontier. The latter included the Wakaya, whom he encountered in the Georgina River Aboriginal trading camps on particular stations, including Lake Nash. These were the type of 'human specimens' that best fitted Meston's brief to enlist 'Wild Australians'!

---

25   Fysh, *Taming the North*.

Enter Kudajarnd

Kudajarnd and his party came off the edge of the red-sand spinifex desert plain, Country of the eastern Wakaya people, and, taking a sip of water from their kangaroo-skin waterbag, rested under a clump of Acacia trees. He commented on being able to smell the scent of the long lake of Ilpirrereleleleme even though it was still a half day's walk away. Kudajarnd's two wives drank first, Langinkab, the elder wife, then Kulindab, who was not full Wakaya like the others but also Indjalandji of the upper Georgina River people proper. The two women then passed the bag over to Kudajarnd's brother-in-law, Narinbu, and Narinbu's son Dangakura. The latter two came from the estate [or Country] of Kurntubulangu, of Emu and Wild Orange Dreaming, on the top of what white people were now calling the Ranken River and where a white man's run or station named Soudan was formed. Langinkab, being Narinbu's brother, was also from this Country. Kudajarnd himself was boss for the next Country down the river, Juwanyingera, which was Rain and Devil Dreaming. Narinbu began straightening his spear shafts, forecasting the catch of a fat red kangaroo as they approached the lake that lay within the Georgina River. He wished to present his father-in-law, Pipakarinya, with fresh meat upon their arrival at the lakeside camp; it would bring happiness to his mother-in-law. Out of a string bag hung around his neck he took his unkwupiya, a short dowel, bound with human hair string, and inserted it into his nasal septum to bring him hunting prowess.

As they rested, Kudajarnd began singing the Wantju song cycle of Pitungu, the Dreamtime Flying Fox. For it was under this tree in the ancient past that Pitungu first sighted the Nyumala or Rat ancestors of Ilperereleleleme, or Lake Nash as it was now called, the new name for the cattle station on the big lake to where the party were heading. Dangakura was joking about the cheeky Pitungu who was famous in the sacred histories for lustily stealing two adolescent sisters from Ilperereleleleme and repeatedly projecting them long distances with his woomera, which he hooked around their hair, and then flying after them.

The party moved on as they wished to reach the station camp before dark and greet their Wakaya relatives who had married into the local Bularnu people under the headship of Pipakarinya of the Nyumala [Rat] clan. Joyous laughter and shouting arose from the camp children when the party arrived under the big bloodwood trees, where the fat kangaroo was prepared for the ground oven. The party gazed with pleasure at the ducks and swans cruising at dusk on the lake's serene waters and the passing flocks of budgerigars. Freshly cooked yellowbelly fish, honey and water were assembled next to a warming fire for them, with sheets of bark to sit on. Pituri, the chewing drug, was then shared with coolabah ashes to flavour it.

All of the gossip was about a newly arrived white man named 'Brab' whose family name [Purcell] was too difficult to pronounce [there was no 'S' sound in local languages]. He was being hosted by the station Boss 'Cotello' [John Costello]. Brab was trading bush artefacts—boomerangs, spears, nets, feather tassels—from one and all in the camp in exchange for whitefella things— clothes, foods, tobacco, pocketknives. The Wakaya visitors would meet him the next day. Purcell had been informed of the imminent arrival of the Wakaya thanks to Pipakarinya explaining to him the meaning of the smoke signal that Kudajarnd had sent from the desert in the west on the previous day.

Kudajarnd slept contentedly as he was carrying authoritative message sticks on behalf of other Wakaya clan Elders that represented trading promissories, and it seemed he might be able to arrange profitable bargains from this white man. Little did he know that one of his message sticks would end up two years later in an English museum, or that Purcell was about to take his family group on the adventure of a lifetime, as members of Meston's Wild Australia Show!

Although there is little detailed written description about Purcell's interactions with Aboriginal people on the stations in this vicinity, it seems he encountered the Wakaya Elder Kudajarnd and his party at Lake Nash during this first artefact collecting and reconnaissance expedition undertaken in the early months of 1892. Based on Kudajarnd's 'Devil' (Arrenty) Dreaming (see later), we surmise he had (probably) travelled there from his Juwanyingera (Devil Dreaming) Country on the Ranken River,[26] which was then at the western limit of the colonial frontier. It lay on the eastern edge of the Wakaya Desert, as it is now known, and had not yet been crossed by European explorers, surveyors or pastoralists, and only partially circumnavigated.

While at or near Lake Nash Station, Purcell met one of the Wakaya people, quite probably one of Kudajarnd's party, who had travelled there to exchange two heavy spears and some boomerangs for as many trousers and shirts obtainable. This person was an agent for a third party '60 miles' to the west and was thus carrying a specially prepared message stick authorising

---

26   Juwanyingera was later identified and numbered as Estate 7 during preparation of the Wakaya land claim in the 1980s. It was not until 1980, when the Central Land Council in Alice Springs decided to mount a land rights claim over the vacant Wakaya Desert (unoccupied Crown land), that anthropological attention became systematically focused on what was once the Wakaya world. Paul Memmott was engaged as the senior anthropologist on the claim, which progressed throughout the 1980s involving literature research, fieldwork, preparation of court documents and an on-Country court hearing. This research is, for the most part, so far unpublished (although the documents are largely present in the public domain as court exhibits). See: Memmott, Langton and Stead, *Wakaya/Alyawarra Claim Book*.

their travel for the purpose of trade, a customary practice. The distance of '60 miles west of Lake Nash' (some 96 km) could have placed the origin of the Wakaya sender of the message stick in the Juwanyingera estate on the Ranken River. (The message stick in question, to the best of our knowledge, is in the collections of the Pitt Rivers Museum.)

When its path crossed with Purcell's, Kudajarnd's party was probably intent on travelling downstream along the Georgina River's traditional Aboriginal trade route, possibly as far as the Toko Waterhole, an important Rain Dreaming centre and trading camp, from which the Wakaya would procure the customary drug pituri. Although we cannot be certain, the available evidence does suggest that Purcell arranged to rendezvous with Kudajarnd and his group some time (measured in moons) later, and indeed he returned to collect them around late July or early August 1892. By whatever means, he had established a relationship with them, and convinced them, somehow or other, to join him.

Locating the Wakaya: Contact history in Wakaya Country

The Wakaya (also spelt in the early literature as 'Workii' and 'Akaya'), as they were known regionally, occupied a desert and surrounding country in the central east of what is now the Northern Territory. Their territory included the Frew River, Walkabout and Whistleduck creeks in the west, the Ranken River and Lorne Creek in the east, the internal drainage basin of lakes Sylvester and Corella in the north, and the lower Elkedra River in the south. They actually referred to themselves as Wuka (hence a 'Wooka' tribe reference in a caption to one of the troupe photographs), which also had a feminine form, Wukarr.[27] In his notebooks, Meston renders the Wakaya as both 'Wooki' and 'Wakki', and as being 'west of Georgina River'. In a press report, he stated that:

> Three men and two women come from the Spinifex desert, west of the Georgina. They are from tribes which practise what is known by ethnologists as Sturt's terrible rite ... Those of the tribe on whom the

---

27 Gavin Breen, pers. comm., 6 January 2015; N. B. Tindale, *Aboriginal Tribes of Australia: Their Terrain, Environmental Controls, Distribution, Limits, and Proper Names* (Berkley: University of California Press, 1974), 236.

rite is not practised become a sort of hereditary priesthood. Mr B. H. Purcell was nine months after the north-west men, and it was a most difficult thing to induce them to come.[28]

Putting aside Meston's ethnographic errors, and warning the reader that what is being spoken about is a secretive and restricted men's ceremony that is still practised, what can be said is that 'Sturt's terrible rite' and the 'micka' refer to ceremonial penile subincision, a custom about which both Meston and Purcell wrote and lectured, and that the press sensationalised during the Wild Australia Show's tour.[29]

When Kudajarnd's group met Purcell at Lake Nash, the Wakaya and their neighbours had been encountering whitefellas travelling near their Country for at least three decades. In search of the missing Burke and Wills expedition, the first was William Landsborough and his exploration party, which came through in 1861 and 1862. Travelling southwest from the bottom of the Gulf of Carpentaria, they came to the upper Georgina River with its three large lakes, which Landsborough named Lake Mary, Lake Francis and Lake Canellan. As the sites of the Rainbow Serpent Dreaming, as well as the trading and ceremonial camps of the Indjalandji people who are the eastern neighbours of the Wakaya, these lakes were, of course, already amply named. As it was late December when Landsborough arrived, the lakes were full from the early summer rains, and there were large camps indicating an influx of visitors to this summertime, food-rich part of the interior.[30] As an adjacent tribal group, the Wakaya were regular visitors of the Indjalandji; they shared a tradition of intermarriage and had joint ceremonial interests, so it is feasible that Kudajarnd was present as a youth with his family at the Georgina lakes when Landsborough appeared. Juwanyingara Country on the Rankin River was just a three-day walk from the three lakes.

Landsborough's reports of the country to the west of the Georgina as magnificent open grassland plains catalysed an influx of new settlers, who brought herds of sheep. The first pastoral stations were established from 1864 to 1867 but had been abandoned by 1869 due to 'drought'.[31]

---

28   '"Wild Australia": Some Facts about the Natives. Aboriginals in Queensland—A Dying Race' [interview with A. Meston on the Wild Australia Show], *Daily Telegraph*, 9 January 1893, 4 (reproduced in *Brisbane Courier*, 11 January 1893, 6).
29   See, for example, 'Meston's Wild Aboriginals', *Sydney Mail*, 21 January 1893, 134, 135, 141.
30   W. Landsborough, *Journal of Landsborough's Expedition from Carpentaria, in Search of Burke & Wills* (Melbourne: F. F. Bailiere, 1862).
31   Memmott, Langton and Stead, *Wakaya/Alyawarra Claim Book*. There is a large literature about whether 'drought' is an applicable term.

They were, however, the forerunners to pastoral stations known later as Rocklands, Austral Downs (first called Stony Plains) and Roxbourgh on the Georgina, and Avon Downs on the intermediary tributary of the James River. As a boy, Kudajarnd would have witnessed the arrival of the new settlers and their animals. A widespread concern of the Aboriginal land managers was the bogging of drought-weakened sheep in the clayey basins of the waterholes as the waters receded and the attending pollution of these sacred sites with decaying carcasses.

It took until 1876 for settlers to return to the upper Georgina basin, and, gradually, over 10 years, to restock the old runs and form new ones. This time the impact on the waterholes was worse, as they brought large herds of cattle that trampled the edible plants along the edges of the waterholes. During this period, introduced European diseases caused the death of many Indjalandji and other Georgina people. They also faced the alarming danger of the Native Police, who had arrived at Boulia in 1878 under the command of Sub-Inspector Ernest Eglinton and were known to be shooting and hanging tribespeople of the Georgina both upstream and downstream, including the Warluwarra, Wangkayujuru, Pitta Pitta and the Wangkamanha. These groups were trading partners of the Wakaya who relied on them for many specialised goods that were not available in their own Countries.

When Kudajarnd completed his advanced higher levels of initiation in the 1880s and obtained his second wife, Kulindab, who was of both Wakaya and Indjalandji descent, it is probable that news was arriving from the east of the conflicts between Kalkadungu and Native Police, as the Kalkadungu adopted a style of guerrilla warfare that prevented white men easily taking their Country.[32] News was also coming from the west of a high string on poles built by white people through Kaydej and Warumungu Countries. This was the Overland Telegraph Line erected in 1872. New settlers followed the line up from Adelaide and spread laterally out from it to take up new runs, some of which encroached on western Wakaya Country. This was in the eastern half of the Davenport–Murchison complex of mountains, where perennial waterholes fed intermittent streams that flooded out into the Wakaya Desert. Three cattle stations were formed in this region during

---

32   Fysh, *Taming the North*.

the late 1880s: Murray Downs, Frew River and Elkedra. All of them were to be eventually abandoned due to severe droughts, the problem of getting cattle to the distant markets and sustained Wakaya hostility.[33]

Frew River Station was located inside the mountains, on the middle reach of the Frew River, in a western Wakaya estate known as Thethewe. The station site was at a large waterhole known as yithithuwiy in Wakaya and in Alyawarr as thethewa,[34] with Wallaby and Rainbow Snake Dreaming, and adjacent to an important initiation site. Downstream on the Frew and on Ti Tree Creek and thence north and east were Wakaya lands. The Warumungu tribal or language group were to the northwest on Kurundi Creek and beyond. To the south and southeast were Alyawarr lands. Members of all these groups regularly visited the Frew River for social, economic and ceremonial interaction. The major upland waterholes of the Frew River basin, like thethewa, were occupied and regularly polluted by cattle. This became an acute problem for Wakaya people during drought periods. Grass species with edible seeds were eaten and trampled by the cattle as well as other edible vegetable staples that grew around the waterholes. Sacred places like the elelaturu ceremony ground became isolated from their Aboriginal owners.[35]

The Wakaya retaliated by spearing cattle. The pastoralists were further infuriated by the burning of the grass plains by the hunters. No doubt some of these fires would have burnt out of control, destroying extensive areas of fodder. Pastoralists, therefore, saw reason for reprisals. Conflict escalated until the execution of bodily harm and murder was considered justifiable to many involved. This pattern of conflict was to continue spasmodically for some years. This especially occurred in the mountainous areas where an effective guerrilla war was carried out. Coulthard, the manager of Frew River Station, made several attempts to discourage cattle attacks but with little success.[36] The Wakaya attacked the Frew River Station in June 1891:

---

33   A. A. Davidson, *Journal of Explorations in Central Australia: By the Central Australian Exploration Syndicate, Limited, under the Leadership of Allan A. Davidson, 1898–1900* (Adelaide: Government Printer, 1905), 6; Memmott, Langton and Stead, *Wakaya/Alyawarra Claim Book*, 51.

34   Gavin Breen, pers. comm., 6 January 2015. The name 'thethew' or 'thithuwa' was well recognised by the new settlers. See, for example, D. J. Gordon, 'A Description of the Country to East of Barrow Creek', in *Our Land, Central Australia*, ed. J. Flynn (reproduced in *Inlander* 1 [1913–14]: 20).

35   Memmott, Langton and Stead, *Wakaya/Alyawarra Claim Book*, 52.

36   'Life in the Heart of Australia', *Adelaide Observer*, 11 July 1891, 34; Memmott, Langton and Stead, *Wakaya/Alyawarra Claim Book*, 53.

about sixty natives surrounded the station fully armed with intent on murdering those on the station. The dogs and lubra gave timely warning. Mr Coulthard called on his men to defend themselves. Three natives were then inside trying to entice the station boy away from the wurley to learn which of the white men slept, the remainder staying outside the fence waiting for the signal 'all clear'. Hearing Mr Coulthard call all three got outside, and Mr Coulthard fired, which dispersed the natives, they [sic] dropping the firesticks and dozens of spears, boomerangs etc. About midday the natives were seen on the hills looking to the action of the whites.[37]

The station bookkeeper suggested the attack was a reaction to police attempts to arrest the most troublesome of the cattle killers.[38]

Exactly six months after the Frew River conflict subsided, a number of Wakaya, led by Kudajarnd, travelled to Lake Nash, where they encountered 'Brab' Purcell and soon found themselves implicated in an unimaginable— or unprecedented—journey. Five of the future Wild Australia Show troupe thus identified as Wakaya, although, as we have shown, one of the women was of shared Wakaya–Indjalandji descent. The Wakaya contingent, led by the Elder Kudajarnd, became the Show's most publicised performers.

The Wakaya travel to the saltwater

In late July 1892, Purcell travelled back to Cloncurry with the five Wakaya troupe members, either by wagonette or coach, and thence to Hughenden, from where they caught the train to Townsville.[39] We can only imagine their emotional response to their first sighting of a steam train and riding in it. However, this was only the first of many encounters with the technologies of the new settlers. There was another unsettling experience: that of seeing the ocean for the first time with its peculiar behaviour of rising and falling tides and unknown mysterious creatures in its depths. Purcell was later to write:

> The blacks of the Spinifex Desert, the Wakii, have a superstitious dread of the ocean, as they imagine that their 'Aranja', or evil spirit dwells therein, and would get them if they went too near the sea … For this reason he had some difficulty in persuading them to

---

37 'Life in the Heart of Australia'.
38 Ibid.
39 'Local and General News', *Capricornian*, 13 August 1892, 20 (citing *Townsville Bulletin*, 8 August 1892).

accompany him on his tour. When they arrived at Townsville, and were asked to drink the salt water, they did so, but on finding it salt they covered their faces with their hands, repeating the word 'Aranja'. However, as soon as they saw that no dreadful results followed, even when they tasted the salt water, their fears were allayed.[40]

As mentioned earlier, 'Aranja' is a rendition of Arrentye, which means 'devil' or 'monster' in Arrerntic languages.[41] It is also a term used by the Wakaya and is a Dreaming associated with the Wakaya estate of Juwanyingera. From this estate, giant devils travelled east into Indjalandji Country, chasing crawling babies in the Dreamtime with an intent to consume them. There are many sacred histories involving this Devil Dreaming.

At this time, Townsville had a population close to 13,000 people with a bustling main street full of horse-drawn vehicles, a sight that must have surely made an impact on the Wakaya. But an even larger metropolis awaited—Brisbane—where they arrived a few days after leaving Townsville. Purcell and the Wakaya contingent caught the steamship *Arawatta* from Townsville, arriving at Brisbane on 3 August 1892. The SS *Arawatta* was a newly celebrated passenger steamship (built 1889). The five conscripts were publicised in the press as both 'Wahki' and 'Peture' tribe (i.e. Wakaya and Pituri).[42] As one report noted:

> Among the passengers by the *Arawatta* yesterday, was Mr. Brabazon Purcell, who has returned with the far north-west contingent of blacks from the famous Wahki tribe … the Australian tribe most interesting of all to the ethnologist. The men brought down are big, powerful fighting men, terribly scarred by the cuts of stone knives. They have arrived in perfect health, and survived their astonished fear of railways and steamers. Mr. Purcell also brings an entirely unique collection of weapons of the Stone Age, and many other new and rare ethnological specimens. Mr. Purcell returns at once for the North Coast blacks to complete the party.[43]

40   B. H. Purcell, 'The Aborigines of Australia', in *Royal Geographical Society of Australasia Transactions* (Victorian Branch) 11 (1894): 19.

41   J. Henderson and V. Dobson, *Eastern and Central Arrernte to English Dictionary* (Alice Springs: IAD Press, 1994), 247; J. Green, comp. *Alyawarr to English Dictionary* (Alice Springs: Institute for Aboriginal Development, 1992), 90.

42   'Local and General News'; 'Our Brisbane Letter', *Queensland Times, Ipswich Herald and General Advertiser*, 6 August 1892, 3.

43   'Our Brisbane Letter'.

Another newspaper explained that Purcell:

> sailed south on Monday in the *Arawatta*, a triumph of civilisation,
> by the way which astonished his aboriginals almost as much as the
> railway which conveyed them to the coast from Hughenden.[44]

Here we have a taste of the rhetorical and exaggerated statements being
made by journalists to suggest the superiority of European invention and
technology and playing on the trope of the encounter between supposed
'primitives' and modernity. The advertising spin for the future Wild
Australia Show had begun.

On 3 August 1892, Purcell arrived back in Brisbane briefly to 'deliver'
the Wakaya contingent to Meston. The *Capricornian* newspaper in
Rockhampton, citing the *Townsville Bulletin*, told its readers that Purcell
had returned 'from the interior' with '5 natives of the Northern Territory—
three men and two women—members of the "Piture" [Pituri] tribe, and an
interesting collection of native weapons and tools of all kinds'. It went on
to claim that: 'Mr. Purcell made himself thoroughly acquainted with the
language of this tribe, and then obtained from its members an immense
amount of information, especially their customs and traditions.'[45] This
information, readers were told, would be used in lectures during the tour
and would be of 'much scientific value' to anthropologists and folklorists.
This suggests the ways in which this group was critical to the Show and
were to be set apart for special study and scrutiny. Purcell's return from
the 'interior' with these men and women was reported with avid and
sensationalised interest.[46]

Conclusion

Earlier during Brabazon Purcell's journey, Queensland newspaper
journalists, probably as a result of Meston's press statements, had insisted on
sensationalising the prospect of his conscripting Kalkadoon performers, who
were by then famous for their frontier guerrilla warfare during 1879–85.
However, when Purcell returned to Brisbane after eight months in the
northwestern borderlands, it was not with Kalkadoon but five Wakaya, who
came from deep within the desert region of the Northern Territory of South

---

44 'Local and General News'.
45 Ibid.
46 Ibid.

Australia. The Wakaya were then engaged, as the Kalkadoon had been, in a frontier guerrilla war. During 1892 and 1893, it was being fought in the western Wakaya territory off the Overland Telegraph Line. Kudajarnd's group were eastern Wakaya, from closer to the Queensland border, where they had their traditional trading partners on the Georgina River. Of all the troupe members who were eventually conscripted, they were the closest to Meston's specification of coming from the 'wild' frontier. Their leader Kudajarnd was highly initiated in Aboriginal law and his status, along with his authoritative presence, was to permeate through the performances and portrayals of the troupe on tour. This group of five—three men and two women—likely lived temporarily with Meston and his family in South Brisbane (see Chapter 7) while Purcell returned to collect other conscripts who had been gathered together by local 'agents'. It is to them that we now turn.

4

In the Gulf of Carpentaria

Paul Memmott

After chaperoning the Wakaya contingent from the western Queensland border to Brisbane via Townsville and leaving them with Meston and his family, Brabazon Purcell had no time to linger. He arrived in Brisbane on 3 August and departed on 6 August 1892, again aboard the SS *Wodonga*. His destination this time was Normanton, and his mission was to collect a further contingent for the troupe from regions in the southern Gulf of Carpentaria.[1] Alighting for a brief stopover on Thursday Island, Purcell met John Douglas, the government resident in the Torres Strait, before travelling on to Normanton, arriving there on 25 August.[2] His entrance into the frontier town was met with a modicum of fanfare: 'Mr Purcell, of showman fame, has arrived [in Normanton] and is said to be collecting some aboriginals for his proposed show.'[3] With the publicised recruitment of the Wakaya, Meston and Purcell's enterprise was garnering notice, and their reputations as 'showmen' were building in parallel.

---

1   Readers are advised that some quotations contain terms and phrases that are no longer in common use, and that are likely to be considered racist and to cause offence. That is not our intention. These terms and phrases are retained within quotations from archival material for the purpose of demonstrating historical ideas and attitudes only. 'Today', *Brisbane Courier*, 5 August 1892, 4; 'Departures', 1892 *Brisbane Courier,* 8 August 1892, 3; 'Shipping News', *North Queensland Register* (Townsville), 17 August 1892, 41.
2   'Queensland News', *Northern Miner*, 25 August 1892, 2.
3   Ibid.

Purcell's time in the south of the Gulf was divided into parts. He first visited Normanton before moving on to Croydon. It is unclear how he conscripted the five troupe members from the Kimberley Town Camp at the mouth of the Norman River or the 11 from the town camps of Croydon, some 150 kilometres to the southeast of Normanton. But evidence suggests that Meston had made prior arrangements back in January 1892, as Purcell was to later report that he carried letters of introduction to local police magistrates. The recruitment of these two groups of mainly young men from the Gulf Country, a couple of whom brought partners with them, had been dependent upon the network of police that increasingly ruled Aboriginal people's lives in the northwest. The fact that Purcell was only very briefly in the region suggests that he was there to 'take delivery' of performers who had already 'agreed' to go.

Due to his connections in colonial Queensland, Meston probably knew that the police magistrate of Normanton was Philip Pears and that the police magistrate of Croydon was Fredrick Parkinson. He might also have encountered them when, as a young adult, he travelled extensively in northern New South Wales and across into southeast Queensland. Pears was from Unumgar Station near Mt Lindesay, and, within two years of each other in the early 1870s, both he and Meston had ascended that mountain. Parkinson had been sugar farming at Beenleigh in the later 1860s. As younger men, he and Meston had been attracted to two young attractive sisters living at the Coomera Store and Post Office. Parkinson was to marry one; Meston's fate was to write about them in later life.[4]

---

4   J. Richards, 'Croydon and Normanton Policing up to 1892', Aboriginal Environments Research Centre, University of Queensland [unpublished manuscript].

Enter Yungkwa

'Left-hand Charlie, sub-inspector want talk you. Come.'

Yungkwa still had anxiety, fear and grief in his body when dealing with a native policeman so he did not hesitate to obey this instruction to him, despite its brevity. He climbed on the wagonette with the three armed black para-military. Normanton was a two-hour trip by wagon to the wharf, then by steam boat up the Norman River, so he grabbed his billy can of water, his blanket, a spare pair of trousers, tobacco, pipe and some cooked barramundi wrapped in paperbark. The wagonette then went to several other humpies in the Aboriginal camp at the Norman [River] Mouth Telegraph Station camp, where the three Native Police sought after Yungkwa's cousin-brother Jerang and his full cousin Kuthanta. Like Yungkwa, these two were also local traditional owners of the Kuthant saltwater people. Next was Yalanga, who was a refugee from Kalkadungu Country a long way to the south, adopted into the Kuthant people. Then, to Yungkwa's surprise, the Native Police collected a fifth man, Kungkardi, a brother-in-law to Yungkwa, being partnered with his cousin-sister. He was not a local but a Kurtjar speaker from the northeast and inland, the freshwater river country of what whitefellas now called the Gilbert River.

Yungkwa was watching Kungkardi closely as he emerged from his ramshackle humpy, looking to see how he was carrying himself. Was he still stooped heavily in mourning, and with fear too? For it had been some of these same Native Police who had killed five of Kungkardi's close male relatives near the Norman Mouth camp here; it was now four years on, but the sadness had not yet lifted.

Yungkwa stood with Jerang on the front of the steamboat as it chuffed up the winding Norman River, often sighting crocodiles as they slithered from under the shady green mangroves and down the muddy banks to surveil the intruders passing through their habitat. Yungkwa could not fail to wonder whether these Native Police had fed the bodies of those Kurtjar men to the crocodiles, as it was well known that they were disposed of without a trace under orders from sub-inspector Poingdestre when it was announced that an inquiry was to take place. Poingdestre had since left and been replaced, but memories of his evil ways were still strong; one of the three black women whom he'd kept locked up for sex was Yungkwa's own auntie.

Upon reaching the Burns Philip Store wharf at Normanton town, a steamer was to be seen tied up and loading wool bales for southern ports. The party were met by another police wagonette that drove them to police headquarters in the bustling regional town of Normanton. Here, they were surprised to see a group of 11 Bama [Aboriginal] people sitting outside waving at them. Kularinga and his smiling wife Ramurra jumped up and came over to them, excitedly explaining that a white man named Purcell had arrived and was taking them all on the steamer *Wodonga*, which was to leave for 'TI' [Thursday Island] that afternoon! As Yungkwa gazed over the whole 11, he realised they were all from the Croydon camps and must have travelled here on the morning's mining tram [rail train]. There were distant relatives from the Bugulmara, Walangama, Ariba, Kurtjar and other 'mobs'.

Locating the Gulf performers: Contact history of the Gulf Country

The completed contingent of performers from the Gulf was composed of some 16 individuals, mainly young men but also two women, from tribal groups in the southeast Gulf of Carpentaria, including Kuthant, Kurtjar, Ariba, Walangama and Mayikulan, but who were mainly residing in a camp on the lower Norman River and in the Croydon town camps. Of these, we have concluded,[5] one was Mayikulan, from south of Normanton but residing with his spouse in Croydon; three were Kuthant from a camp at the Kimberley Telegraph Station near the mouth of the Norman River; six were Wallangarra and/or Bugulmarra of the Gilbert River basin and residing in Croydon town camps; one was Ariba and who was also residing in the Croydon town camps; three were Kurtjar from the coastal area to the south of the Gilbert River, either living in the Kimberley Telegraph Station camp or in Croydon, and two others were from miscellaneous regional groups who were also living in the Croydon camps.[6]

---

5   We know from the return journey that 5 of the 16 returned to Normanton and 11 to Croydon (see Chapter 10).

6   In the mid-1990s, Paul Memmott developed a relationship with an elderly consultant Kurtjar man, Peter Campbell (born 1912), in Normanton. Campbell had a clear memory of the Aboriginal camps in the vicinity of Kimberley Telegraph Station in the period from about 1928 to 1940. He identified some 10 or more camps as being Kurtjar, Kuthant and some mixed with Walangama. His evidence verifies the mix of individuals of different tribal descent in these semi-sedentary camps due to a variety of reasons, especially intermarriage as well as kinship and local employment links.

Burketown, founded in 1865, was the first settlement in the Gulf to service the pastoral industry, but was eclipsed as the principal port by Normanton once the latter was established on a superior site in 1867. Conflict between the incoming pastoralists and Aboriginal people was a frequent occurrence in the 1860s and 1870s. The traditional owners resisted the invasion of their lands, but their resistance was met with the counter force of the Queensland Government's Native Police. For example, in 1868, a correspondent wrote:

> Everybody in the district is delighted with the wholesale slaughter dealt out by the native police, and thank [Sub-Inspector] Mr Uhr for his energy in ridding the district of fiftynine (59) myalls.[7]

Once the conflict escalated, Aboriginal people responded by spearing pastoralists' cattle. The Crown land commissioner's report of 1870 stated:

> Besides sheep, horses and cattle actually washed away [in floods] numbers have perished from wet, cold, hunger and incursions by blacks who have become very bold as the ground got boggy.

The Aboriginal groups of the region were soon severely depleted in all areas of the southern Gulf; in some parts, they were virtually wiped out, as the following details testify:

1. The Country of the Mayikulan people was first settled by whites in 1864. The group then numbered 400. By the mid-1880s it had dropped to 200 due to the rifle and syphilis.[8]

2. Kuthant ('Karrandee') Country was first occupied by whites in about 1866. In 1875, this group comprised 250 persons, but by the mid-1880s it had been reduced to 160 by rifle and syphilis. Ninety men were allegedly shot.[9]

3. The Mayi-yapi population was 1,000 when whites first settled. Only a few years after, in 1868, there were but 250 persons remaining. In 1879, the Native Police, measles and venereal disease had further reduced the population to about 80.[10]

---

7   'Carpentaria', *Brisbane Courier*, 9 June 1868, 3.
8   W. E. Armit and L. Poingdestre [both officers of the Native Police], 'Middle Norman', in *The Australian Race: Its Origin, Languages, Customs, Place of Landing in Australia and the Routes by Which It Spread Itself over the Continent*, vol. 2, ed. E. M. Curr (Melbourne: J. Ferres, 1886), 310, 311.
9   W. E. Armit, 'Mouth of the River Norman', in *The Australian Race*, 306, 307.
10   Palmer and Anon., 'The Cloncurry Tribe', in *The Australian Race*, 330–5.

Writing to the *Queenslander* from Normanton in 1880, an anonymous correspondent alleged that Aboriginal people in the Gulf were generally inclined to be peaceful. However, he complained that the police were always:

> rounding them up and shooting them for the purpose of kidnapping gins and little boys and making them travel to some station or else to the township of Normanton, where they are made to work and slave against their will.[11]

In one particularly gruesome account of a kidnapping,[12] a Normanton police magistrate had been riding through the countryside when he was joined by another horseman who had a pair of bloody hands dangling from his stirrup. This second rider explained that he had captured an Aboriginal woman and handcuffed her to his side, but due to her incessant 'howling', he had detached her by severing her wrists with a tomahawk and left her to bleed to death. The police magistrate had the man arrested.

In a book titled *Memories of Normanton*, a Kurtjar descendant Charles Bynoe, drawing upon the linguist Paul Black's research as well as the oral history of his own people, gives the following account of conflicts in his ancestors' Country in the early contact period:

> In the 1860's [sic] Europeans were already beginning to come to the Normanton area in large numbers, and by the 1880's [sic] the territory of the Kurtjar had been divided among several cattle stations. Even though water was plentiful, much of it was undrinkable. The rivers for example can be tidal as far inland as 20 or 30 km. The settlers accordingly competed with the Kurtjar for sources of freshwater near the coast and drier inland areas. Even though these sources of water were often soaks dug by the Kurtjar themselves. Whenever disputes arose the Europeans always ultimately won the fight by using firearms.[13]

One of Bynoe's sources was Kurtjar Elder Rolly Gilbert (since deceased), a knowledgeable oral historian who told of what was known as the 'no good' time:

---

11 'White v. Black', *Queenslander*, 24 July 1880, 113, cited in D. May, 'From Bush to Station: Aboriginal Labour in the North Queensland Pastoral Industry, 1861–1897', *Studies in North Queensland History* 5 (Townsville: History Department, James Cook University, 1983), 67.

12 C. D. MacKellar, *Scented Isles and Coral Gardens: Torres Straits, German New Guinea, and the Dutch East Indies* (London: John Murray, 1912), 19–20.

13 C. Bynoe, *Memories of Normanton: An Aboriginal Perspective* (Normanton: Normanton State School, 1992), 2.

The white men would drive us away from the places they wanted. They drove us away from our soak at [site name] or Skull Hole, so that their cattle could have the water. They shot many of our people there, and you could still see the bones in recent years, before the last flood. The white men or the Native Police also shot up whole camps of our people at such other places as [gives four placenames]. Butcher Pallew's father was shot at [placename] but by playing dead he was able to get away later and live to tell what happened. Sometimes white people left poisoned flour for our people to take, and some of our people died from that too … The neighbouring tribes were probably worse off than ours was—at least there seem to be fewer of these people left today.[14]

By the early 1870s, as the black resistance was being increasingly subdued, surviving local Aboriginal people were being rapidly absorbed into the north Queensland pastoral economy. The historian Dawn May elicited the advantages of Aboriginal labourers to the pastoral industry during this period, the most obvious being 'that they were on the spot … a labour exchange situated on the property: squatters were able to obtain [seasonal] workers without delay or recruitment cost'.[15] The second and most important advantage was that their labour was cheap. May writes:

> This was important in the north where returns were often lower and costs greater than in the less remote areas. Initially Aborigines were paid in kind—in food, clothing, blankets and perhaps tobacco. The quantities issued were determined by the individual employers as no regulation existed. Such a system was obviously open to abuse.[16]

It was not only Aboriginal men who were employed and exploited but also Aboriginal women. Indeed, the women were made equally, if not more, subservient to the Gulf pastoral industry, as May explains:

> Aboriginal women … performed those tasks traditionally assigned to European females such as domestic duties and childcare. On the male-dominated frontier domestic work often went hand in hand with sexual services and the acquisition of a permanent Aboriginal female companion considerably enhanced the lives of many European males.[17]

---

14 R. Gilbert and P. Black, *About Kurtjar* (Canberra: Australian Institute of Aboriginal Studies, 1980), 2, 3. Redaction of some information in this quote has been done for the sake of brevity.
15 May, 'From Bush to Station', 54, 55.
16 Ibid., 55.
17 Ibid., 83.

In the early decades of occupation, it was recorded that some pastoralists shot the local Aboriginal men and used only women as labour for all duties, including as 'stockmen' and for sex.[18]

Pastoralists justified their exploitation of Aboriginal people on the grounds that they were contributing to their wellbeing by 'civilizing' them and providing protection.[19] For instance, Percival Walsh of Iffley wrote that his:

> boys are very willing to leave their tribe and go with the white man: and is this not better than their running about the bush living from hand to mouth and a prey for the native police.[20]

Walsh made judgements about the possible benefits to Aboriginal boys and men of leaving their people, but he did not countenance the reasons they might have had for entering into such arrangements or their apparent preference for station life, with its promises of adventure and autonomy. What motivated the young men to whom Walsh and others referred might well have had parallels in the 'decisions' and 'choices' that the young men who went with Purcell were also making.

Normanton prospered when the Etheridge goldfield was opened up (in the vicinity of the Etheridge River) in the 1870s; it was active until the Palmer River strike in Cape York of 1873.[21] According to G. P.,[22] gold was first discovered in the vicinity of Croydon in 1886 (although it may have been 1885). The railway was connected to Croydon from Normanton in 1891.[23] We believe that the Croydon members of the Wild Australia Show troupe travelled on this railway to meet up with the other 'conscripts' in Normanton. The cosmopolitan population of Normanton quickly grew to 3,000.[24] By the 1890s, both Croydon and Normanton were thriving centres:

---

18   Swan, Floraville, to Lilley, Justice Department, 21 December 1891, complaining about Hann using only female workers, Colonial Secretary's Office, Inwards Correspondence, QSA ITM847444, 1892/10383; Alex Douglas, Normanton, to colonial secretary, 4 October 1892, concerning claims made by Swan against Hann, Colonial Secretary's Office, Inwards Correspondence, QSA ITM847444, 1892/12790.
19   May, 'From Bush to Station', 92, 93.
20   P. Walsh, 'Slavery in Queensland', *Queenslander*, 16 February 1884, 259.
21   E. Palmer, *The Early Days in North Queensland* (Sydney: Angus & Robertson, 1903), 136, 137.
22   G. P. (pseud.), 'The Gulf Country', in *Cummins and Campbell's Monthly Magazine*, October 1944, 13, 31, and November 1944, 11, 31. [G. P. stands for Glenville Pike.]
23   Palmer, *The Early Days in North Queensland*, 159.
24   Normanton Centenary Committee, *Normanton Centenary 1868–1968* (Normanton: Normanton Centenary Committee, 1968), 5.

A rush quickly set in and in a matter of months, the town of Croydon was laid out and there were 10,000 people on the goldfield. In a year, Croydon boasted twenty hotels, many stores, three banks, and a newspaper … Carriers were soon on the road from Croydon to Normanton, and the latter place grew in size and importance as the nearest seaport to the goldfield. By 1886, Normanton was a municipality … there were four large general stores, eight hotels, and a number of Chinese stores. There was a newspaper and two banks. There was a police force of twelve.[25]

Following the establishment of Normanton in the late 1860s, the mouth of the Norman River was to increasingly fulfil a function as both a port and a communications centre. Larger vessels from Brisbane had to unload their cargo into smaller vessels, which then ferried up the river. To effectively perform these operations, a system of communications had to be maintained with Normanton. An Overland Telegraph Line was installed but it is not clear exactly when.

In January 1883, it was reported that the only structure at the mouth of the Norman River was a telegraph station, known as Norman Mouth Telegraph Station or 'The Flinders'. A ship could anchor there or, if not too large, could proceed further upstream to the Baffle group of islands where it could be met by the steam launch *Truganini* to carry passengers and cargo on to Normanton.[26] In 1887, the telegraph station had become known as the 'Kimberley Telegraphic Office'. A semi-sedentary Aboriginal camp had been established nearby.[27]

Aboriginal people who had chosen to maintain their traditional economy found the resources of their estates to be shrinking as they were taken over by the pastoralists. In 1886, a correspondent complained that the Aborigines of the Gulf were 'being slowly starved to death' because they were being chased away from their usual hunting grounds.[28] One ridiculous justification for this practice was that cattle were disturbed by 'the smell

---

25   G. P., 'The Gulf Country'.

26   Emily C. Creaghe, 'The Diary of Emily Caroline Creaghe: Diary of the Exploration Party Partnered by Ernest Favenc and Harr A. Creaghe and Accompanied by Lindsay Crawford', 1883, Mitchell Library, MLMSS 2982, 4.

27   'Kimberley Telegraph Station', *Telegraph* (Brisbane), 5 June 1885, 4. See also: Governor's address to Queensland Parliament, *Queensland Government Gazette* 14 (1873): 1093; H. Stockdale to NSW Government, Colonial Secretary's Office, Inwards Correspondence, QSA ITM846930, 1874/2424.

28   'The Niggers Again', *Queenslander*, 26 June 1886, 109.

of blacks'.[29] Inspector Galbraith of Normanton was to later comment on the loss of Aboriginal hunting rights, also indicating the increasing propensity of people to move between pastoral, town camp and bush economies:

> Another contentious matter which must be approached with great care is the right of the aboriginals to hunt and fish on the watercourses. It is their right, and it is their only means of existence when in their natural state. They must camp by water to appease their thirst ... Their food (i.e. game) is nearly always found by or in the water. To deprive them of this right simply means wiping them out or driving them into the smaller townships, where the women must prostitute themselves in order to enable the men and children to live. Those that are myalls will naturally kill cattle, or even commit murder, if driven away from their hunting grounds. The station owner or manager claims that his stock have to go to water—so have the aboriginals' game—and that the sight of the blacks disturbs his cattle. The result is that the blacks are often dispersed by the station hands. Of course, such dispersals are not reported to the police.[30]

This, then, is the grim and harsh background to the recent lives and experiences of the Wild Australia Show performers conscripted, probably by local police and with some degree of coercion, in August 1892 at town camps in Normanton and Croydon. As they departed by steamship to commence a tour that would take them further away from their Country than they had presumably ever been before, more of their people were dying from a measles epidemic,[31] and venereal disease was also on the increase.[32]

Conclusion

Of the 14 men and two women from the town camps who were enticed, coerced or both to join the Wild Australia Show, all had been born before or just after the arrival of frontiersmen in the late 1860s and early 1870s. They had grown up in an environment of land usurpation, hostility, massacres and reprisals, as well as widespread disease, increasing poverty and limited access

---

29 May, 'From Bush to Station', 96.

30 W. E. Roth, *Annual Report of the Northern Protector of Aboriginals for 1902* (Brisbane: Government Printer, 1903), 23.

31 Telegram, R. Riley, police magistrate, Cloncurry, to colonial secretary, Colonial Secretary's Office, Inwards Correspondence, QSA ITM 847481, 1893/11827 & 11958; 'Measles at Normanton', *Week*, 15 September 1893, 13.

32 W. E. Roth, *Annual Report of the Northern Protector of Aboriginals for 1900* (Brisbane: Government Printer, 1901), 7.

to resources. The lower Norman River group had experienced violence and shootings only a few years prior to their recruitment, while the Croydon group had experienced a massive mining invasion on their lands. We can only surmise that the offer of a part in the Wild Australia Show, and the promise of a world tour, attracted this younger group of performers led by Yungkwa. A journey to distant places was probably seen as an escape.

At less than a month, Purcell's time in the Gulf Country was quite brief compared with the time it took him to work along the western Queensland border recruiting the five Wakaya and making a large collection of artefacts (Chapter 3). As Meston had likely used his networks to secure assistance from local police, who, it appears, took charge of selecting, recruiting and transporting the performers at Normanton and Croydon, less time was no doubt needed. (Similar arrangements were in place at Thursday Island, as we outline in the following chapter.) Purcell's trek through the pastoral stations of far western Queensland, by contrast, was done largely on his own with little to no advance warning nor preparation. Certainly, he did not report any assistance from police stationed at Boulia nor Urandangi, although Meston was well acquainted with Sergeant Whelan in the latter town. In that vast region along the Georgina basin, power largely rested in the hands of 12 justices of the peace, most of whom were pastoral station managers or owners. Here in the Gulf, the strong arm of the law, and the long hand of government, was mainly vested in police, who also operated as so-called protectors of displaced and exploited Aboriginal people.

Already this indicates that the various troupe members entered the enterprise with different experiences and expectations—not to mention motivations. The nature of the encounter and relations between the Wakaya, the Normanton and Croydon peoples, and the Kaurareg contingent (who we will meet in the following chapter) will become even more apparent once the tour proper is underway (see chapters in Act II). Before it could commence, Purcell had another small cohort to collect from Thursday Island en route to Brisbane.

5

In the Torres Strait

Paul Memmott

After securing 16 performers (14 men and 2 women) in the Gulf Country, Purcell returned to Thursday Island, where he had touched briefly on 6 August 1892 and met with Government Resident John Douglas, presumably to confirm arrangements that had already been made. Purcell's evidence at the 1893 court case over liabilities after the Wild Australia Show had unravelled (see Chapters 9 and 10) provides clues to, although not always absolute clarity about, his sojourns to secure performers willing to travel the world with him. At one point in the court proceedings, Purcell explained that he:

> saw the Hon. John Douglas and arranged for 5 Prince of Wales Islanders, also saw Inspectors Douglas and Savage together with the various P.M.s [police magistrates] to whom I deliver my letters of introduction obtained by Mr Meston, selected 21 men and women and brought them to Brisbane.[1]

The 21 men and women he mentions comprised the five recruited on Thursday Island and the 16 mainlanders met in the preceding chapter. Purcell's abbreviated account provides a few vital details about how the bulk of the recruitment of the Wild Australia Show troupe was achieved.

---

1 Readers are advised that some quotations contain terms and phrases that are no longer in common use, and that are likely to be considered racist and to cause offence. That is not our intention. These terms and phrases are retained within quotations from archival material for the purpose of demonstrating historical ideas and attitudes only. B. H. Purcell to colonial secretary, 21 July 1893, Colonial Secretary's Office, Inwards Correspondence, QSA ITM847483, 1893/8474.

First, it indicates the sequence with which Purcell went about his commission; he travelled initially to Thursday Island (6 August) and then on to the Gulf Country (for less than a month) before returning to Thursday Island (where he remained until around mid-September). The forward stop at Thursday Island had given him the opportunity to meet and negotiate with local senior public servants there. What this makes clear is that Purcell picked up the Kaurareg (Prince of Wales Islanders) from Thursday Island on his return voyage, meaning that they joined the Normanton and Croydon contingents who were already aboard the outbound ship.

Second, Purcell's brief report names some of the middlemen who were conduits to securing the conscripts Purcell had come to collect, and the offices, positions and authority they held. This illuminates how Purcell and Meston operated and, at the same time, tells us something about the particular contexts from which the recruited performers came. There were not only differences between the town camps and the islands, but also between the sparsely populated western pastoral borderlands and the coastal regions experiencing gold rushes and rapid population increases centred on growing townships. On the western frontier, from where the Wakaya came, Purcell had had to rely on a network of cooperative pastoralists (not all of whom were well disposed to his designs) to secure talent. On the islands and in the Gulf, his intermediaries were government-appointed officials and police magistrates and the men under their charge.

Third, Purcell's testimony reveals that he carried letters of introduction *only* from Archibald Meston (a private citizen) and not from the Queensland Government's colonial secretary or other government officials and politicians, as might have been expected. This was to become a controversial issue once the tour was underway. It serves as a reminder that, at this time, Queensland had no specific legislative structure governing Aboriginal people, unlike some of the southern colonies (as will become clear in later chapters on the troupe's tour). Rather, Purcell, as Meston's agent, operated via a mix of private interests and was reliant on the local authority of senior bureaucrats, police officers and justices of the peace. The lack of a clear central government authority for what Meston and Purcell were undertaking would be an element of their undoing.

Conditions had developed differently in the Torres Strait compared with the far north and northwest. Although Queensland was created as a separate colony to New South Wales in 1859, the Torres Strait Islands were not fully brought under the jurisdiction of the Queensland Government until 1879. As part of that arrangement, John Douglas had become a government resident at Thursday Island in May 1885[2] as well as special commissioner for New Guinea. Writing in 1899, a journalist provided insight into the resident's authority, pointing out that:

> the affairs of the township are managed by a divisional board, part of the machinery of Queensland local government, and so, as regards the township, Mr. Douglas is a constitutional sovereign.

The writer noted the presence of a 'military garrison' funded by New South Wales, Victoria and Queensland, but concluded that the source of Douglas's authority was legal and moral. 'On Thursday Island', he explained:

> [Douglas] sits on the bench and administers justice tempered by mercy, and outside the Thursday Island limits he periodically, or when occasion arises, travels by schooner or steamer and settles matters of high policy, even being able, if need be, to, like a modern Warren Hastings, 'depose legitimate princes'. But his sway is milder than that of his celebrated prototype: he rules by suasion and example as much as by anything else, and has imbued with respect surrounding potentates, such as the Mamoose (king) of Prince of Wales's Island and the Mamoose of Mabuac—the island blacks, unlike their kinsmen of the greater part of the mainland, have hereditary rulers. Prince of Wales's Island is about one and a half—or it may be two miles from Thursday Island; there is a boat house and one white family on it, and a few cattle are run upon it occasionally.[3]

Charles Savage was acting sub-inspector of police on Thursday Island during the early 1890s at the time the Wild Australia Show troupe was being assembled. Presumably in response to Meston's request, Douglas had agreed, with the assistance of sub-inspector Savage, to bring together a small group of performers from Prince of Wales Island.

The villages of Prince of Wales Island (or Muralag) were also the source of the territory's Aboriginal police whom Douglas appointed for tasks such as street patrols and court duties on Thursday Island.[4] Douglas and Meston were old acquaintances, having served overlapping terms in the Queensland Parliament. Douglas was the colonial secretary from 1877 to 1879, while Meston was the member for Rosewood (in the vicinity of Ipswich) from 1878 to 1882.

---

2   S. W. Griffith to Colonial Secretary's Office, *Queensland Government Gazette* 36 (1885): 1250.

3   'White and Brown. Where They Meet. Men of Many Colors', *Evening News* (Sydney), 9 September 1899, 1.

4   J. Douglas, government resident, Thursday Island, to chief secretary, 15 July 1890, 'Re duties of Black Troopers at Thursday Island', Colonial Secretary's Office, Inwards Correspondence, QSA ITM847354, 1890/8096 Benches T.

Colonial government incursion into the Torres Strait had initially been for shipping surveillance and territorial defence, but the economic role of the region was to become firmly established through the advent of the pearling industry. These various threads, overlapping interests and personal networks helped to make possible the recruitment of the final five people for the troupe that Purcell had come to collect.

Enter King Gida

'King' Gida was in his long dugout outrigger canoe propelled by six oarsmen from his village of Kiwain on the north of Muralag [Prince of Wales Island, Torres Strait]. He was following behind the water police longboat rowed by the government crew from Waibene [Thursday Island], and standing in the prow was the water policeman, Billy Norman, wearing his former Native Police cap. Billy Norman was a Yagara tribesman from somewhere west of Ipswich and was a known assassin when in the Native Police, killing many Aboriginal people in Queensland and eventually being convicted of murder and put for a time in the jail at the mouth of the Brisbane River [St Helena], a place that Gida knew had a hard and harsh reputation. Whenever Gida saw Billy, he shivered as he had childhood flashbacks to the day when the white man John Jardine had raided his island with his fierce posse of Native Police, Tanna Islanders and Gudang [mainland Aboriginal] assassins, and massacred his people, killing three in every four. Gida's memory of over 20 years ago still haunted him; he could vividly see, hear and smell the screaming Countrymen, women and children, fleeing, bleeding and dying from carbine, club, cutlass and spear. That massacre had happened following the wreck of the *Sperwer* [1869] and the decapitation of its crew by a group led by islanders from the central islands of the Strait. Nevertheless, it was Gida's own people, the Kaurareg, who took the brunt of the wild revenge, with many innocents slaughtered in the village of Yata on the southeast of Muralag. The Kaurareg had never recovered their numbers; now [in 1892], only 100 from the original 500 or so remained.

The party were now almost across the channel between Muralag and Waibene, running with the tidal current, and Gida could see the administration township and pearling port of Thursday Island coming up large. He was being taken to meet with the Queensland Government boss man, Mr John Douglas. Curiously, he could make out a party of strange black people in a makeshift camp on the foreshore. Who were they? As the shore loomed larger, his keen eyes counted 14 black men and 2 women; John Douglas was sitting with them alongside another whiteman whom he'd never seen before.

Upon landing, the two white men approached Gida. John Douglas, arms outstretched, immediately greeted him and shook his hand, then introduced him to Brabazon Purcell as the 'Mamoose King Gida of the Kauraregas', better known locally by his nickname 'Tarbucket'. 'Meet Tarbucket', he said, as he introduced the two men. Douglas explained to Gida that the party of travellers had come by steamship from Normanton in the southern Gulf of Carpentaria, and that Mr Purcell was taking them on a round-the-world adventure for 24 moons to dance and show off their customs to white people. Gida was impressed by the clean uniforms the party wore. Purcell was talking about how the dancers would receive meals, clothes, shoes and blankets for the tour.

Gida noted that two men from the Gulf party seemed to be the recognised leaders: Yangala for the Norman River group of four and Kularinga [who had an attractive wife Ramurra] for the inland [Croydon] party of 12. From their chest scars, they were clearly initiated warriors. But Gida could see he was older than all of them and most of the men seemed quite young.

John Douglas now asked Gida if he would like to go on the tour that would start in Brisbane, Sydney and Melbourne before going to England to meet Queen Victoria, and whether he could take some Kaurareg dancers. They were all to go to a place called America, which Gida had heard about from pearl fishermen. Douglas added that the Gulf group needed a strong leader to keep discipline and he told Purcell that Gida's experience in charge of pearler crews and dancing men amply qualified him. Douglas went on to explain that the big boss for the tour was Mr Archibald Meston, working on behalf of Queensland Government [somewhat of an exaggeration as will be seen], who would meet them in Brisbane for rehearsal camp.

Gida's heart leapt at the thought of such an adventure. Noting the presence of two women among the Gulf people, Gida asked Douglas if he could take his young wife, Kemaliya. He said he would also need to take two good dancers, one mask leader from each ceremony group; he also would need his biggest drum and would have to take his recently adopted son, Kawara, as he would fret for his new daddy if left behind. John Douglas and Brabazon Purcell confirmed these requests. Gida promptly called forward two of his canoe oarsmen, introducing them as Bula or Willie and Dugum or Bazu. He added that Dugum was a police tracker but did not divulge that he was also a former native policeman who had endured a number of mass spear attacks in his time. Dugum, he said, would perform in his renowned ceremonial dingo mask.

Locating Kaurareg: Contact history in the southern Torres Strait

The twentieth-century anthropologist Norman Tindale described the Kaurareg of Prince of Wales Island (Muralag) and the southwestern islands of the Torres Strait, including Hammond and Thursday, as 'a blended group of Australian and Torres Strait Island people speaking an Australian language'. This was his attempt to reconcile the group's Aboriginal identity with the large corpus of customs held in common with Torres Strait Islander groups.[5]

Muralag was an island in a cluster traditionally owned by the Kaurareg.[6] Their Country included all the islands to the immediate north of Cape York, including Tuined (Possession Island), Palilug (Goode Island), Nurapai (Horn Island), Gialug (Friday Island), Keriri (Hammond Island), Waiben (Thursday Island), Maurura (Wednesday Island) and Zuna (Entrance Island). Muralag itself was almost 20 x 13 kilometres in size, with rocky ridges, green valleys and flats, and permanent water sources in several places. The Kaurareg were sometimes termed 'Wera Kauwagal', meaning 'Island Aborigines' by other Torres Strait Islanders, and were closely connected to the adjacent mainland Aboriginal people on the tip of Cape York, the Gudang, by intermarriage and as trading partners.

According to the anthropologist Michael Southon, based on research he did with Horn Island consultants in 1994 and 1995, the Kaurareg archipelago was divided between a number of clans and each clan had a headman or chief, in later times called a 'mamus'. However, there was also an overarching headman or mamus who had a level of governance over the Kaurareg fishery known as Waubinin Malu ('Sea of Waubin'). Waubin was an ancestral hero.[7]

The Kaurareg provided a vital link in the cross-strait trade route as far as the Gulf of Papua coast. Their principal exports to the north were dugong harpoons (wap); arm guards (kadig); scrap metal such as bars; flat pieces of sheet metal; nails and so on, which were obtained from shipwrecks on reefs

---

5   N. Tindale, *Aboriginal Tribes of Australia: Their Terrain, Environmental Controls, Distribution, Limits and Proper Names* (Canberra: Australian National University Press, 1974), 175.
6   Also variously recorded as 'Kauralgal', 'Kawalgal', 'Kowieragas'.
7   M. Southon and Kaurareg Elders, 'The Sea of Waubin: The Kaurareg and Their Marine Environment', in *Customary Marine Tenure in Australia*, ed. N. Peterson and B. Rigsby (Sydney: University of Sydney, 1998), 221–2.

in Kaurareg waters; a range of marine products (turtle shell, shell armlets, necklaces, pendants); and spears and woomeras, these last two being traded from their Gudang neighbours on the Cape York coast. From Papua, the Kaurareg imported bows, reed arrows, cassowary and bird-of-paradise feathers, drums, stone clubs and, most importantly, dugout outrigger canoes. An order for a canoe from Muralag had to be verbally sent via Moa (an intermarrying island), Badu, Mabuiag, Saibai, thence east along the coast from village to village to those at the Fly River delta (Wabuda and Dibiri) where the source of logs was located. Each intermediary might require a fee, and at Saibai, embellishments were added such as outriggers, gunwales and figureheads. The British anthropologist A. C. Haddon described the payment system for canoes as occurring in instalments over three years and commented on the remarkable regional commercial morality underpinning the reliable success of such long-term transactions.[8] The Kaurareg not only traded and intermarried with the Gudang but also, according to Southon et al., shared turtle-hunting areas with them around the islands south of Muralag.[9]

The capacity for status in the Indigenous trade region seems to underlie the Kaurareg enthusiasm for looting shipwrecks for scrap iron as well as other exotic artefacts during the early and mid-nineteenth century, which in turn contributed to their ill-repute and perceived threat among European voyagers, traders and colonists. Haddon does not mention the taking of heads from particular categories of people for trade, but Southon says his consultants asserted they were traded up to Papua.[10]

One of the first well-documented foreign contacts with the Kaurareg was that of 16-year-old Barbara Thompson, a survivor of the shipwrecked cutter *America* in December 1844, who was adopted by a Muralag leader named 'Pacquey'[11] or 'Peaqui'. She was rescued by the crew of HMS *Rattlesnake* in October 1849.[12] Thompson left valuable ethnographic accounts of the Kaurareg, including about the laws regulating ownership of every part of Muralag.[13]

---

8   A. C. Haddon, 'Manners and Customs of the Torres Strait Islands', *Nature* 42 (1890): 641; A. C. Haddon, 'Trade', in *Reports of the Cambridge Anthropological Expedition to the Torres Straits. Vol 6. Sociology, Magic and Religion of the Eastern Islanders* (Cambridge: Cambridge University Press, 1908), 185–8.

9   Southon and Kaurareg Elders, 'The Sea of Waubin', 221.

10   Ibid., 224.

11   Packe Island, close to Muralag, may have been named after Pacquey.

12   David R. Moore, *Islanders & Aborigines at Cape York. An Ethnographic Reconstruction Based on the 1848–50 'Rattlesnake' Journals of O. W. Brierly & Information He Obtained from Barbara Thompson* (Canberra: Australian Institute of Aboriginal Studies and New Jersey: Humanities Press, 1979), 5–9.

13   Ibid., 262.

In response to shipping security concerns, the settlement of Somerset was established on the tip of Cape York by 1862.[14] Originally planned as a ship coaling and stores depot and the base for 'British colonisation',[15] in 1887, it became the northern link of a telegraph line from Brisbane. Dispatches mention shipwrecked passengers in Melanesia being eaten in the mid-1860s and the perceived threat of cannibalism was clearly an ongoing vivid fear for new settlers in this region.[16] Somerset was seen to provide a critical function as a rescue base for such shipwrecked people.

John Jardine, as the first officer in charge of Somerset, was appointed police magistrate and Crown lands commissioner.[17] Official dispatches from Somerset between 1865 and 1867 clearly indicate that, as police magistrate, he had identified the different tribal groups in the region, in particular the Gudang around Somerset on the tip of the Cape, and the Kaurareg ('Kororega', 'Kororigas') on the offshore islands, including Prince of Wales Island. From 1864, Jardine was requesting detachments of Native Police for Somerset.[18] In May 1865, his son Frank Jardine succeeded him as police magistrate after the family had established a cattle station at nearby Newcastle Bay.[19]

A pivotal event for the Kaurareg occurred in April 1869 when Captain J. Gascoigne and his crew of the cutter *Sperwer*, aka *Speerweer*, were executed at Muralug by what seems to have been a mixed group of Torres Strait

14   G. F. Bowen, governor, to Duke of Newcastle, regarding Cape York, Letterbook of Despatches to the Secretary of State for the Colonies, QSA ITM17671, 1862/57.

15   'Northern Settlements', *Brisbane Courier*, 16 April 1864, 6.

16   G. F. Bowen, governor, to E. Cardwell, MP, Letterbook of Despatches to the Secretary of State for the Colonies, QSA ITM17672, 1865/80; G. F. Bowen, governor, to E. Cardwell, MP, Letterbook of Despatches to the Secretary of State for the Colonies, QSA ITM17672, 1866/54; Letterbook of Governor's official letters to various persons, QSA ITM17659, 1866/54.

17   G. F. Bowen, governor, to E. Cardwell, MP, Letterbook of Despatches to the Secretary of State for the Colonies, QSA ITM17672, 1864/31.

18   E. W. Lamb, chief commissioner of Crown lands, to secretary of works and lands, Lands Department, Correspondence Received, QSA ITM22049, 1864/1431; J. Jardine, police magistrate, Somerset, to colonial secretary, Colonial Secretary's Office, Inwards Correspondence, QSA ITM846794, 1865/495; J. Jardine, police magistrate, Somerset, to colonial secretary, Colonial Secretary's Office, Inwards Correspondence, QSA ITM846798, 1865/1533 Z6536; H. G. Simpson, police magistrate, Somerset, to colonial secretary, Colonial Secretary's Office, Inwards Correspondence, QSA ITM846813, 1866/2491.

19   J. Jardine, police magistrate, Somerset, to colonial secretary, Colonial Secretary's Office, Inwards Correspondence, QSA ITM846797, 1865/1451.

Islanders.[20] This was followed by a retaliatory massacre of the Kaurareg led by Jardine junior, as well as the execution of several Kulkalgal from the central Torres Strait, which Gida may have witnessed as a boy.[21]

The majority of historical sources on this violent episode are told from the perspective of the colonists, who frame the actions of the islanders as 'savagery' and 'cannibalism'. Archaeologist Ian McNiven, however, has attempted to construct the islanders' underlying value system to better understand and explain it. He describes a range of threatening behaviours that strangers could unintentionally manifest in the spiritually charged cultural landscapes and seascapes of the Torres Strait.[22] The island geography included such dangerous places as the creation sites of ancestral beings (e.g. Waubin), increase ritual sites, animal bone storage sites and men's ritual lodge centres (Kwod).[23] Ritual violence occurred towards such strangers to remove their spiritual threat to local traditional owners, particularly when they were present in the littoral and near-shore zone. As McNiven writes:

> While Europeans mostly essentialized these brutal actions as typical of 'savages', Torres Strait Islanders saw their actions as appropriate to either neutralizing the spiritual danger and potential destructive power of spirits of the dead, intruders, and castaways (for example, hand removals) and/or enhancing spiritual power and status (for example, head removals).[24]

20   Receipt of report from J. Jardine, police magistrate, Somerset, Colonial Secretary's Office, Register of Letters Received, QSA ITM6913, 1869/4015; 'The Massacre at Prince of Wales Island', *Brisbane Courier*, 9 November 1869, 3; Receipt of letter from acting police magistrate, Somerset, to colonial secretary, Colonial Secretary's Office, Register of Letters Received, QSA ITM6913, 1869/3946; 'Country News, by Mail. Somerset, Cape York. The Massacre at Prince of Wales Island. The Wreck of the Tynemoth. The Booby Island Robberies. Difficulties with the Blacks', *Queenslander*, 6 November 1869, 10.

21   For a fuller account of the *Sperwer* incident, see: P. Memmott, J. Richards and J. Kane, 'A Man of the "Wild" Queensland Frontier: King Gida of the Kaurareg', *Memoirs of the Queensland Museum—Culture* 12 (June 2021): 27–71, doi.org/10.17082/j.2205-3239.12.1.2021.2021-03.

22   Ian J. McNiven, 'Ritual Mutilations of Europeans on the Torres Strait Maritime Frontier', *Journal of Pacific History* 53, no. 3 (2018): 229–51, doi.org/10.1080/00223344.2018.1499007.

23   N. Sharp, *Footprints along the Cape York Sandbeaches* (Canberra: Aboriginal Studies Press, 1992), 105–8; S. McIntyre-Tamwoy, 'Hunting Magic, Maintenance Ceremonies and Increase Sites Exploring Traditional Management Systems for Marine Resources in Northern Cape York Peninsula', *Historic Environment* 23, no. 2 (2011): 19–25.

24   McNiven, 'Ritual Mutilation', 251.

In August 1875, dispatches from Somerset recorded a devastating measles epidemic spreading on Cape York and Prince of Wales Island, resulting in 'numerous deaths'.[25] This epidemic spread throughout the Torres Strait, reducing the population of some islands by half. The Kaurareg population, already severely depleted by Jardine's massacre, was further decimated by disease.

By the 1870s, the informal pearl and trepang industry throughout the Torres Strait was having an adverse impact on island populations.[26] In 1880, 102 fishing boats were operating in the strait, serviced by about 800 men, of whom about a quarter were Indigenous, and a station with four boats had been established in Kaurareg Country on Muralug.[27] Official reports from the early 1870s regularly commented on the pearl shell industry,[28] and on the use of local Indigenous people from both the mainland and the islands as pearl divers.[29]

In 1877, the Queensland Government authorised Henry Chester, resident magistrate at Somerset, to establish an official settlement at Thursday Island as a port for the export of pearl shell and other resources found in the Torres Strait.[30] The economic and administrative reasons for the establishment of Thursday Island were described 50 years later in a jubilee exposition of the town, as follows:

> It is known that the vessels engaged in pearl-shelling in the early days made this harbour, then officially known as Port Kennedy, a place of shelter and refuge; and it is most probable that this fact led the Queensland Government to make the change to Thursday Island from Somerset, to secure closer administration and control over those engaged in the industry, for coloured men were being employed in greater numbers, and there was a tendency to subvert good order when they were so far distant from administrative centres.[31]

25   C. Aplin, police magistrate, Somerset, to colonial secretary, Colonial Secretary's Office, Inwards Correspondence, QSA ITM846943, 1875/2350.

26   J. Beckett, *Torres Strait Islanders: Customs and Colonialism* (Cambridge: Cambridge University Press, 1987), 33.

27   J. Singe, *The Torres Strait: People and History* (St Lucia: University of Queensland Press, 1979), 160.

28   F. L. Jardine, police magistrate, Somerset, to colonial secretary, Colonial Secretary's Office, Inwards Correspondence, QSA ITM846905, 1872/2260.

29   C. E. Beddome, police magistrate, Somerset, to colonial secretary, Colonial Secretary's Office, Inwards Correspondence, QSA ITM846917, 1873/2194.

30   'Jubilee of Thursday Island—1877–1927', *Sydney Mail*, 12 October 1927, 14–15.

31   Ibid.

Dispatches from Thursday Island through the early 1880s include various reports of conflicts and killings in the region. One, in November 1881, noted that 29 men had deserted their employment with Joseph Tucker, apparently because they refused to dive in a place where a Countryman had been taken by a shark.[32] It is clear, then, that Kaurareg men were becoming absorbed into the emerging pearling industry and were formally organised into labour pools to service pearling enterprises that operated from leases on many of their islands. Prior to this, in the 1870s, it seems the Kaurareg had more of a trading relation with pearlers. Gida grew up in this industry.

In 1888 and 1898, Alfred C. Haddon led Cambridge University expeditions to the Torres Strait.[33] In 1898, he described Gida (using his pseudonym 'Tarbucket') as a 'chief' and a 'mamus' of Muralag, as well as a pearling lugger worker. Haddon recorded significant Kaurareg sacred histories from Gida, including that of the Kaurareg ancestor Kwoiam and his epic travel to Mabuiag in the western Torres Strait, along with the various sacred sites he created.[34] Gida was clearly an authority in Kaurareg 'Law' (religious doctrine).

Haddon had first visited Muralag towards the end of 1888 and described aspects of village life. For example, he wrote about a family sitting on mats around a fire within a yard enclosure in the evening outside of their house, playing a Malay card game with the male head smoking from a bamboo pipe. According to his description, this was in a village directly opposite Thursday Island, presumably Kiwain (Blue Fish Point). Haddon also described dances that some old men had travelled 13 miles (20.8 km) from another village (possibly Yata [Port Lihou] if they travelled via the coast) to perform for him. He described a 'war dance' that, he said, 40 years previously would have been performed to commemorate 'some deed of valour or treachery'. At least eight other secular dances, which he termed 'festive dances' or kap, were also performed.[35] Historian Nonie Sharp has since confirmed these two villages as Kiwain (Blue Fish Point) and Yata (Point Lihou), respectively.[36]

---

32   H. M. Chester, acting police magistrate, Somerset, to colonial secretary, Colonial Secretary's Office, Inwards Correspondence, QSA ITM847057 1881/5118.
33   A. C. Haddon, ed., *Reports of the Cambridge Anthropological Expedition to Torres Straits. Vol 2. Physiology and Psychology* (Cambridge: Cambridge University Press, 1901), v.
34   A. C. Haddon, ed., *Reports of the Cambridge Anthropological Expedition to Torres Straits. Vol 5. Sociology, Magic and Religion of the Western Islanders* (Cambridge: Cambridge University Press, 1904), 80–1; W. H. R. Rivers, 'Vision', in *Reports of the Cambridge Anthropological Expedition to Torres Straits, Vol 2. Physiology and Psychology*, 59, 62.
35   A. C. Haddon, *Head-Hunters, Black, White and Brown* (London: Methuen & Co., 1901), 186.
36   Sharp, *Footprints*, 109.

Another Cambridge Expedition team member, W. H. R. Rivers, compiled a list of Muralug persons who were adopted into another totem.[37] These included the adoption by Gida, who was Kursi or hammerhead shark totem (*Zyoera* [now *Sphyra*] genus), of his son 'Kaur' (Kawara), of Omai or dingo totem (*Canis dingo*) (Rivers' spellings). Rivers reported that 'King Tarbucket' of Muralug said: '*Tati* [father[38]] take thing, me growl; *apu* [mother] take thing, me growl; *wadwam* [*waduwam* is mother's brother or father's brother] take thing, me no speak; *ngaibat* [father's father's] take thing, me no speak.'[39] Clearly, Gida was explaining appropriate and inappropriate behaviours according to Kaurareg kinship principles. Rivers also mentioned a drawing made for him in 1898 by 'King Tarbucket'.[40]

As a grown man and young leader, it would seem Gida was taken to the newly formed administrative centre of Thursday Island (c. 1891) to be trained as a government liaison person for his new village and bestowed with the status-forming title of 'King Gida' by John Douglas. By the time he left the Torres Strait to join the Wild Australia Show in the middle of 1892, he was well acknowledged as 'King'.[41] Douglas and Gida were, or were to become, close allies. Gida was accompanied on the Show's tour by his wife and their adopted son.

Back to Brisbane with 20 new recruits

On 14 September 1892, the *Cairns Post* reported that Purcell had returned as a 'through passenger' on board the *Quiraing* from Normanton in company with 'some 30 blackfellows collected from Normanton, the Gilbert River, Flinders groups, and inland'.[42] The number 30 was probably a misprint, since, as we have indicated, the correct figure was 20 (or 21 if we count Gida's young adopted son). The report went on to say that:

---

37   W. H. R. Rivers, 'Kinship', in *Reports of the Cambridge Anthropological Expedition to Torres Straits, Vol 5. Sociology, Magic and Religion of the Western Islanders*, 152.

38   Kinship terminology identified by Milton Savage, 28 November 2018, Thursday Island.

39   Rivers, 'Kinship', 147.

40   Rivers, 'Vision', 62.

41   For more detail of how this was achieved, see: Memmott, Richards and Kane, 'A Man of the "Wild" Queensland Frontier', 46–7.

42   'General News', *Cairns Post*, 14 September 1892, 2.

The boys in Mr. Purcell's troupe supply, in most cases, the missing
links between the various tribes, and show the connection between
the different casts and stamps of the race as a whole.[43]

This conjecture alludes to popular notions of evolutionism triggered by
Charles Darwin's writings, and gives a taste of the kinds of claims on which
the Show would come to trade.

A week later, on 20 September 1892, it was reported that Purcell travelled on
the *Leura* from Townsville to Brisbane with '20 aboriginals', a more accurate
report this time.[44] Adding further detail of Purcell's return trip, the *North
Queensland Register* (citing the *Cooktown Courier*) reported, replete with
racist language, that:

Mr Purcell (of nigger fame) returned last Monday from his trip
North on his way South, and brought with him seventeen blacks,
three gins and one picinini recruited from Croydon, Percy River,
[Normanton], Kuramanga, Prince of Wales and Thursday Islands,
who have agreed to go with the party. They all look very well and
jolly in their new uniform dresses.[45]

This report is interesting for the way in which it distinguished the (17) men
from the (3) women and (one) child. The new uniform dresses referred to
suggests that the group was already being formed into a collective—that
is, wearing the same clothes. These were probably styled on what Meston
liked to wear when he performed: a body stocking with bloomers. The 'new
uniform dresses' were designed not only to set them apart as a troupe, but
also to make them presentable and modest as they began to journey into
population centres and settler towns.

When the *Leura* arrived in Brisbane, a small announcement was printed in
the *Telegraph* under the heading 'Meston's Tour. Twenty more Aboriginals':

Mr. B. H. Purcell arrived in Brisbane on Tuesday night
[20 September] by the *Leura* steamer, bringing with him 20
aborigines intended for the tour round the world, now being
organised by Mr. Meston.[46]

---

43 Ibid.
44 'Shipping Intelligence', *Queenslander*, 24 September 1892, 614. See also: 'Miscellaneous', *Gympie
Times and Mary River Mining Gazette*, 1 October 1892, 6.
45 [Untitled], *North Queensland Register,* 21 September 1892, 19.
46 'Meston's Tour', *Telegraph* (Brisbane), 22 September 1892, 2.

Conclusion

After nearly a year, Purcell's recruitment drives in the far west and far north were finally over. By late September, the 16 Gulf people and the five Kaurareg joined the five Wakaya who had been living in Brisbane since early August. Now assembled in the city, they were to establish a rehearsal camp at St Lucia, a farming pocket of the Brisbane River (see Chapter 7), upstream of Brisbane proper and not far from the village of Toowong.

The *Cairns Post* article that had covered some of this story finished by claiming, somewhat optimistically as it turned out, that preliminary arrangements would be finalised in a month. The Show would then open its tour in Brisbane. As it was, the Wild Australia Show did not open to the public until the start of December, two months later than anticipated (Chapter 7). During the extended rehearsal period, bookings for appearances in the southern cities were being made and contracts drawn up. Yet, there was one last troupe member still to arrive—a Kabi Kabi man whom Archibald Meston had probably personally invited to join. His story is told in the following chapter.

6

On the Mary River

Paul Memmott

On 31 October 1892, the last member to join the troupe, Kabi Kabi man Yamurra or Bob, arrived in Brisbane.[1] He travelled independently of the other troupe members, probably coming by rail from Maryborough (or perhaps from the nearby village of Tiaro). His trip was likely to have been organised by Meston, whom he knew. This happened a good month and a half after the others, accompanied by Purcell, had arrived. This may have contributed to the later difficulty Yamurra experienced in relating to Purcell as the manager on the tour, and may also explain his abiding support for 'Mister Meston' right to the end, even as the troupe's situation deteriorated (see Chapters 9 and 10). As far as it is possible to tell, Yamurra joined the Wild Australia Show not so much as a performer, although he did take to the stage, but more as a broker, intermediary or right-hand man upon whom Meston relied in his dealings with the troupe.

---

1   Readers are advised that some quotations contain terms and phrases that are no longer in common use, and that are likely to be considered racist and to cause offence. That is not our intention. These terms and phrases are retained within quotations from archival material for the purpose of demonstrating historical ideas and attitudes only. Meston n.d., Meston Papers, OM64-17/13, John Oxley Library, State Library of Queensland.

Enter Yamurra

Yamurra was standing on the deck of the steamship *Myora*, which plied and pulsed up and down the Brisbane River from Petrie Bight Wharf in the city to the coal mining centre of Ipswich, some 70 kilometres upstream. He felt out of place among the whitefellas in their flash clothes on the roofed deck and stood to one side as his new boss, Mister Meston, spruiked to ladies in long dresses buffed out by layers of petticoats and balancing teacups, and gestured to besuited gentlemen in bowlers and top hats. Some were drinking bottles of beer in the noonday heat of late October as the steamboat chugged against the current. Mister Meston seemed a cut above them all, talking in his 'long wind' style with his pointy moustache ends quivering in accompaniment to his ever-flowing words and occasionally emphasising a point with a click from his brown leather riding boots.

Yamurra gazed to the low bank on the south side of the big river with its patches of thick scrub [rainforest] punctuated by bunya pines penetrating up and above the dark-green figs. The sight of the ripening bunya nuts saddened him; he envisaged the laden branches in the bunya forests of his mother's father's Country where, by rights, there should be a triennial intertribal feasting and ceremonial festival this season. But his people were too frightened to call for any more festival times due to the ruthless invasion of the white men who had killed his grandparents and had been shooting his Countrymen for 25 years. Yamurra saddened to reflect that he had been in the last Kabi Kabi bora run from the Frilly Lizard Mountain of Bopal, up the Murrabukala, what white men now called the Mary River, learning the Mimburi ceremonies for growing the Country at each story place: Gudiya [Clever Goodbye Stone], Guji [Goanna fat], Thilbain [Lungfish], Miva [Chestnut]. A flock of white corellas rose from the scrub to greet Yamurra and his mind was momentarily distracted from his young-man-time songline. But then his anger welled up again thinking of all his dead people and damaged sacred sites. And the aftermath of violent people who trod the streets of the settlers' big town of Maryborough, built where the saltwater meets the freshwater boundary on Murrabukala. The dangers still stalking in his Country had induced him to accept Mr Meston's invitation to join the dancing troupe so that he could start afresh in his life.

The steamship jerked and the engine slowed. They must be getting close to the rehearsal camp now. What would the other warriors and songmen be like, who were waiting for Mister Meston at the camp at Tu-wong? They were from two-moon walkabout places, a long way away … Would their people still be living the old way? Or most killed, same as his own people, by the white man's disease and their terrorist Native Police?

Then he saw them. Coming around a bend, the steamship veered back to the opposite bank towards a short jetty on which a number of bare-chested warriors stood waving. Behind was a broken-down, chimney-topped house where a few older women were standing waving green branches, the greeting sign of all the old people. Yamurra felt warm at the thought of meeting new Countrymen and joining in a new camp. He reached for his swag-roll. As the boat was tied to the wharf, a tall, red-haired whitefella came forward down the jetty and helped Mister Meston alight, shaking his hand vigorously as he regained his footing. 'Brab, meet Bob, blackfeller name Yamurra. Bob, meet Brabazon Purcell, your new Manager boss.' Purcell then told him that everyone was waiting for him at the dance ground.

As the steamship pulled away, blowing its whistle, Yamurra found himself at the end of the single-file line walking across an open field to a patch of dense scrub. Upon entering the cooling shade of the rainforest and adjusting his eyes from the glare, Yamurra smelt roasting fish in the fire smoke and heard Purcell announce: 'This is the Kabi Kabi man Yamurra, Bob; welcome to the rehearsal ground of the Wild Australia Show, Bob.' Some 25 performers were arranged in a circle to greet him, variously dressed in motley gear, some scantily clad and adorned freshly in ochre. Kudajarnd came first, clearly revered as the leader, called his name and rubbed his underarm perspiration on Yamurra; Yamurra reciprocated. The others followed one by one, variously shaking hands or hugging. Then the five women shyly at the end merely nodded, waiting to find out his skin so they could understand how to relate. Meston said: 'In his mob, his skin, Balgunj. He's Fish Dreaming, Lungfish.' Show them your back scars Bob. Mr Meston lifted up the back of Yamurra's shirt to reveal two vertical lines of scars symbolising fish scales. Chatter erupted in four languages simultaneously, none of which Yamurra could understand.

Kudajarnd, whose own chest scars had caught Yamurra's eye, then began to sing. A number of the younger men began preparing for a cockatoo dance to show Mister Meston, who had taken a seat with Purcell on a nearby log. The others sat around the periphery of the ground, resuming various tasks with their dancing paraphernalia. The younger woman, Ramurra, was plucking white feather down from a bag of netted corellas and passing it to several men applying it as balls of white colour to the torsos of the dancers. An older woman, Kulindab, took up a spinning stick and commenced manufacturing waist string from human hair. The older leader, Gida, was painting the bowl of his drum. Others were tying branchlets of leaves to their shins in readiness for a shake-a-leg dancing demonstration. Two heavily scarred warriors entered with firewood and a freshly speared wallaby and busied themselves at a peripheral ground oven pit. Yamurra was passed a tin pannikin of tea from a warming billy adjacent the fire, then a quid of chewing tobacco and ash, and at last he began to relax and watch his new team mates show off their dancing 'tricks', dance actions that they had been practising in their rehearsal camp for the past month.

Locating Kabi Kabi: Contact history on the Mary River basin

The Moreton Bay penal settlement of New South Wales, established in 1824 as a restricted access region, was eventually declared open to free settlers and squatters in 1842. In the same year, Henry Stuart Russell accompanied Andrew Petrie, superintendent of government works in Brisbane (along with a Mr Joliffe), to investigate the bunya pine forests and the lands as yet unoccupied by colonists in the region to the immediate north of Moreton Bay.[2] Russell's party sailed north, ascended the Mary River, and camped to the west of Mt Bauple (in Kabi 'Bau'pval' or 'Boppal').[3] The Kabi Kabi name of the Mary River was found to be Murrabukula.[4] From 1842, squatters spread northerly from Brisbane, very quickly taking up runs on Kabi Kabi Country in and around their heartland of the Mary River basin. The third member of Russell and Petrie's party, Mr Joliffe, was to return with sheep belonging to John Eales of the Hunter River.[5] In 1843, they established Tiaro, initially as a head station with Owanyilla and Gigoomgan as its outstations.[6] By the end of that year, Tiaro Station was abandoned partly due to the hostilities of the Kabi Kabi.[7]

Archibald Meston would later describe this country in his *Queensland Railway and Tourist Guide*, which he had researched in the late 1880s, as follows:

> Passing Kooringa we arrive at Bopple [Boppal], in full view of the mountain bearing that name. 'Bopple' is what the natives call the frilled lizard. In the vicinity of this mountain lived [escaped convict] Davis the white man, the 'Thurrimby' or 'kangaroo rat' of the blacks … Next to Bopple, a dark isolated mountain covered from base to summit by dense pine scrub, comes Gunidah ('Goodiah', good-bye) station, in spotted gum and ironbark country. Here is a large sawmill operating in the midst of splendidly timbered country. This station is

---

2   Henry Sturt Russell, 'Old Times in Wide Bay', *Mackay Mercury and South Kennedy Advertiser*, 21 June 1873, 3.
3   Ibid.
4   Russell gives 'Morrobocoola' in 'Old Times in Wide Bay', and 'Monoboola' in his *Genesis of Queensland* (Sydney: Turner & Henderson, 1888), 285, while Meston gives 'Morrobocoola' and the variation 'Monobooloo' in his *Queensland Railway and Tourists' Guide* (Brisbane: Gordon & Gotch, 1890), 89, as well as 'Numabulla' in his *Geographic History of Queensland* (Brisbane: Edmund Gregory, Government Printer, 1895), 54.
5   Russell, 'Old Times in Wide Bay', 3.
6   Ibid. F. McKinnon, 'Early Pioneer of the Wide Bay and Burnett', *Journal of the Historical Society of Queensland* 3, no. 2 (October 1940): 91.
7   McKinnon, 'Early Pioneer', 92.

half way to Gympie. Two miles beyond is 'Gootchie,' a native name
of the iguana, and passing 'Kayan' arrive at the Kilkivan junction, in
the midst of a hoop pine scrub.[8]

Ongoing colonial occupation was marked with violence,[9] setting the pattern
that was to recur time and again as the frontier moved north and west at
an average rate of 300 kilometres per year.[10] The Kabi Kabi underwent a
marked population collapse with deaths due to conflict and disease, and later
alcohol and opium abuse. Colonial settlement and Aboriginal displacement
were further catalysed by the gold rush at Gympie in 1867.[11]

There is regular reference in the early white settler literature to meeting
Aboriginal people seasonally en route to the 'bunya district' between
November and February.[12] Aboriginal visitors flooded into this locale for
bunya festivals (especially during January–February), but most frequently in
the triennial cycle of abundant nut production coming from the Richmond,
Dawson and Macintyre rivers.[13] As Malcolm Prentis explains:

> the whites believed that the tribes were conspiring against them,
> that the blacks were especially troublesome at this time, and
> even that they greatly hungered for human flesh in the bunya
> season … The common thread through these two local factors is the
> feeling of threat engendered in the white intruders by the coming
> of unfamiliar blacks, especially in large groups. Partly as a result of
> these factors, racial conflict was particularly prolonged in the Wide
> Bay – Burnett region.[14]

Yamurra would have grown up hearing the recent oral history of his older
Countrymen and women, recounting these conflicts during the first
quarter-century of contact history. Yamurra's particular clan, the Tawarbura,
was one of the first to have had their Country occupied—in their case by
the Tiaro sheep station.

---

8   A. Meston, *Queensland Railway & Tourists' Guide* (Brisbane: Gordon & Gotch, 1891), 94–5.
9   J. Richards, *The Secret War: A True History of Queensland's Native Police* (St Lucia: University of
Queensland Press, 2008).
10   Receipt of despatch from G. F. Bowen, governor, Letterbook of Despatches to the Secretary of State
for the Colonies, QSA ITM17670, 1860/90.
11   George E. Loyau, *The History of Maryborough and Wide Bay and Burnett Districts from the Year
1850 to 1895* (Brisbane: Pole, Outridge & Co., 1897), 44.
12   Russell, 'Old Times in Wide Bay'; Frederick Wheeler (1863) cited in J. Richards, 'Frederick
Wheeler and the Sandgate Native Police Camp', *Journal of the Royal Historical Society of Queensland* 20,
no. 3 (2007): 117.
13   M. D. Prentis, 'John Mortimer of Manumbar and the 1861 Native Police Inquiry in Queensland',
Journal of the Royal Historical Society of Queensland, 14 May 1992, 469.
14   Ibid.

An informative account of the demise of the first pastoralists at Tiaro has been provided by George Beardmore. He records the property of Tiaro as being first taken up by an absentee lessee, a 'Mr Eames [Eales]', who employed seven armed men to look after his sheep. One evening, a local Aboriginal man was caught fleeing with a bag of flour. A 'couple of charges of buck-shot' were poured into him as he escaped. Several months later, the station hut was stealthily invaded at early dawn by an Aboriginal revenge party and all but one of the work team was killed with tomahawks. The Native Police then took revenge for this attack, killing 'not a few', implying very many. Eales removed his sheep and abandoned his run.[15] As Beardmore tells it:

> In later days the Native Police were invoked to disperse the blacks, which was done by surrounding their camps, blazing into them and giving no quarter. These Native Police were aboriginals drilled to ride and shoot, and officered by a white man. There were about fifteen in a squad, and they gloried in the work of slaughter—it was nothing else, as they [the Aboriginal victims] could not face gunfire.[16]

George Beardmore was familiar with the detail of the Tiaro massacres as he and his brother were the next of the new settlers to take up the Tiaro run in late 1854, which by then had an 'evil name as far as the blacks were concerned'.[17] The Beardmore brothers adopted a policy of 'no shooting except in self-defence' for their staff of four. Nevertheless, Aboriginal men were regularly sighted, keeping shepherds scared. Eventually, a Kabi Kabi party, which included women and children, came to visit, indicating no hostile intentions. An Elder of the group requested tobacco, which initiated a pipe-smoking session, followed by a conversation in which the Kabi Kabi visitors were led to believe that the Beardmore brothers were reincarnated kinsmen whose 'skin' or class names were Barang and Terwoi, respectively:

> It was a belief among the Wide Bay Tribes that every blackfellow who died jumped up a white fellow! I noticed our bulky friend regarding us intently, and, presently, as though he had a sudden inspiration, he questioned 'You jump up?'… I nodded, which at once caused quite a commotion. His next question was 'You long time catch possum (opossums) here?'… I again nodded, which was a signal for the gins to set up a wail … Our friend, bursting with enthusiasm, turned first to me and then to my brother Sam, and said 'You Barang, you Tarwan' [Terwoin], whereupon we both nodded, accepting the names we

15 G. O. Beardmore, *Glimpses of Early Australia* (Brisbane: E. J. Beardmore, 1964), 475.
16 Ibid., 293.
17 Ibid., 445.

answered to in our previous state of existence! We were then formally introduced to our sooty relatives. 'Me Bungaree, boss', explained the bulky one and, pointing to a wrinkled old hag scantily clothed, added, 'Mine Coobythinmin' (wife) ... Our dusky brothers were made known to us under their English names as David and Jonathan—'Brothers belonga you'! Our two sisters as Sally and Lizzie, aged about 8 and 10, and dressed in necklets of beads and shells.[18]

Like all language groups in the surrounding region, the Kabi Kabi classified their people as well as their 'Dreamings' or totems into four classes: Barang, Terwoin, Balgunj and Banda. The relation between a Barang man and a Terwoin man was father–son.

The Beardmore brothers correctly predicted that they would be claimed as relatives by this group who could potentially provide them with a protective capacity, but also with a labour pool for shepherding and stripping bark for cladding buildings. The Beardmores decided they should learn as much as possible about their new relatives' customs:[19]

A few days later old boss 'Bungaree', as anticipated, made a second appearance—this time with all his camp outfit, etc. He had not waited for an invitation, and on arrival merely announced 'Me make um camp longa Barang, Terwan, budgeree fella, got um plenty bacca' [tobacco] ...

As soon as the blacks' gunyahs were fixed up, we at once started them at bark-stripping, work they are remarking clever at. We grasped the many opportunities, as time went on, of gaining information from our coloured relatives regarding our 'previous existence' in black skins, so that before long we accumulated sufficient data to enable us to confirm them in their weird belief.[20]

The rainforest, including the tall bunya pines growing along the banks of the Mary River, had economic value to the new settlers. However, in felling suitable rainforest timber, such as silky oak and hoop pine, to construct their buildings, the Beardmore brothers took care not to cut down bunya trees, as they bore fruit highly prized by their Kabi Kabi co-residents, and because an act of Parliament had been passed protecting them.[21] No attacks occurred under the protection of their Kabi Kabi relatives, and the Beardmores never fired at any Kabi Kabi person.

---

18   Ibid., 476.
19   Ibid., 476, 477.
20   Ibid., 477.
21   Ibid.

A little before the time of Yamurra's birth, two extreme, violent events occurred in the central-eastern region to the immediate north around the upper Fitzroy River basin. The Hornet Bank massacre took place in late 1857 and the Cullin-la-ringo massacre in late 1861. Each could be characterised as a reverberating tit-for-tat exchange of homicides, in which Aboriginal parties exterminated entire groups of settlers (11 in 1857; 19 in 1861, including women and children) as revenge for the growing numbers of their people being killed.

At the time of Yamurra's infancy, then, Kabi Kabi society was depopulated and dispersed. Key families and Elders held their shrinking society together from within safe-refuge camps, either on friendly pastoral stations or in Maryborough town camps and other small town camps. Survivors from other groups were mixed in with the Kabi Kabi in these camps. In his analysis of town camps in nineteenth-century Queensland, the historian Henry Reynolds cited the author G. E. Loyau in an early history of Maryborough:

> in the perilous times of 1850 to 1860 it was imperative for the settler, however humble, to carry firearms and be on his guard against treacherous foes, and I believe I am not wrong in stating that every acre of land in these districts was won from the aborigines by bloodshed and warfare.[22]

Commenting on this situation, Reynolds wrote:

> These remarks should emphasise that while life in towns was not normally as threatening, for Europeans, as it was in the more remote districts, some communities experienced periods of acute collective anxiety ... Settler insecurity meant that Aboriginal camps had to be a safe distance away and the blacks themselves kept out of town after dark—and on Sundays in some places—even if the de-facto curfew had to be enforced with the stock-whip. But the Aborigines could not be so far away as to prevent their utilization for cheap labour and casual sex. The camps had to be near enough for their younger and more active members to walk to work and for the local gin jockeys to ride in the opposite direction after the pubs had closed at night.[23]

---

22 Loyau, *The History of Maryborough*, 3.
23 H. Reynolds, 'Fringe Camps in Nineteenth Century Queensland', Section 25 of the 47th ANZAAS Congress, Hobart, May 1976 (published 1979), 2–3.

New settler town residents regularly voiced a range of complaints about Aboriginal town campers, including begging, drunkenness, noise and 'indecency', a term referring both to nakedness and 'public displays of overt sexual behaviour'. The white citizens of Maryborough became so concerned about the undesirable presence of Aboriginal labourers that things 'reached a well-orchestrated climax in 1865 with a large protest meeting and despatch of petitions to Parliament'.[24] At the end of the 1860s, the *Maryborough Chronicle* remarked that Aboriginal burglars carried out their trade 'as though they had served an apprenticeship in London or New York'.[25] This was the frontier context within which Yamurra came of age.

As noted, available evidence indicates that Yamurra was from the Tawarbura clan[26] whose Country was located in the vicinity of the Mary River townships of Tiaro and Owanyilla, the first sites of settlement on the Mary River. Meston commented on the 'famous lily-covered lagoons of Tiaro'— possibly a significant Aboriginal seasonal food resource that would have assisted in hosting a large regional ceremonial gathering.[27] According to Watson's Kabi Kabi dictionary,[28] the edible waterlily was *Nymphaea gigantea* or 'magum', a plant with blue flowers. Meston noted in 1890 that the population of Tiaro was about 1,000.[29] He gave the Aboriginal name for Owanyilla Station as 'Wanya', but this might have been an abbreviation of a longer Aboriginal name such as Awanyanyila. It is also known that Yamurra was connected to Gootchie Station, as he told the press that he was returning there after the Wild Australia Show was over, stating he was looking forward to returning to his 'sweetheart' Katie there (see Chapter 10).[30] Meston reported that Gootchie was an Aboriginal name meaning 'goanna'.[31] It is a little upstream on the Mary River from Tiaro and was leased by Henry Missing at this time.

24 Ibid., 4.
25 Ibid., 11; 'Maryborough', *Queenslander*, 6 March 1869, 6 (and *Moreton Chronicle*, 23 February 1869, 2).
26 'Wild Australia', *Queenslander*, 22 July 1893, 180; J. Mathew, *Two Representative Tribes of Queensland* (London: T. Fisher Unwin, 1910); A. W. Howitt, *The Native Tribes of South-East Australia* (London: Macmillan, 1904), 824.
27 Meston, *Queensland Railway and Tourists' Guide*, 94.
28 F. Watson, *Vocabularies of Four Representative Tribes of South Eastern Queensland* (Brisbane: Royal Geographical Society of Australasia, 1944), 27.
29 Meston, *Queensland Railway and Tourists' Guide*, 94; Loyau, *The History of Maryborough*, 196.
30 'Wild Australia', *Queenslander*, 22 July 1893, 180.
31 Meston, *Queensland Railway and Tourists' Guide*, 95.

Yamurra's back displayed geometrically incised cicatrised scars that were most certainly received in an initiation ceremony. Historical evidence from Kabi Kabi consultant Alex Bond estimates that the last 'bora runs' on the Mary River occurred in the mid-1870s. In a genealogy of his Kabi Kabi consultant Fred Embrey (Alex Bond's great-grandfather), the anthropologist Norman Tindale recorded that the:

> *Kabi Kabi* start from Gympie takes in all of Mary River head and right down to the sea. From Gympie to Tin Can Bay. Tin Can Bay was place where had last bora runs up to heads of Brisbane River … and Kilkivan is in Kabi Kabi country.[32]

The 'Brisbane River heads' is a reference to the mountain saddle near the top of the east branch of the upper Brisbane River where the Brisbane Range intersects with the Jimna (extension of Conondale) Range and the Coast and Kandanga ranges. This intersection divides the creeks of the Mary, Burnett and Brisbane rivers. Proximate stations were Manumbar and Barambah on upper Barambah Creek (Burnett River side), and Yabba on upper Yabba Creek (Mary River side). Alex Bond has described this area as the 'head office' of the Bunya Pine Dreaming.

These last bora runs would have occurred when Yamurra was aged about 11 or 12. As youths were usually initiated at puberty, we hypothesise that Yamurra was initiated in one of the last bora runs. As Alex Bond explains, the bora run involved undergoing key rituals on particular bora grounds, as well as the initiands being taken on an educational tour of their Country to impart both practical survival knowledge as well as geographic and religious knowledge. Further, this travel took them from the mouth of the Mary River upstream to the various upper tributaries that flow down from the Conondale Range and its peaks, including the upper Mary, Yabba and Obi Obi watercourses where there is an intensification of sacred sites and ceremonial grounds. On the top of this range is also the area where the concentrated bunya forests grew, and this was the site of the famed bunya festival feasts that the Kabi Kabi hosted triennially, attracting up to several thousand people, mostly from within a radius of 250 kilometres[33] but also from further afield.

---

32   N. B. Tindale, 'Cherbourg', Tindale Genealogical Collection 1928–1960, South Australian Museum, Adelaide, Sheet 30.

33   R. Kerkhove, *The Great Bunya Gathering: Early Accounts* (Enoggera: Ray Kerkhove, 2012); H. Sullivan, 'Aboriginal Gatherings in South-East Queensland' (BA thesis, University of Queensland, 1977); R. Evans, 'Against the Grain: Colonialism and the Demise of the Bunya Gatherings, 1839–1939', *Queensland Review* 9, no. 2 (2002): 47–64, doi.org/10.1017/S1321816600002956.

The entire troupe assembled at last

By the end of October 1892, then, nearly a year since Meston and Purcell had first departed Brisbane heading north and northwest, respectively, to begin the process of recruitment, the 27-member troupe, consisting of 21 men, 5 women and 1 child, was finally gathered in Brisbane. The troupe was, as this and the preceding chapters have shown, composed of performers from different parts of Queensland who brought with them distinct experiences and cultural knowledge, individual hopes and desires, and unique personalities. The troupe's backers often claimed that the Wild Australia Show represented 9 or 10 'tribes' and that the performers spoke a number of dialects. Our research shows that the performers were drawn from the following language groups (sometimes referred to as 'tribes'): Wakaya, Mayikulan, Walangama, Kuthant, Ariba, Kutjar, Kalkadungu, Kaurareg and Kabi Kabi, and there were possibly links to other Gulf groups as well.

As the Wild Australia Show took shape, and as its tour through Australia's eastern colonial capitals got underway, it is worth keeping in mind the heterogeneity of the troupe. Within its overarching story, there was a constant pull between difference and unity. Differences among troupe members, some of which were highlighted (even if crudely) in Wild Australia Show publicity and advertising, were not an obstacle to the group becoming one. While they might have been 'thrown together' by happenstance, they also quite quickly became bonded through the shared experience of performing and touring. This is a leading theme in the following section of the book, Act II, as we reconstruct the story of the Wild Australia Show from late 1892, when rehearsals in Brisbane began, to the middle of 1893, when the troupe members returned to their homes. We write the story of the troupe by shadowing it as it travels from place to place, teasing out as best we can the performances given, the experiences had and the challenges faced in Brisbane, Sydney and Melbourne, before returning to Sydney and then home again, at which point we lose, apart from an occasional glimpse or two, clear sight of the performers.

ACT II
TOURING

7

Beginning in Brisbane

Paul Memmott

With the recruitment of the performers from three key regions in north and northwest Queensland, and joined by Yamurra as intermediary and interpreter, the Wild Australia Show was taking shape. Over the next few months, as it prepared for its first season of public performances, its repertoire of dances would be worked out and its demonstration of weapons and skills honed. This phase in the Wild Australia Show's formation was foundational, as the disparate troupe members gradually cohered into a successful performance troupe that would perform together for seven or eight months, even as they faced unimaginable challenges along the way. In the various written descriptions and visual representations of the performers and their acts, we come to see and know the 'recruitees' more intimately and personally.

Before the troupe was fully assembled in Brisbane, the Wild Australia Show publicity machine was already operational. Archibald Meston's intention to take an Aboriginal performance troupe on a world tour had been announced as early as late 1891 (see Chapter 2). And so, while Purcell was still out recruiting and transporting the Wild Australia Show troupe members, maestro Meston was in the city laying the groundwork for their joint enterprise. From then on, public statements about the enterprise were regularly made whenever an opportunity arose. As we have seen so far, Mr Meston was masterful at using whatever platforms were available to promote his various schemes and ventures—and, in the process, himself.

June 1892

In early June 1892, a couple of months before the Wakaya contingent chaperoned by Brabazon Purcell was dropped off in Brisbane, Meston gave a presentation to the Royal Society of Queensland on Aboriginal material culture, in which he told his audience that 'the ethnological collection with which he would start on his European tour and to Chicago would include many specimens never collected before'.[1] The touring collection would most likely have combined numerous objects that Meston had procured during recent sojourns in the Cairns region with two Italian travellers (see Chapter 3) and on other occasions,[2] as well as what he described as the 'immense collection' that Purcell would bring to Brisbane when he 'returns with the far northwest specimens'.[3] (Here it is not clear whether 'specimens' refers to the performers, items of natural history, material culture or a combination of all three.) As earlier chapters have shown, reports of Purcell's activities in Queensland's northwest as he sought to recruit performers regularly mentioned his parallel efforts to acquire artefacts (see Chapters 3 and 5 especially). By the time Purcell was preparing to return to Brisbane with the bulk of the recruited troupe members, a newspaper report gushed that:

> Mr Purcell has secured a large quantity of selected beautiful native birds and also a large assortment of all kind of native war and other implements which he is taking with him, and which will no doubt prove of great value to the multitude at Chicago next year.[4]

The quantity of objects, probably exaggerated, that Purcell and Meston were reported as having amassed suggests that northwest Queensland was effectively being emptied of its Aboriginal material culture. What has happened to these seemingly vast and hugely valuable collections remains unclear, although it is likely Meston dispersed and disposed of them through various donations and direct sales, mainly to museums, particularly the

---

1   Readers are advised that some quotations contain terms and phrases that are no longer in common use, and that are likely to be considered racist and to cause offence. That is not our intention. These terms and phrases are retained within quotations from archival material for the purpose of demonstrating historical ideas and attitudes only. 'Royal Society of Queensland', *Brisbane Courier*, 14 June 1892, 7.

2   Meston collected very few Aboriginal artefacts prior to 1891, and mainly from the Mulgrave, Russell and Johnston rivers region of northeast Queensland. For further details of Meston's collections, see: S. Price, L. Allen and C. Knowles, '"The (Not-So) Sacred Ibis": Archibald Meston, The Colonial Collector, and the Queensland Museum', *Memoirs of the Queensland Museum—Culture 12* (June 2021): 73–121, doi.org/10.17082/j.2205-3239.12.1.2021.2021-04.

3   'Royal Society of Queensland', *Brisbane Courier*, 14 June 1892, 7.

4   [Untitled], *North Queensland Register*, 21 September 1892, 19.

Queensland Museum, in the decade after the Wild Australia Show.[5] Efforts to trace the current location of Meston's collection have not been successful, although we do know that he sold over 400 objects to the Australian Museum in Sydney (see Chapter 9 for more detail). Had the reported collection been taken wholesale to the Columbian Exposition in Chicago in 1893 as intended, it might well have become part of the Field Museum there.[6]

Not only were the collections assembled by Purcell and Meston vast, they were also diverse and comprehensive. According to Meston's lecture to the Royal Society of Queensland in mid-1892, they included:

> fighting and throwing nullas, fighting and throwing boomerangs, broad-bladed spears from Boulia, spears from Cape York pointed with cruel-looking clusters of stingaree barbs, heavy hand spears barbed with shark teeth, 10ft. heavy hand spears made from black brigalow, finely made woomeras from the Russell River, Mackinlay Ranges, and Cape York, some of them ornamented with nautilus shell and red seeds, 15in. 'paddiemella' sticks used chiefly for killing game, small shields from the far west and turtleshell shields from the east coast bearing the double red cross on a white ground, the war mark of the old Minyahgo-Wallo tribes.[7]

In addition, Meston showed his audience 'the fire-stick of Cape York, a double wand with the ends in a waterproof cover', and described its methods of use, as well as displaying 'a large 6lb. wooden sword used exclusively by the blacks in the tropical jungle country of the Cape York Peninsula north from the Herbert River'.[8]

As this inventory indicates, some objects in the Wild Australia Show's collection came from regions beyond where the troupe members themselves hailed and may have originated with Meston or been acquired from other collectors. As will become evident as the tour progresses, only a fairly small selection of objects were used regularly in the stage show. This suggests that there was not a complete nor clear correspondence between the objects and the people that Meston and Purcell were gathering up for exhibition

5   No documentation has been located that links any Aboriginal artefacts directly to the Wild Australia Show's collection; however, they are likely to be among the thousand or more objects that Meston donated and sold to museums—the Australian Museum in 1893, Queensland Museum between 1897 and 1904, and Linden Museum in Stuttgart in 1899—and the collection of over 1,110 items sold at auction in Brisbane in 1904. See: Price, Allen and Knowles, 'The (Not-So) Sacred Ibis'.

6   Field Museum, 'About the Field Museum', www.fieldmuseum.org/about.

7   'Royal Society of Queensland', *Brisbane Courier*, 14 June 1892, 7.

8   Ibid.

purposes. Quite commonly within the scope of the Show, performers from the Gulf regions, or from the arid borderlands, appeared on stage with rainforest shields, suggesting that items in the collection were used as theatre props and were distinct from the personal possessions that troupe members brought with them.

The emphasis that Meston and Purcell gave to 'ethnological' objects, and the various claims they made about them, remind us that the performers in the Wild Australia Show were seen as an extension of—or complement to—other forms of ethnographic display. Within the Show's parameters, the performers worked to animate the objects; however, they themselves could just as easily be 'objectified'. If the artefacts were valued for their demonstrative capacity about other cultures and technologies, then so too were the bodies of the men who held and used them on stage.

In the story of the formation of the Wild Australia Show, the collection of artefacts came first and the recruitment of the performers second, both in a temporal sense and within a hierarchy of value.[9] But it would be a mistake to generalise too much about either. Various kinds of judgements, distinctions and discernments were constantly being made and revised over time and according to context. In terms of the artefacts that travelled with the troupe once its tour commenced, it is important to distinguish between the objects brought along by troupe members and those that had been sourced from various unnamed Aboriginal people who did not become part of the troupe (and probably had no interest or intention to join), but who were clearly participating in a valuable frontier economy by selling, bartering and exchanging their material culture.[10]

The high value placed upon the ethnographic collection amassed for the Show's planned world tour is evidenced as well by the ways in which it became a source of conflict between the business partners. There emerged disagreement about to whom the objects belonged and, thus, who had rights to them. As the conflict between Meston and Purcell sharpened, a key difference appeared. While Meston rushed to realise his investment in objects, Purcell remained faithful to the Show's 'living exhibits' (Chapter 9).

---

9   For discussion of museum collections and the politics of value, see: H. Morphy and R. McKenzie, eds, *Museums, Society and the Creation of Value* (London: Routledge, 2023).
10   For examples of such economies and exchanges, see: G. Sculthorpe, M. Nugent and H. Morphy, eds, *Ancestors, Artefacts, Empire: Indigenous Australia in British and Irish Museums* (London: British Museum Press, 2021).

August 1892

As already noted, the five Wakaya people (three men and two women) led by Kudajarnd were the first members of the troupe to arrive in Brisbane. They alighted around 2 August 1892. There is evidence that they resided first in South Brisbane before moving in mid-September to the main rehearsal camp that was set up at St Lucia. From August until mid-September, while Purcell was again travelling through the northern regions on recruitment drives, the Wakaya were under Meston's personal care and oversight. It seems most likely they stayed at his rented residence at Sussex Street, South Brisbane, in what is now West End. In the later court case, from which much of the evidence of the Show's tour comes, Purcell reported that rehearsals had occurred 'at South Brisbane ... [as well as] Indooroopilly [St Lucia] Pocket'.[11]

In August 1892, Brisbane received a visit from a popular French author and journalist, Leon Blouet, a literary celebrity who had written a hugely successful, humorous account of English society under the pen-name Max O'Rell. He had already been in Sydney and Melbourne, and his popularity did not wane in Brisbane. Historian Jana Verhoeven observes that 'the French lecturer's presence in the Queensland capital was celebrated as a major cultural event'.[12] And it was quickly grasped as an opportunity to put the Wakaya performers to work. Organised by Meston, the Wakaya entertained O'Rell and entourage with a display of boomerang throwing at South Brisbane. As one newspaper reported:

> a party, including Monsieur, Madame, and Mdlle. Blouet, R. S. Smythe, Mr. Thomas Mylne and Miss Mylne, Mr. H. I. Blake, Mrs. and Miss Meston, and a representative of the *Telegraph*, went out to a little valley on the bank of the river at South Brisbane, where a display of boomerang throwing was given by a Nerang Creek black-fellow and two wild myalls from the Wahki [Wakaya] tribe in the Northern Territory of South Australia.[13]

---

11 'Supreme Court ... in Civil Jurisdiction Purcell v. Meston' [account of trial before His Honour Mr Justice Reed], *Brisbane Courier*, 22 November 1893, 7.
12 J. Verhoeven, '"The Biggest Thing in Years": Max O'Rell's Lecture Tour in Australasia', *Explorations* 44 (2008): 3–24, www.isfar.org.au/wp-content/uploads/2016/10/44_JANA-VERHOEVEN-The-Biggest-Thing-in-Years-Max-ORells-Lecture-Tour-in-Australasia.pdf. O'Rell's tour was organised by R. S. Smythe who also had a hand in the Wild Australia Show.
13 'M. Blouet's Doings', *Telegraph* (Brisbane), 17 August 1892, 5.

Michael Aird believes that the Nerang River Aboriginal man referred to in the report was Billy Keogh, aka Yoocum Billy, aka Lumpy Billy. Meston had first met him at the Benowa Sugar Mill (inland from Southport) and, in the 1880s, had commissioned him to manufacture 50 throwing boomerangs. Years later, Meston wrote of him:

> Many Brisbane people in present years will remember a black known as 'Lumpy Billy', who threw the boomerang some times in George-street and other places and always wore a coloured handkerchief round his head … He was called 'Yoocum Billy,' because he spoke the Yoocum dialect of Nerang, but the name given to him in the Bora Circle was 'Dilmianu'. He went to the scrubs of Logan, and made 50 return boomerangs for me, under contract, and they were all first-class specimens. He was the Nerang youth of 1870.[14]

Given the prospect that hundreds of boomerang throwing demonstrations would be performed on the Wild Australia Show's world tour, and the likelihood of a fair proportion of breakages requiring a considerable stockpile, 'Yoocum Billy' might again have been contracted as a boomerang maker for Meston.

The journalist reporting the event briefly described the spear and boomerang throwing by both the Wakaya troupe members and Meston, the latter apparently throwing both right- and left-handed, and reputedly 'better than the blacks'. Presumably, for this demonstration they were using some of the spears that Meston had described and displayed in his Royal Society lecture in June.[15] According to available ethnographic evidence, the language groups around the Brisbane region and Moreton Bay did not utilise the woomera,[16] hence the interest shown in its propulsive capacity from both Aboriginal and non-Aboriginal people alike. As one reporter noted:

> One of the blacks—they were all remarkably fine looking intelligent fellows—also threw a primitive spear by means of a concave woomera peculiar to the tribes of the north-west of Queensland.[17]

The occasion must have been a success since a second newspaper report described another entertainment afternoon hosted by Meston for Max O'Rell. This time, the party included Horace Tozer, the Queensland colonial

---

14   A. Meston, 'Lost Tribes of Moreton Bay', *Brisbane Courier*, 14 July 1923, 18.
15   'M. Blouet's Doings'.
16   'Royal Society of Queensland', *Brisbane Courier*, 14 June 1892, 7.
17   'M. Blouet's Doings'.

secretary. 'On Saturday week [i.e. 27 August 1892] Mr and Mrs A. Meston entertained a party of visitors at Norridge Villa, South Brisbane', a report began. Present were Max O'Rell, Mrs Keightley, the Hon. Horace Tozer, Hon. Mr and Mrs P. Perkins, Mr A. J. and Miss Thynne, Dr Hirschfeld and Mr Ross. They were entertained by a 'grand boomerang throwing contest by ten aboriginals'.[18] This was just 11 days after the earlier Max O'Rell event but still before the balance of the Wild Australia Show troupe arrived. If all three Wakaya men were participating this time, who then were the other seven Aboriginal men providing the demonstration? We can only surmise that they were Goori people from the Moreton Bay groups, perhaps from the Bribie Island Mission where Meston had hitherto been active (see Chapter 2).

September and October 1892

The remainder of the troupe members were brought by Purcell to Brisbane in mid-September 1892, along with the large collections of artefacts, birds and other natural specimens amassed (and discussed above). The company travelled first on the *Quiraing* and then on the *Leura*, via Townsville and ports, during which the separate contingents from Thursday Island, Croydon and Normanton had time to get acquainted. According to the shipping intelligence column in the *Queenslander*, there were '17 [passengers] in the steerage, and 20 aboriginals', indicating they were confined to the least salubrious part of the ship and probably sharing that space with seasonal labourers. Purcell, by contrast, was listed with all the other named passengers, enjoying a more comfortable above-deck trip.[19]

In Brisbane, a campsite was established for the entire troupe on the city's outskirts at the St Lucia reach of the Brisbane River, where the University of Queensland campus is today. One newspaper article referred to it as the 'St Lucia Estate'.[20] This estate was initially advertised in 1883 but proved to be a 'white elephant', as the land was not sold, being too isolated and without any services. The St Lucia Pocket area of the river had been used for mixed farming and pastoral grazing, and the access roads from the nearby village of Toowong were rough and vulnerable to flooding by rising creeks.

---

18   'Social Doings', *Week*, 2 September 1892, 27.
19   'General News', *Cairns Post*, 14 September 1892, 2; 'Shipping Intelligence', *Queenslander*, 24 September 1892, 614.
20   'To-morrow—December 18', *Brisbane Courier*, 17 December 1892, 4.

A sugar farm had been tried for a number of years but had failed, leaving an unoccupied millhouse (on what is now known as 'Mill Road' on the edge of the University of Queensland campus). Meston had, in fact, worked in the mid-1870s at another sugar farm on the opposite side of the river at Oxley Creek. We assume he knew of the derelict St Lucia sugar farm and mill, and chose it as a base and rehearsal site for Purcell and the troupe.

As noted, Meston was living with his family in South Brisbane at this time. From there, he was able to walk to the opposite side of the river across from the St Lucia camp and catch a ride across with a ferryman in a rowboat. Steamships also plied upstream from Brisbane to Ipswich, stopping at various farm jetties along the way. Hence, Mill Road was then known as 'Jetty Road' according to early maps, and St Lucia Pocket was at that time occupied by dispersed farmhouses.

Besides the old millhouse, which would have given protection from rain, there were two freshwater creeks, fed by springs and possibly fringed in places by patches of forest, where shady daytime dance grounds could be established. The upper ridges also probably retained some open forest and some game, such as wallabies, possums and echidna, as well as wild bee honey. Fish could have been speared or netted in the two creeks and off sandspits in the river. Probably, the troupe members engaged in hunting, fishing and collecting locally available foods within the limits of accessibility in the local semi-developed farmlands to supplement the supplies provided by Purcell and Meston.

Very little has been recorded about what occurred in the rehearsal camp once the entire troupe was gathered there at the end of September 1892 (see Figures 7.1 and 7.2). Almost all records relate to when the Show had opened to the public and was on the move. But, similar to our emphasis on the Country and contexts from which the performers came (Act I), the Brisbane base where the troupe lived together and rehearsed for a matter of months is also a vitally important site and cultural space to try to imagine and understand. As 'knowledge men' and 'master dancers', troupe members would have understood processes of rehearsal and preparation, and would have enjoyed and respected displays of each other's knowledge and prowess. As such, the camp on the river where they lived with each other for two or three months is at the heart of the Wild Australia Show.

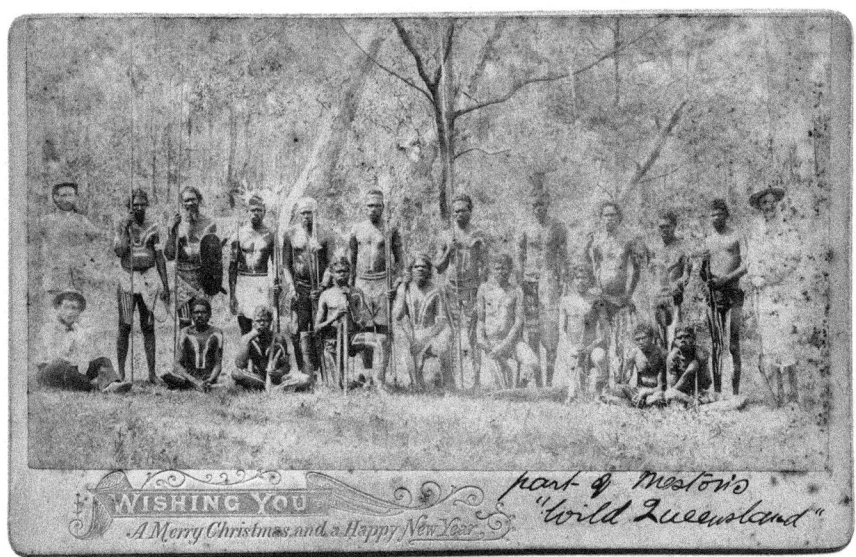

Figure 7.1: Members of the Wild Australia Show troupe with Archibald Meston (left), Meston's son Harold (sitting) and Brabazon Purcell (right) during the troupe's rehearsal period, probably at their camp at St Lucia, in late 1892

Source: University of Sydney, Chau Chak Wing Museum, Macleay collections, HP83.3.13. Photographer: Will Stark [attributed].

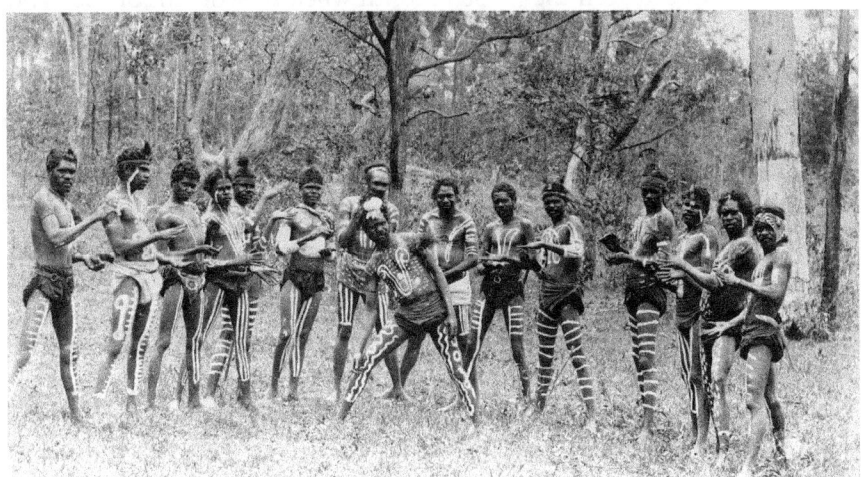

Figure 7.2: Members of the Wild Australia Show troupe, including those from the Gulf region, during the troupe's rehearsal period in Brisbane in late 1892

Source: Pitt Rivers Museum. Photographer: [likely] Will Stark.

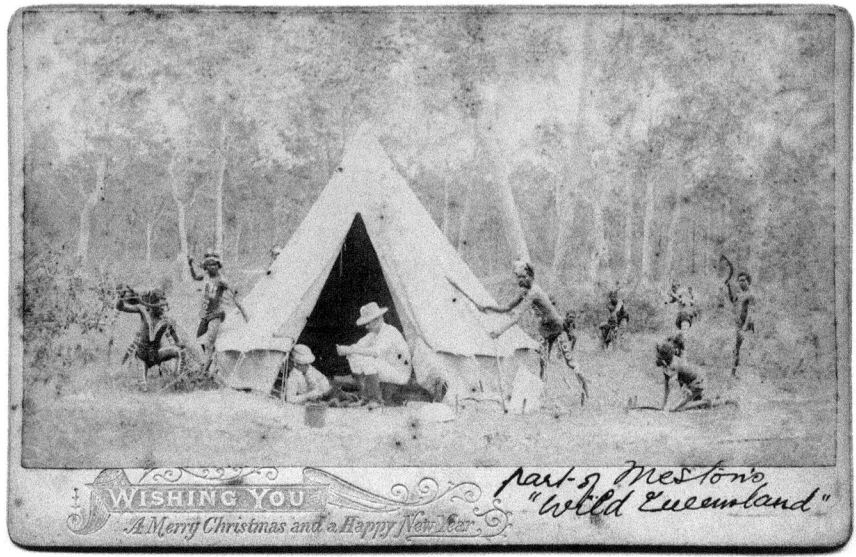

Figure 7.3: A staged scene of frontier conflict performed by the troupe. Archibald Meston and his son Harold shown in the tent

Note: This is one of six images used on greeting cards sold by Tuttle and Company.

Source: University of Sydney, Chau Chak Wing Museum, Macleay collections, HP83.3.14. Photographer: Will Stark [attributed].

October must have been the pivotal month when the content of the Wild Australia Show was devised, prepared and practised. In the middle of that month, photographs of the troupe acting out various scenes were offered for sale as cards carrying Christmas and New Year greetings. A set of six could be bought from Tuttle and Company in Brisbane.[21] The copy in the newspaper explained:

> These depict scenes in aboriginal life as depicted by the party of natives collected by Mr. Meston from North Queensland … The pictures represent corroborees, combats, attacks on white men, and war dance.[22]

Only a few examples of the six original cards survive, including one showing two unsuspecting settlers sitting in a tent (Meston and his son) about to be ambushed (see Figure 7.3). The cards not only provide a visual rendition of the Show's developing program, but also serve as rare documentation of the

---

21 'Advertising', *Brisbane Courier*, 14 October 1892, 4.
22 Ibid.

rehearsals then underway as the Show was taking shape; they capture the performers learning and practising the repertoire, some of which, as in the case of the 'attacks on white men', was imposed upon them.

Among the fragmented and scattered sources of this period are two small clues—mere hints—that all was, perhaps, not proceeding as smoothly or as quickly as Meston hoped. As will be recalled from Chapter 6, by the end of October 1892, Yamurra (or Bob), a Kabi Kabi man (see Figure 9.1), had been brought into the rehearsal camp and onto the planned tour, most likely at Meston's behest. What had prompted Meston to invite Yamurra at this stage in the proceedings? Had this been part of the plan from the outset? Or had Meston seen a need to bring Yamurra in? One response might be that Meston and Purcell were struggling to keep the troupe together and on track, and so an Aboriginal person who could serve as an intermediary or broker between the troupe members and the Show's managers was required.

The second hint that all was not smooth sailing at this point is that the opening date for the Show's Brisbane season was pushed back by some weeks—from November to December. More time, it seems, was needed to prepare.

November 1892

Come November, while the troupe continued in rehearsal mode at the St Lucia camp, Purcell and Meston pursued their program to promote and publicise the Wild Australia Show (still sometimes referred to as 'Meston's Wild Australia'). In the middle of November, the two men each delivered lectures to the Royal Society of Queensland in Brisbane. Purcell's special topic was 'Pituri' and 'Pituri Blacks', and he would deliver the same lecture again in Sydney and Melbourne later in the tour (see Chapters 8 and 9). His talk made quite an impact in the press and caused a stir among amateur ethnographers. Purcell's style was personal: he provided a firsthand account drawn from his travels to the Mulligan River (see Chapter 3). Here was frontier experience being alchemised into authoritative expertise. To add further authority to his presentation, the Wakaya performers accompanied him to the lecture hall and assisted him in demonstrating pituri use.

For the lecture, Purcell started by describing the pituri plant's habitat in sandhills in the east of the Simpson Desert, before asserting that:

> All attempts to cultivate it had so far proved futile. The plant grew
> to about 8 feet or 10 feet in height, but was very seldom met with
> at such a height.[23]

Aboriginal fire management was given as the reason for the plant's stunted growth—'so that they would be able to obtain the young branches shooting up from old roots'. Once picked, it subsequently underwent a cooking process, Purcell explained.[24] He went on to describe the preparation of pituri for chewing, stating:

> the blackfellow took a quantity of the cooked pituri and placed it in
> his mouth to moisten. After it had been sufficiently wetted he placed
> it on a curiously shaped implement which combined the triple
> purpose of spear thrower, tool fashioner, and board for burning his
> pituri. He then burned over it gidyea leaves, allowing the ashes to
> drop on to the chewed pituri. After dipping it in the ashes so as to
> use the whole, he placed it in a fibrous substance and the drug was
> ready to use. After the first man had taken his 'chew', he passed it to
> the next, and so on. When finished with, the preparation was placed
> behind the ear until again required.[25]

The lecture continued with various details about the effects of chewing pituri (a sound slumber and a warming effect); the trade in the substance (dominated by only one or two tribes who control its distribution); and concluded with a practical demonstration from one of the Wakaya members of the troupe, who prepared some and chewed it.

In his comments on the lecture, the Royal Society's president took pains to review previous research and lectures on pituri, such papers having been given over the last 20 years or so. Perhaps this was a subtle way of showing that Purcell had not, in fact, discovered or contributed anything new on the topic. Soon afterwards, Purcell was to receive additional critical comment by an established expert on pituri, Thomas L. Bancroft, a botanical collector and son of Dr Joseph Bancroft. Bancroft senior had pioneered the pharmaceutical research on pituri. His son wrote a short note to the *Queenslander*, which was published a week after Purcell's lecture, exclaiming:

---

23   'Aboriginal Customs', *Leader*, 26 November 1892, 31; 'Royal Society of Queensland', *Brisbane Courier*, 14 June 1892, 7.
24   'Aboriginal Customs'; 'Royal Society of Queensland', *Brisbane Courier*, 14 June 1892, 7.
25   Ibid.

Sir,—I am afraid Mr. Purcell was 'had' by some one out West when he was led to believe that 'white people were using the pitchery [pituri], and that headache could be cured by smelling and neuralgia by chewing it'. A few stock-owners keep a supply, not for their own use, but to encourage their blackboys to work. The blacks look upon pitchery as a great luxury, and can be induced to do almost anything by promise of a handful.[26]

Had Purcell himself offered pituri as a lure for recruiting young men to his travelling troupe during his time in the northwest? Regardless, the level of debate that always surrounded pituri indicates colonial scientific and pharmacological interest in it. It was a coup for Purcell to have Aboriginal trader-consumers of the substance on stage, and to be able to give an account of the main managed harvest area on the Mulligan River in far western Queensland on the edge of the Simpson Desert. This interest was to continue when the Wild Australia Show reached the southern colonies, and Purcell would continue to present himself, with mixed success, as an expert on pituri.

Purcell's pituri lecture to the Royal Society of Queensland was followed by a presentation on 'Dugongs and Their Oil' by his business partner, Archibald Meston. Meston's lecture made little mention of the Wild Australia Show, except to say that the Prince of Wales Islanders' name for dugong was 'dahmal'. Once more, however, Meston used a public lecture as an opportunity to promote the promised world tour that he and Purcell were in the throes of organising, explaining that he would be taking 'five barrels of the [dugong] oil … to America' as well as other commodities. As this indicates, Meston's sights were not solely on the ethnographic show that was in rehearsal. Nor was he focused solely on the ethnographic collection he had previously proudly trumpeted in the very same venue. He still burnished hopes to be colonial Queensland's leading booster and promoter. Meston would only gradually focus his attention on the Wild Australia Show when support for him as a champion for colonial Queensland and its resources began to dissipate.[27] Throughout his chequered career, Meston never enjoyed the complete confidence of the colonial men in Brisbane who mattered most when it came to realising his ambitions and schemes.

---

26   Thomas L. Bancroft, 'Letters to the Editor: Mr Purcell on Pituri', *Queenslander*, 6 November 1892, 1018.

27   'Royal Society of Queensland', *Brisbane Courier*, 14 June 1892, 7.

The day following the double-header at the Royal Society, the troupe was ready to give a 'dress rehearsal' for the Queensland Press Club, of which Meston was also an active member. The occasion for this tryout in front of a live audience was the Press Club's annual picnic. Its members travelled by boat upstream from Brisbane for the occasion. Among them, as a guest of honour, was the travelling journalist Flora Shaw, recently returned from a tour through western Queensland, where she had reported on the shearers' strikes.[28]

The picnic's paddle steamer, *Natone*, picked up Purcell and the troupe at St Lucia before going on to Chelmer for the main event. This was where and when the only group portraits of the entire 27 members of the Wild Australia Show troupe, taken by a government photographer, were created (see Figure 7.4).

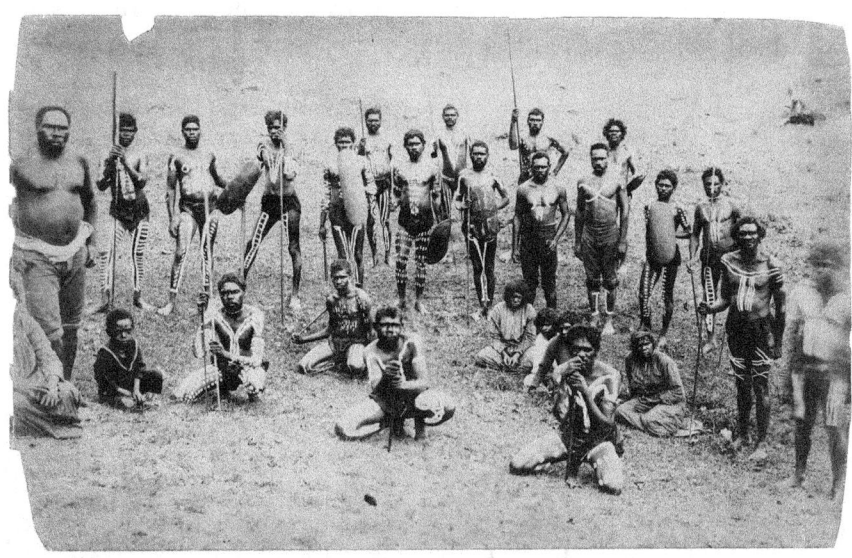

Figure 7.4: The whole troupe photographed by a government photographer in Brisbane in late 1892

Source: Michael Graham-Stewart.

28   At this time, Flora Louisa Shaw was colonial editor and special correspondent to the colonies for the *Times* in London. She was one of the first eminent female journalists in the world. See: P. Clarke, *Bold Types: How Australia's First Women Journalists Blazed a Trail* (Canberra: NLA Publishing, 2022), 40–59.

The journalist Flora Shaw, observant but also inclined to rely too heavily on common tropes about Aboriginal people, provides a vivid description of the press picnic:

> The journey was continued as far as Chelmer, where the steamer anchored at a short distance from the bank, and Messrs. Meston and Purcell, with the blacks, went ashore in boats, and gave a capital exhibition of boomerang and spear throwing. Mr. Purcell, who looked after the spear throwing, fixed a paper target, and the blacks soon riddled it, throwing the spears from their woomeras or throwing sticks. After this they threw light spears by hand at one another. To give some idea of the keenness of their vision, it may be mentioned that the men at whom they were thrown, although without shields, did not attempt to get out of the way of the spears, but simply knocked them aside, often smashing them with their woomeras. The wonderful force obtained by the use of the woomera was demonstrated by the great height to which the spears could be thrown. The guest of the occasion took great interest in the flight of the boomerangs and spears, and, indeed, all on board were much pleased with the exhibition.[29]

With the first outing declared a success, anticipation of the opening public performances of the Wild Australia Show began to mount, and the local Brisbane press (no doubt with Meston's influence through the Press Club) did much to foster interest and build expectation. A correspondent in the *Brisbane Courier*, for instance, wrote in late November:

> It was not to be supposed that savages gathered as these have been from districts separated by many hundreds of miles, speaking dialects and practising customs which render them as strange to each other as they are to the white man, could be brought at once to act in concert. They are now well acquainted with each other and with what is required of them and no doubt when they have settled down to their work the whole entertainment will be particularly interesting.[30]

The writer suggests that truly something innovative was about to happen: the integration of a number of distinct groups from different parts of the colony, each with their own customs and practices, into a single, seamless and cohesive performance. It is possible that this, then, was the first 'trans-tribal' performance by Aboriginal people in colonial Australia.

29 'Queensland Press Club Picnic', *Queenslander*, 19 November 1892, 967.
30 'To-day—November 23', *Brisbane Courier*, 23 November 1892, 4.

The rehearsal period that had stretched over more than two months from September to November 1892 had been critical. It is understandable that the troupe had needed to spend months learning to communicate with one another, sharing their cultural practices as well as choreographic and performance skills, and then developing a repertoire in which all were showcased that would suit both open-air and indoor stage venues. For such apparent cohesiveness to build, we suggest that the troupe members had been active in creating the various components of the Show rather than being solely manipulated by Meston like puppets. Important here is that the performers had the freedom or scope to present their own dances rather than to create a melange. They worked, in a sense, as an ensemble, each presenting with integrity dances and ceremonies from their own cultures, and presenting them in an agreed-upon sequence. Further evidence for this performer-centred creative control would accumulate as the tour proceeded.

December 1892

With its widely reported dress rehearsal in the middle of November, and the production and circulation of descriptions and depictions of the Wild Australia Show repertoire, the troupe, then still camped at St Lucia, began to attract more notice and a steady stream of curious visitors. In early December, for instance, the artist Oscar Friström paid a visit. While there, he made a portrait of a member of the troupe, Wedbura (see Figure 7.5).[31] Why he chose Wedbura, or why Wedbura volunteered, is not clear, but what resulted is a quite sympathetic portrait, as the following description indicates:

> Mr. Friström, who has been very successful in the past in depicting aborigines, has taken advantage of the presence of Mr. Meston's blacks to secure a model. He has chosen a young man, 19 years of age, named Werpoora [Werdbura], who belongs to the Boo-gool Murra [Bugulmara] tribe in the Croydon district, and has produced a life-size bust portrait of him. The dark flesh tint is very cleverly manipulated, and the face beams with intelligence. While the artist was painting this portrait at the blacks' camp, St. Lucia Estate, Werpoora's mates watched the operations with considerable interest, and as it was approaching completion they used to stand before it and gaze on it with astonishment.[32]

31 'To-morrow—December 18'.
32 Ibid.

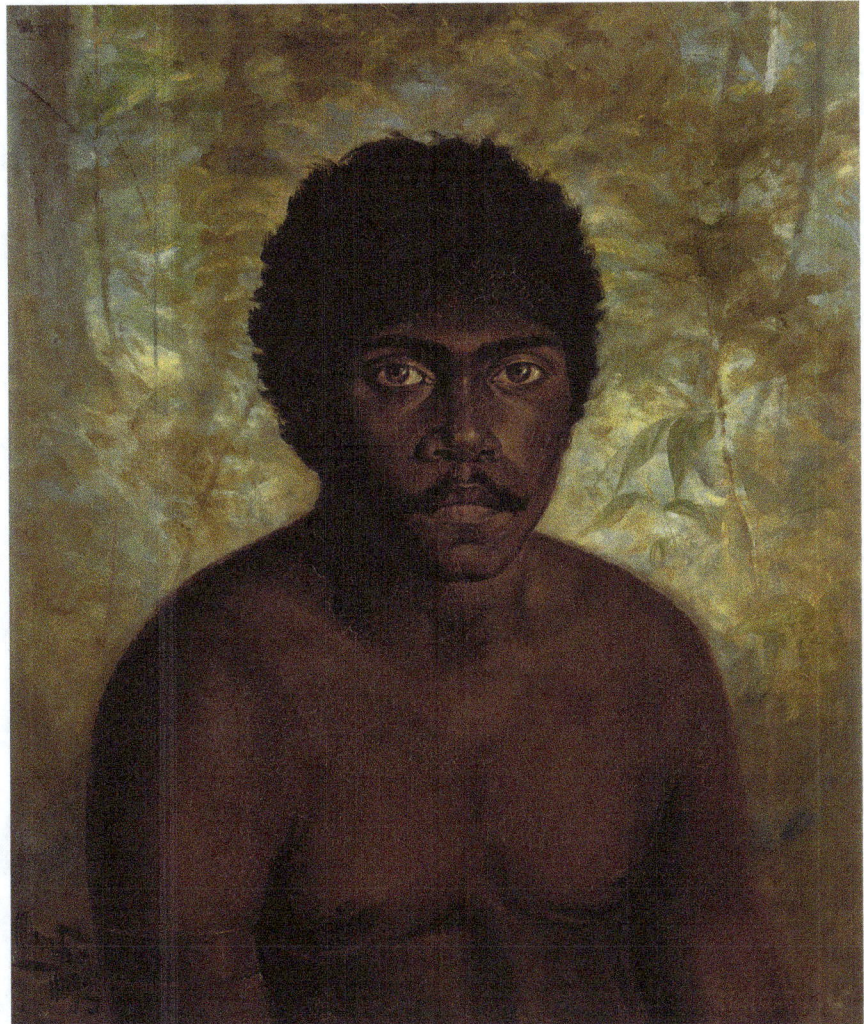

Figure 7.5: Werpoora (Wedbura), portrait by Oscar Friström (b. Sturko, Sweden, 1856, d. Brisbane, 1918)

Notes: Oil on canvas, 61 x 50.8 cm.

Source: Gift of E. T. B. Hutchinson, 1897, Art Gallery of South Australia, Adelaide, 0.116.

The report of the portrait turns the gaze from the artist to the onlookers, casting them as being in awe of settler forms of image production.

Later, Friström would produce a series of paintings of several members of the troupe based on photographs taken by Charles Kerry in Sydney (see Chapter 11). They were part of a corpus of portraits he did of Aboriginal subjects during his artistic career from the 1880s to the 1910s. Friström's genre involved portraying the Aboriginal performers as unique Australian individuals as opposed to stereotyping them through racial attitudes.[33]

After some delays, the opening date for the Wild Australia Show was finally settled. 'The first lecture', it was announced, 'will be given in Her Majesty's House on Monday week, 5th December'. Describing it as a lecture suggests that it was to follow the format that Meston and Purcell had favoured when they brought Bribie Island people to Brisbane back in 1891 (see Chapter 2). But this particular announcement of the opening night performance came with a veiled message for the verbose Archibald Meston:

> and if Mr Meston can but place before his audience the life history of the tribes represented in his group of thirty two[34] aboriginals, leaving them to tell their own story as far as possible in their own graphic way, the entertainment will be both attractive and instructing.[35]

His reputation preceded him. Meston was a man well known for loquaciousness and for a tendency to self-aggrandisement (see Chapter 2). Here, the writer suggests, quite gently but directly, that he might well be advised to take a different tack and allow the performers to tell their own stories—a suggestion with which we would have strongly concurred. A wrestle for artistic control was, it seems, already underway even before the Show properly began. That same struggle for performative space and creative control would occur behind the scenes. As the tour continued, it would be the troupe members who elbowed Meston out of the way as they grew in confidence and showed metropolitan audiences 'in their own graphic way' the value of their own lives, societies, ceremonies and cultures.

The making of the Show

In anticipation of the December opening date, during all of November, newspaper advertisements for Wild Australia began to be printed with considerable frequency in the Brisbane papers. Many referred to the group who practised 'Sturt's "terrible rite"' [penis subincision], which was explicitly

33 Ross W. Johnston, 'Reviving Oscar Fristrom: His Aboriginal Paintings', *Queensland History Journal* 22, no. 4, (2014): 271–86.
34 Clearly there was still some uncertainty about how many people actually composed the troupe. Was it 32 or 27? If 27, had there been another five at some point? If so, what happened to them? This has been an enduring puzzle in the history of the troupe, one not yet solved.
35 'To-day—November 23'.

designed to attract audiences who might be titillated by strange and painful practices; and it again indicates the ways in which top billing was given to the Wakaya contingent.

The advertisements are also a testament to early ambitions for the Wild Australia Show, referring as they do to various elements and plans that never eventuated. They indicate, for instance, a more expansive itinerary, including Adelaide, Tasmania and New Zealand, than the one ultimately travelled. Mention is also made of Meston projecting 'Limelight Pictures' of Queensland's scenery, but it is not clear whether this was to be a prominent feature in the Wild Australia Shows performed in Australia. Limelight pictures, also known as lantern slides, were an especially popular form of entertainment at this time.[36] During the late 1880s, Meston had been commissioned by the Queensland Government to produce the *Queensland Railway and Tourist Guide* (published in 1890), the first visitor and tourist guide to the occupied parts of Queensland with photographic illustration. From this project, Meston had likely amassed a full set of lantern slides made from the photographs for the publication.

Advertisements ranged from describing the performers as 'doomed' or as 'survivors' or as 'doomed survivors'. Some stressed that the Show would exhibit the 'habits and customs of a doomed race', reproducing the popular ideology of Social Darwinism and the survival of the fittest theory.[37] Others claimed that the Australian public had been misled about 'the true character of the wild tribes of Australia', and that audiences could be enlightened for a one- or two-shilling entry fee. An advertisement printed in the *Brisbane Courier* in early December, for instance, stated:

> These Ethnological Lectures, illustrated by representative men and women from the wild tribes of Queensland, will during the next two years effectually dispel the world's ignorance of the true character of the wild tribes of Australia and save the doomed survivors from the gross misrepresentation to which the whole race has been subjected since first discovery.[38]

---

36   M. Jolly and E. DeCourcy, eds, *The Magic Lantern at Work: Witnessing, Persuading, Experiencing and Connecting* (London: Routledge, 2020), doi.org/10.4324/9780429317576.

37   'Meston's Wild Australia', *Brisbane Courier*, 6 December 1892, 2.

38   Ibid.

Meston was, in fact, developing his ideological policy position on the 'Aboriginal problem', rejecting the popular 'doomed to extinction' theories, recognising the positive attributes of Aboriginal people as humans, and formulating the need for separate Aboriginal reserves to allow slow adjustment to European culture, education and economy. This was reflected in a pamphlet he prepared in 1895 and in his contribution to the drafting of the Queensland *Aborigines Protection and Restriction of the Sale of Opium Act 1897*.[39]

In preparation for the Show's opening and subsequent tour, stage settings had been commissioned and created, and these also provide insight into what Meston, in particular, had in mind as he went about realising his own version of what 'Wild Australia' was. To paint backdrop scenery of 'surroundings representing as close as possible those in which the blacks have lived', Meston had contracted the well-known scenic artist Carl William Vennermark (who had immigrated from South Africa).[40] That the backdrop portrayed where the 'blacks have lived' is a curious assertion, since the only backdrop of which a photograph survives shows Mt Bellenden Ker in rainforest country, an area from which none of the troupe actually came (see Figure 7.6). Was Meston speaking of the past? Or had he expected to include rainforest people within the troupe?

Other details about the scenic backdrops come from later reports on the Show's various performances. For instance, one critic wrote:

> The background was a scene showing the Bellenden-Ker range, with the Mulgrave River at its foot. It was a faithful picture, and was much admired when seen by a good white light. By clever manipulation of lights various parts of day and night time were illustrated.[41]

---

39 A. Meston, 'Queensland Aboriginals. Proposed System for their Improvement and Preservation', report to H. Tozer, colonial secretary, in *Queensland Parliament, Legislative Assembly, Votes and Proceedings* (Brisbane: Government Printer, 1895); A. Meston, 'Report on the Aboriginals of Queensland', addressed to Horace Tozer, home secretary, in *Queensland Parliament, Legislative Assembly, Votes and Proceedings*, 4 (1896): 723–38; P. Memmott and J. Richards, '"Where Is the Aboriginal Act?": Archibald Meston and the Emergence of Aboriginal Policy in Queensland', *Memoirs of the Queensland Museum—Culture* 12 (2021): 123–46, doi.org/10.17082/j.2205-3239.12.1.2021.2021-05.

40 'To-day—November 23'.

41 'Theatrical Topics, Wild Australia, 32 Aboriginals on Show, Corroborees and War Dances', *Week*, 9 December 1892, 6.

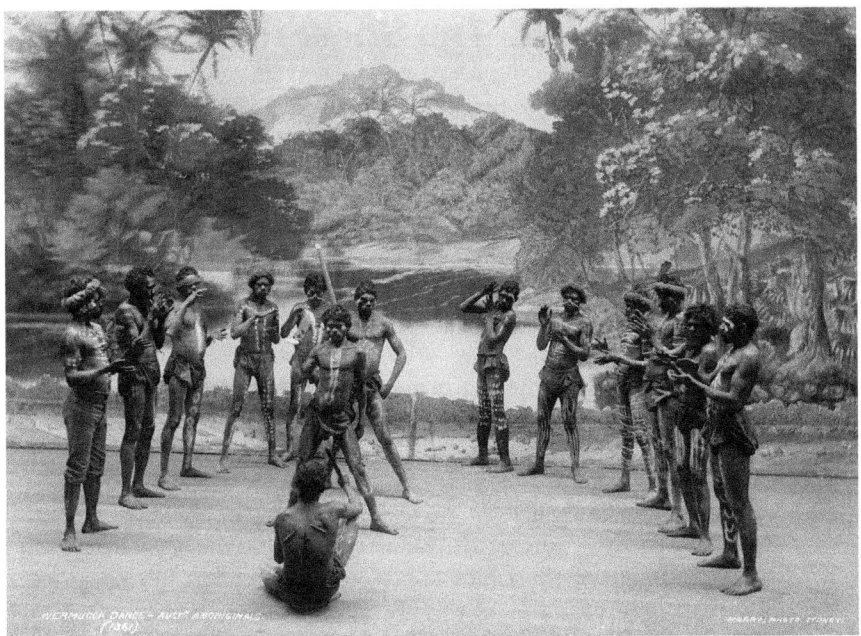

Figure 7.6: Wild Australia Show troupe members performing on an indoor stage in front of Vennermark's painted backdrop of Mt Bellenden Ker

Source: Powerhouse Museum. Gift of Australian Consolidated Press under the Taxation Incentives of the Arts Scheme, 1985. Photographer: Kerry and Co., Sydney. Object no. 85/1284-634.

This gives a sense of the ways in which the backdrops were designed to create the scene and mood on stage, evoking different atmospheres and effects, and how the stage show might have transitioned from daylight to dark or from night-time to day.

There is mention in other press coverage of two other backdrops painted by Vennermark: one of a tropical view of the Russell River and another that was not described. But it is the Bellender Ker backdrop that received the most attention. Meston later suggested that Purcell could sell the backdrops to generate funds for the return of the troupe to Queensland.[42] That two of the three backdrops were of the northeast rainforest region—Bellenden Ker and Russell River—suggests that Meston had supplied photographs for Vennermark to copy, photographs that were likely to have been taken for Meston's *Queensland Railway and Tourist Guide* book.

---

42   A. Meston to colonial secretary, 12 June 1893, concerning Aboriginal people taken from Thursday Island by B. H. Purcell, Colonial Secretary's Office, Inwards Correspondence, QSA ITM847483, 1893/6869.

5 December 1892: The Show finally opens

The first performance at Her Majesty's Opera House on Monday, 5 December 1892, was liberally described in the local press, indicating that it was a notable occurrence worthy of considerable commentary. The language used to evoke the stage show suggests that it was an immersive experience for audience members. One writer referred to 'stirring, actual, and engrossing scenes of native life [portrayed] under the comprehensive title of "Wild Australia"'. This version of the Show included Archibald Meston as master of ceremonies, providing 'descriptive addresses ... interspersed between the various exhibitions'. While the performers acted, Meston spoke, assuming the status as an expert and educator. 'The opening remarks made by the lecturer', the reviewer continued:

> were in the way of a rough sketch, in which he told of the different districts whence the band of natives came, of the fact that they were the third troupe of aborigines to set out on a world-embracing tour, that those in charge of the preceding companies knew not the Australian, but this inferentially, that between his colleague and himself and the natives there existed a confidence begotten of mutual understanding, and that the show in its peregrinations would be a grand advertisement for Australia in general and Queensland in particular.[43]

Although it is not absolutely clear, it can be surmised that the other two troupes that Meston mentioned, and in the same breath denigrated, were those organised by R. A. Cunningham (discussed briefly in Chapter 1). Cunningham was an American who was working under contract to P. T. Barnum. The first troupe he assembled had travelled to Europe and North America in the 1880s. Once the Chicago Exposition was announced, Cunningham had quickly organised another troupe, and it had already left Australia before Meston and Purcell had got their act together. Controversy had dogged Cunningham's first troupe and tour, and concern was regularly expressed about the conditions his latest troupe would experience this time around.[44] Meston never missed an opportunity to criticise his competitor.

---

43   Ibid.
44   R. Poignant, *Professional Savages: Captive Lives and Western Spectacle* (New Haven: Yale University Press, 2004).

It is clear from the early newspaper coverage, including in the lengthy report published in the wake of the opening Brisbane performance at Her Majesty's, that the entire scheme known as Wild Australia had been planned as an unapologetic advertisement for the colony of Queensland. Aboriginal people and their culture were only part of what Meston wished to exhibit. Equally important, in his view, was the colony's diverse landscapes and regions, its natural beauty and resources (both above and below the ground), and the promise it held out to immigrants. According to one report, throughout his repartee, Meston shared:

> enlightening statements … as to our [i.e. Queensland's] resources and the display of Australia's industrial and commercial possibilities through the exhibition of collections of products such as timber, dugong oil, and other articles.[45]

In some ways, Aboriginal people were displayed as the colony's 'ancient' past, and its natural resources as a path to its 'anticipated' future. It is clear, then, that Meston and his audiences had to manage a fair amount of dissonance and denial, as it would be increased settlement and migration to Queensland's frontier regions that posed the greatest threat to Aboriginal people like those he was touring.

Not everyone savoured Meston's stage commentary, and it seems that some reviewers would have preferred the Aboriginal performers to be allowed to represent themselves without Meston's incessant drivel. One noted it was 'interesting but his digressions of a reminiscent and historical character were rather long'.[46] Another journalist referred to 'Mestonian speeches' that were 'long' and 'digressed'.[47] Indeed, Meston was a target of sarcasm and jibes among journalists, becoming known as a flamboyant and loquacious orator who had earned himself the sobriquet of 'The Sacred Ibis' after he mentioned it in a speech as a parliamentarian in the late 1880s.

Leaving Meston to one side, what is valuable about the long and detailed report describing the opening performance of the Wild Australia Show at Her Majesty's Theatre is the insight it gives into the program and repertoire. Indeed, the press report must serve as a proxy theatre program. It provides the 'master repertoire' against which later descriptions of performances can

---

45   'Theatrical Topics, Wild Australia, 32 Aboriginals on Show, Corroborees and War Dances'.
46   Ibid.
47   Ibid.

be compared to detect adjustments, additions or deletions. What the report clearly reveals is that the Wild Australia Show's program fell into three key components: dance, display and drama.

Dances — both particular and 'pan'

The stage show opened with 'a presentation of camp life, introducing a war dance'. 'On the stage', the writer explained, 'was a camp with gunyahs at either side in which women reclined'. Reclining on stage and lighting fires was, it seems, about the extent of what the women on the tour were permitted to do. They observed the action; in turn, they were observed. 'A kangaroo and a cassowary formed the rest of the audience', and we presume that these were taxidermied specimens made to appear as lifelike as possible. Likely, these stage props were on loan from Queensland Museum, since Meston had requested the loan of such specimens from there to use in his lectures. In a letter to the museum's director, Charles de Vis, Meston further explained that he had been 'disappointed of receiving my expected skins of kangaroo and emu from the west in time for lecture'.[48]

With the onstage onlookers in their positions, and the curtains drawn back, 'the dancers, painted, feathered and armed, rush on in an effective manner'. The action—and accompanying sound show—begins:

> One man stood in front, beating time, and others formed a kind of circle, maintaining a dance and hand-clapping to a rhythmical chant. Into the ring came individuals, in turn, who performed strange steps and adopted stranger postures. Two men sat down to kindle fire by means of sticks revolved in the palms of their hands, and there was a hearty round of applause when one of them, after some minutes careful work, set a small handful of shavings in a blaze.

After the fire had been lit, there was another dance, its remarkable feature being 'the extension of the legs till at every moment the upper muscles of the limbs quivered like so many steel springs'.

This was immediately followed by a series of corroborees performed in the following order: the Wermugga (Cockatoo), Rengwinna (Goanna), Fish, Waka Linga (Crocodile) and Rah Min (Adolescents). Unfortunately,

---

48   A. Meston to C. de Vis, 1 December 1892, Inward Correspondence 1892, Queensland Museum Archives.

newspaper columnists writing on the performances failed to identify which performers enacted which dance, indicating the propensity of the media to dehumanise the cultural individualities of the troupe and homogenise them as all simple 'blacks'.

The liveliness of the performances is indicated by the author's comment: 'Some blacks in the pit found it difficult to keep calm during the corroborees, and they frequently returned the cries of their fellows on the stage.' There is a strong sense that they are 'in' ceremony and 'in' performance even when they are not actually on stage. This works to break down a sense of artificiality. What has been created in the theatre, and by and among the troupe members, is a performance space. It is a space that spills off the stage, composed as it is both by the dancers who occupy the inner ring and those on the outer ring who support them. They adapted the stage and the orchestra pit to their own purposes.

What this also indicates is that different corroborees were performed by different members or groupings of the troupe, and that those assignations were not random or arbitrary but made according to knowledge and expertise. As one reviewer noted, 'these all had peculiar variations in action, the one from the other, and also in the not unmusical sounds which the performers made simultaneously'.[49] Here again, local specificity and cultural regionalism is on display—although it might have been missed by all but the most discerning audience members. The cockatoo corroboree, or the shark dance, for instance, were not the prerogative of all; they belonged to particular performers. As the tour progressed and newspaper reports multiplied, further details would be added to these various corroborees, underlining even further that corroboree was not a generalised nor uniform dance (despite the all-encompassing name that had been ascribed by settlers to such performances). Rather, it was replete with cultural and geographical particularities.

Although reports of the Brisbane show listed about seven distinct dances, from the numerous press clippings, and from photographs and their captions taken from across the entire tour, we have been able to compile details of some 11 dances. This represents a minimum of the dances that the troupe had in its repertoire; we suspect that there were probably more that were performed but went undocumented. As we explain in subsequent chapters,

---

49   'Wild Australia. 32 Aboriginals on Show. Corroborees and War Dances', *Telegraph*, 6 December 1892, 3.

what is abundantly clear is that the performances evolved over time—to appeal to new audiences, to suit new venues, and in ways that reflect the shifting desires, and growing confidence, of the performers themselves.

Displays — of skills, weapons and bodies

The Wild Australia Show's version of the conventional and popular display of warrior skills and bodies began with 'a nulla combat between two parties of men [that] was full of movement'.[50] This was sometimes a duel between two equally armed men that then turned, according to one reviewer, into a 'melee' when everyone got involved. Perhaps this provided a safe or contained space for grievances between troupe members to find expression; or perhaps it served purposes similar to 'sham' fights that are well documented within colonial records.[51]

Various men in the troupe also provided duelling exhibitions using fighting sticks. For this, each proponent would take turns raining blows while his adversary attempted to block them using his own stick. Duelling with stone knives was also a topic alluded to in the press, although it is not clear whether it was a common feature of the Show's repertoire. According to Purcell, the Wakaya men duelled with stone knives while sitting down.[52] The evidence suggests this practice was described on stage by Purcell as performers, like Kudajarnd, displayed their bodies to show the results of stone knife duels.[53] Indeed, body scarification became a key visual attraction of the Wild Australia Show. Certainly, the men's and women's cicatrices were highlighted in many of the portrait photographs taken in studios in Sydney and Melbourne, which typically involved the men and women posing naked from the waist up and at different angles to show, to the best effect, chest, arm and back scarring.

Combat with clubs (or nullas) was followed in the stage show by 'spear-throwing with woomeras and without [which] was done with precision, and two men showed their skill in manipulating spears with their toes'.[54] Duelling with spears was another regular feature in the program: picture

---

50 Ibid.
51 See: G. Karskens, *The Colony* (St Leonards: Allen & Unwin, 2009), 369.
52 B. H. Purcell, 'The Aborigines of Australia', *Royal Geographical Society of Australasia Transactions* (Victorian Branch) 11 (1894): 17–21.
53 For example, see: 'Our Australian Blacks', *Australian Star*, 1 July 1893, 8.
54 'Theatrical Topics, Wild Australia, 32 Aboriginals on Show, Corroborees and War Dances'.

two men standing facing one another at about 36 metres apart, each taking a turn to throw at his opponent, who either dodges or deflects with a shield or fighting stick. As earlier descriptions indicate, spears were also thrown at a target from some 20 or 30 metres away; or, when space permitted, they were thrown for longer distances, either horizontally or arcing high into the air. A final show of physique and agility brought the second act to a close.

Drama — a historical scene of frontier conflict as the finale

The final act of the Wild Australia Show crossed from 'timeless' or 'ancient' culture into recent colonial history as the troupe members performed a scene of frontier conflict and violence (see Figures 7.3, 8.2 and 8.3). It was described in advertising in Brisbane as 'A Thrilling Tragedy … The Shepherd's home attacked in Still Night—a Terrible Death—Burning of the Hut—Avenged by the Minions of the Law'.[55] This is just one of a number of pieces of evidence indicating that the finale or climax of the Show was the depiction of conflict between Aboriginal warriors and supposedly innocent white settlers that was resolved in the mortal punishment of the Aboriginal perpetrators by members of the Native Police. One report described it thus:

> A tableau representing the murder of a swagsman by a native, and shooting of the criminal by a black trooper concluded the programme. The display of tracking the approach of the murderer to his victim, the death struggle of the swagman and the cautious pursuit of the murderer by the trooper were watched with concentrated interest.[56]

The Native Police in Queensland were widely reputed to have been the most violent police force on the Australian frontier and consisted of detachments of armed, mounted Aboriginal troopers led by European officers. They played a central role in the dispossession and punitive treatment of Indigenous people in Queensland from the 1860s to the early 1900s. They were conscripted, often forcibly, from districts at a considerable distance from where they were sent to operate so as not to have any loyalty to their targeted victims.[57]

---

55   *Brisbane Courier*, 21 December 1892, 2.
56   'Theatrical Topics, Wild Australia, 32 Aboriginals on Show, Corroborees and War Dances'.
57   J. Richards, *The Secret War: A True History of Queensland's Native Police* (St Lucia: University of Queensland Press, 2008).

The troupe members from the Kimberley Camp were only too familiar with the operations of the Native Police, as Normanton was a police administrative base for the Gulf districts. And at least one of the Kaurareg performers had some history of being employed in the Native Police, and perhaps others did as well. This means that the closing act in each night's performance, which brought the distant but still ongoing frontier onto the metropolitan stage, very possibly drew on troupe members' own experiences, memories and inherited stories. Yet its inclusion in the repertoire most certainly came from Meston, since it drew on the famous American 'Wild West' shows that had provided him with inspiration in the first place.

In those American shows, like Bill Cody's Wild West Shows, the historical scene or tableau staged an attack on a settler's hut or homestead. For the Wild Australia Show, by contrast, the scene was typically described as the 'death of a swagman', and involved 'the representation of a stealthy approach upon the tent of a swagman and the murder of the occupant', followed by retributive killings by the Native Police. All of the parts were played by Aboriginal troupe members. They performed as the ambushed 'swaggie' (with hat pulled low), as the 'murderers' and as the Native Police, who supposedly brought about justice by shooting the culprits. It was a telling of recent history and ongoing experience that excused settlers of being in any way responsible. In this little drama, whites were exclusively cast as victims. As such, it served as a popular form of settler denialism. Aboriginal people, by contrast, were shown as aggressors twice over—first as the murderers of the (apparently innocent and unsuspecting) swagman and then as the 'law' responsible for punishing the crime with death. This colonial fantasy played into convenient mythologies about frontier life. The concluding drama worked to introduce historical and contemporary time into the Show, and thus the content that preceded it—the dances and demonstrations of skill—that conveyed embodied and enduring knowledge were undercut, threatening to become of the past.

A newspaper report, referring to the Show just two or three nights after opening, stated that attendance at the Opera House was only moderate but nevertheless there was 'warm applause'.[58] Another newspaper report proposed that the moderate attendance was due to the 'oppressive heat' being suffered in Brisbane, stating that Saturday night was to be the last theatre performance. Perhaps due to dwindling audiences, the Wild Australia

---

58   *Telegraph* (Brisbane), 9 December 1892.

Show was moved outdoors. It was soon being advertised as showing at the Breakfast Creek Sportsground before moving to the Exhibition Grounds, where subsequent weekly performances were offered until the troupe's departure for Sydney around Christmas Day. The outdoor version seems to have attracted more interest and larger crowds, and was more suited to the demonstrations and dances that the troupe performed. This was to set a pattern of a dual performance style: one indoors that combined a lecture by either Meston or Purcell with an onstage performance (and a program in the order outlined above), and one outdoors that sometimes included some lecture content but gave more space and freedom for athletic display as well as pyrotechnic spectacle. For example, advertisements for the night-time Exhibition Ground performances featured 'campfire displays', 'aerial flight of fire-tipped spears and boomerangs', and spear and boomerang fighting. All performances included fire making with sticks, corroborees (for both 'peace and war'), fighting displays (nulla-nulla and stone knives on stage) and the climax event of the Aboriginal attack followed by the revenge of the Native Police. The burning of the hut in this scenario was more readily achievable in the outdoor settings than inside a theatre.

The *Brisbane Punch* announced that Meston's 'Wild Australia' would include 'a grand outdoor exhibition' in the 'Breakfast Creek Grounds' on the 'Separation Holiday', which was held annually on 10 December from 1860 to 1920. This specifically colonial Queensland holiday refers to the formation in 1859 of Queensland as a colony by formally separating from New South Wales. Outdoor performances occurred at the Exhibition Grounds (Bowen Hills) on 12, 17 and 21 December, according to newspaper advertisements and news items. A journalist wrote of the Exhibition Ground performance on 17 December that the 'ground will be kept clear by troopers, so that all will be able to view the performance without risk, and a brass band will be in attendance'.[59] The reference to risk appears to have been in response to logistical and crowd control issues during an earlier performance. An article in the *Brisbane Courier* described the ways in which the audience followed the performers around the grounds as they performed different feats, but noted that 'had the events been marshalled more closely together [they] would have merited warm praise'. As it was:

> The performers were arranged in different parts of the ground for various events [so] the spectators found it necessary to follow them. There was accordingly a continual shifting of the populace. At one

---

59   'To-morrow—December 18'.

time there was a stampede toward the racing track; at another men, women and children ran helter-skelter to the shores of the lagoon on the opposite side; and at other times they congregated in a wide sweeping ring in the centre of the oval.[60]

The commentator conceded that the 'continual movement of the people added to the liveliness of the scene', but it seems to have caused some concern for visitor safety. Nevertheless, an 'open-air' exhibition was announced for Monday, involving 'boomerang and spear throwing', as well as 'some of the blacks [showing] their skill in diving in the lake'.[61]

Conclusion

Brisbane was, in many ways, where the Wild Australia Show came into being as a stage show. The Brisbane performances set a template, but the story of the Show's beginnings also reveals a certain disjuncture between the vision that Archibald Meston as maestro had, and how the performers, both together and singly, projected themselves and their cultures to metropolitan audiences. While Meston probably insisted on the historical tableau, most revealing of the performers' own contribution is the seven or more corroborees that made up the spine of the Show. These showcased each group that made up the troupe. But the repertoire was never completely fixed: repertoires rarely are. By the time they reached Sydney and Melbourne, the repertoire was stretched, cut and adapted to suit changing circumstances. In one key aspect, the Brisbane season was distinct, since it was here, in Queensland's capital, that the still liquid, and expectant, backers of the Show could provide the most support to the performers. Gradually, as the tour got underway, that support would begin to dissipate, and the Show's backers would put pressure on Meston and Purcell to deliver a return. No longer camping together on a river bank, but experiencing various other kinds of accommodation, as well as more intense surveillance, the troupe had to adjust to survive. The following chapters explore the effects these various changes, and broadening experiences, had.

---

60 'Meston's Wild Australia', *Brisbane Courier*, 13 December 1892, 6.
61 Ibid.

8

Summer in Sydney

Maria Nugent

The troupe departed Brisbane by steamer for Sydney just before Christmas 1892, in time to open at the Bondi Aquarium on Boxing Day.[1] There had been tentative plans to tour regional towns in northern New South Wales before travelling to Sydney, but a commitment to perform in Melbourne in late January had scotched any detours.[2] To prepare their way, a man named J. R. [possibly I. R.] Webster, who was described in the press as Meston's business manager, was in Brisbane.[3] He was another investor in the enterprise; Brabazon Purcell later testified in court that: '£100 paid by J. R. Webster enabled Meston to get to Sydney with the troupe'.[4] No doubt Webster hoped to profit once the Show opened in Sydney; however, that, like his investment, is only speculation. He is a rather shadowy (in both senses) figure in the troupe's history, coming fleetingly in and out of view. We have looked for him in the records, but have been unable to really track him down.

---

1   Readers are advised that some quotations contain terms and phrases that are no longer in common use, and that are likely to be considered racist and to cause offence. That is not our intention. These terms and phrases are retained within quotations from archival material for the purpose of demonstrating historical ideas and attitudes only. 'To-day—December 26', *Brisbane Courier*, 26 December 1892, 4.
2   '"Wild Australia" Entertainment', *Sydney Morning Herald*, 29 December 1892, 6.
3   'Shipping News', *Daily Telegraph*, 1 December 1892, 7, lists J. Webster on the *Cintra*—Sydney to Brisbane; 'Meston's Wild Australia', *Telegraph* (Brisbane), 3 December 1892, 4, reports that 'Mr Meston's business manager arrived from Sydney by the Cintra yesterday'.
4   B. H. Purcell to colonial secretary, 21 July 1893, regarding his association with A. Meston and Aborigines in north, west and south Queensland, Colonial Secretary's Office, Inwards Correspondence, QSA ITM847483, 1893/8474.

Another shadowy figure mentioned in passing in press reports as travelling with the troupe is Meston's son, Harold Meston, who appears to have travelled with Purcell and the troupe on a steamer from Brisbane to Sydney. A newspaper report explained that: 'Mr. A. Meston's "Wild Australians", accompanied by Mr. Purcell and Harold Meston, left for Sydney in the Barrabool for a week's engagement at the Bondi Aquarium, commencing Monday night.'[5] If young Harold did travel to Sydney with the troupe, he may not have gone any further than that; he is not again mentioned in reports of the tour.

Meston's friend, Robert Browne, is another spectral figure. Browne, like Meston, was a member of the Queensland Press Club and had attended the Press Club Picnic at Chelmer Reach on the Brisbane River, described in the previous chapter. A report of another Press Club picnic in Brisbane noted that 'during the evening the health of Mr Robert Browne, secretary of the [Press] club, who is accompanying Mr A. Meston as advance agent for "Wild Australia" was honoured'.[6] However, hardly anything is known about Browne's involvement in the enterprise or, indeed, how effective he proved to be as an 'advance agent'. In early December 1892, the local newspaper in Maryborough north of Brisbane announced that Browne, described as an 'old Brisbane pressman', had arrived by the mail train to:

> arrange for the appearance at the Town Hall on Thursday, December 15, of the male and female aborigines, selected from the wild tribes of the far west and north west to illustrate the well-known explorer Mr. Archie Meston's lectures on Wild Australia.[7]

It is unclear whether this appearance went ahead.[8]

---

5   'To-day—December 26'.

6   'Press Club Picnic', *Telegraph* (Brisbane), 5 December 1892, 5.

7   'Local News', *Maryborough Chronicle, Wide Bay and Burnett Advertiser*, 10 December 1892, 2. See also: 'Local News', *Maryborough Chronicle, Wide Bay and Burnett Advertiser*, 12 December 1892, 3, warning local residents of Maryborough that 'Mr Archibald Meston's Wild Australia Show will swoop down upon Maryborough on Thursday, appearing at the Town Hall that night'.

8   The only performance at the Maryborough Town Hall on Thursday night that the newspaper reported upon was by 'the stranded members of the Jenny Lee "Jo" Company, assisted by local amateurs', which was described as 'not a financial success, the house being a very small one'. See: 'Local News', *Maryborough Chronicle, Wide Bay and Burnett Advertiser*, 16 December 1892, 2. The evening before, 22 local school children from the Convent School had had their faces 'blackened … and dressed in "nigger" character'. See: 'Local News', *Maryborough Chronicle, Wide Bay and Burnett Advertiser*, 15 December 1892, 2.

While Purcell travelled with the troupe on the steamer to Sydney, Archibald Meston went by train.[9] This seems to have been a common pattern of the tour's logistics; when the troupe subsequently travelled from Sydney to Melbourne (see Chapter 9), it was Purcell who would take the overland route while the performers travelled by steamer. This might have been so that the Show's paraphernalia—the props, collections and stage sets— could travel as rail cargo.

The Show's first Sydney season, spanning late 1892 and early 1893, is revealing, particularly for the ways in which the troupe developed once it was on the move and had travelled beyond the borders of colonial Queensland. Not only were Brisbane and Sydney quite distinct cities—of different sizes and colonial histories—but also, the governments in each had a different approach to Aboriginal people within the colonies of which they were the capitals. The New South Wales and Queensland authorities would increasingly come into conflict over the question of who was responsible for the Wild Australia Show players. Moreover, in Sydney, men like Meston did not enjoy quite the same cachet as they did in colonial Queensland. Nor were they as tolerated or indulged. And so, in New South Wales, the Show and its showmen came in for greater scrutiny and the troupe members for increased surveillance. At a time when the New South Wales Government wanted to keep Aboriginal people quite literally in their place and out of sight, it was the *mobility* of the performers that caused a minor panic for authorities. Such unwelcome and clearly unanticipated governmental attention threatened to hobble the tour before it had made very much progress at all.

Amid these swirling forces, and as the troupe's managers and backers sought to mollify various agents who wanted to see the Wild Australia Show closed down or moved on, the performers went about putting on daily and nightly shows. And, as in Brisbane, they were again photographed, this time by a leading photographic studio, and soon their images were being offered for sale. For most of the first month of 1893, they were perpetually on show: performing their dances, giving demonstrations, delivering dramas and entertaining audiences, at times with more reported success than at others. Although short, this initial Sydney season was formative, strengthening the

9   *Brisbane Courier*, 26 December 1892, 4. He had also planned to remain in Sydney for the week only, before returning to Brisbane to attend to his own affairs.

bonds between the various cohorts that made up the troupe and cementing the cohesiveness that would be critical to its survival under increasingly difficult and challenging conditions.

26 December 1892 – 3 January 1893: A week of shows at Bondi Aquarium

The Wild Australia Show troupe began a week of shows on 26 December 1892 at the Bondi Aquarium. Advertisements appeared regularly in the papers before the troupe's arrival and every day that it performed, emphasising its novelty, expense and greatness, and again highlighting the supposed 'wildness' of the performers. Exaggerated extraordinariness was in keeping with the usual fare that appeared at Sydney's seaside entertainment precincts in this period. As a privately owned entertainment precinct covering a large and open area, where a panoply of amusements, attractions and spectacles were on offer, the ostentatiously named Royal Bondi Aquarium and Pleasure Grounds provided the noisy and fairground-like performance space for the troupe and their 'native village'. One advertisement offered a challenge: 'Any person desirous of hitting one of the Aboriginals with a cricket ball at a range of over 10yds can try.'[10]

The relatively new Bondi Aquarium was one of three seaside entertainment precincts in Sydney to open from the mid-1880s onwards. Manly, on the northside of Sydney Harbour, had led the way in 1885. Within a year or two, the beachside suburbs of Bondi and Coogee to the east of the city centre had followed. Although it traded on the famous Bondi name, the venue where the troupe performed was actually located at Tamarama, a small beach immediately to the south of its more famous counterpart.

Sydney's pleasure grounds were designed along the lines of popular British seaside resorts, such as those found at Brighton and Blackpool. Bondi had a reputation as being the most 'elaborate of the three'.[11] Its landscaped oceanside grounds encompassed 'a skating rink, merry-go-round, camera

---

10   'Advertisements', *Daily Telegraph*, 28 December 1892, 2. Daily notices appeared in the advertisement sections of the *Daily Telegraph*, *Sydney Morning Herald* and *Evening News*, highlighting different aspects of the Show and promising novelty in the program.

11   C. Ford, 'A Summer Fling: The Rise and Fall of Aquariums and Fun Parks on Sydney's Ocean Coast, 1885–1920', *Journal of Tourism History* 1, no. 2 (October 2009): 97, doi.org/10.1080/1755 1820903353454.

obscura, shark pond and a concert hall' as well as an aquarium.[12] The grounds were open during the day and also at night, 'lit up by electric lights … still a great novelty and source of attraction, and also hosted fireworks'.[13] A description from 1893, around the time of the Wild Australia Show's season, gives a taste:

> The place was provided with various modes of amusement. There was the inevitable Merry-Go-Round with its wooden horses ready for mounting, swinging round and round under a large umbrella-shaped canopy. There was the ever-exciting Switchback Railway, with its lofty undulatory ride, which is unsafe for people of weak nerves. It was funny to see how hats flew off the heads of the riders, as they descended violently down the slopes of this aerial railway. The greatest favourite of all was the Skating Rink, which was patronised by crowds of both young and the middle-aged, who vied with each other in gliding quickly on the wooden floors, with roller skates on.[14]

Historian Caroline Ford notes that the:

> Sydney sites combined working class 'sideshow' type amusements such as illusionists, comics, minstrels, rides and acrobats, like those found at Blackpool and Coney Island, with more educative pastimes more strongly associated with the Aquariums of Brighton.[15]

The emphasis at the Bondi Aquarium was on the unusual, the weird and the daring. Audiences came to be entertained and titillated—and they had to travel some distance for the pleasure. In the 1890s, it took 40 minutes in a tram from the city to reach the Bondi terminus with a further 10-minute trip to the aquarium 'over a road at present not provocative of piety to the pedestrian', according to one report.[16] With its focus on bodily exhibition and daring display (primarily as a means for imparting knowledge and information), the Wild Australia Show should have easily fit the bill, although visitors to the pleasure grounds were clearly there for entertainment more than edification. If it were to be successful, the Wild Australia Show had to dial up its spectacle, danger and wonder to capture Sydney audiences.

---

12   Ibid.
13   Ibid.
14   Nundo L. Doss, *Reminiscences, English and Australasian: Being an Account of a Visit to England, Australia, New Zealand, Tasmania and Ceylon, etc* (Calcutta: M. C. Bhomick, 1893), 195, cited in Ford, 'A Summer Fling', 100.
15   Ford, 'A Summer Fling', 98.
16   Viator, 'At the Bondi Aquarium', *Sydney Morning Herald*, 1 October 1887, 8.

Precursors and panics: The 1888 'centennial corroboree' and a desire for 'white' Sydney

While the arrival at the Bondi Aquarium and Pleasure Grounds of the Wild Australia Show from the far reaches of colonial Queensland was much anticipated and widely publicised, it was not, in fact, the first Aboriginal troupe to perform there or at its competitor sites in Coogee and Manly.[17] Early in Sydney's centennial year, 1888, when the Bondi Aquarium had only recently opened its doors, a 'grand aboriginal corroboree' was listed among the entertainments on the bill.[18] Some press reports described it as an 'Aboriginal troupe from the back blocks of Queensland consisting of 60 stalwart warriors and 20 lubra musicians all in full war paint'; others vaguely rendered the performers' origins as 'the far interior';[19] while yet other accounts claimed that many of its members came from New South Wales,[20] including Singleton in the Hunter region north of Sydney, and Warren and Narrabri in the northwest. One reminiscence, for instance, recalled: 'Aboriginals from all parts of the State were gathered in, with their gins and piccaninnies, and I suppose there were fully 100 of them in all.'[21] This guess is reasonable. Reports at the time were imprecise about the size of the group, which numbered anywhere from 60 to 150.[22] While some other Aboriginal performance troupes were known to be working in the 1880s, such as the small family troupe from far north Queensland that R. C. Cunningham toured in Europe and America,[23] an ensemble of this size, even at the lower end of the estimate, was unusual. However, unlike the Wild Australia Show that would, in a handful of years, also play at Bondi Aquarium, the 'centenary players' was not a troupe per se. Rather, it appears to have been a loose gathering of people and groups from different regions

17   In 1889, Harry Stockdale brought Aboriginal men from north Australia to perform at both the Coogee and Manly aquariums. See, for instance: 'N.T. "Exhibits" at the Coogee Aquarium', *North Australian*, 23 February 1889, 3; 'Coogee Aquarium', *Sydney Morning Herald*, 8 March 1889, 8; 'The Aquaria', *Australian Star*, 11 March 1889, 8; 'The Music Halls', *Sydney Morning Herald*, 15 June 1889, 12.
18   [Untitled], *Freeman's Journal*, 28 January 1888, 8; 'Advertising: The Royal Aquarium, Bondi', *Sydney Morning Herald*, 25 January 1888, 2; 'Amusements', *Sydney Morning Herald*, 3 February 1888, 8.
19   *Newcastle Morning Herald and Miner's Advocate*, 1 February 1888, 3.
20   'Advertising: The Royal Aquarium, Bondi', *Sydney Morning Herald*, 25 January 1888, 2.
21   Mr Gilchrist, cited in F. J. Wuhrer, *A Short History of Bondi Aquarium and Wonderland City: Pleasure Places of the Past* (Local Studies, Waverley Library, Sydney), 10.
22   'Late News, New South Wales', *Newcastle Morning Herald and Miner's Advocate*, 2 February 1888, 3; 'Corroboree at Bondi', *Daily Telegraph*, 4 February 1888, 5.
23   R. Poignant, *Professional Savages: Captive Lives and Western Spectacle* (New Haven: Yale University Press, 2004).

brought together for a one-off commemorative event. And, unlike the Wild Australia Show, a fair amount of government sponsorship had brought it together, as this snippet in the *Australian Star* reveals:

> About 60 or 70 aborigines are camped at Bondi, under the charge of Mr Reuben, who has been appointed by the Government to look after them. Contingents from all parts of the country districts are in the camp, and supplied daily with provisions, tobacco, and a 'nobbler' each.[24]

Reuben and his business partner, a Mr Willis, were, it seems, in the business of exhibiting and touring Aboriginal people, although, like Webster and Browne, they are difficult to trace. One report notes that the idea for a centenary corroboree had originated with them and, like Meston and Purcell, they were described as having 'spent many years amongst the natives, and have not only acquired several of their languages but made themselves acquainted with their modes of living'.[25] The veracity of this claim is not validated, but it was certainly a common feature of the schtick used in these kinds of enterprises. A month later, Reuben was reportedly in charge of an Aboriginal cricket team, some members of which might well have been earlier involved in the centennial show since they came from some of the same places—Narrabri, Manning River, Singleton—as performers in the 1888 gathering.[26]

In a way that anticipates coverage of the Wild Australia Show, the remainder of the *Australian Star*'s report on Reuben and Willis's exhibition enterprise was delivered in an ironic or satirical style, commonly used by journalists to question and lampoon Aboriginal people's 'cultural credentials' and their performance as 'authentic':

> Many of them are half caste, and others civilised so much that they have never beheld a corroboree in their lives. Monday next a corroboree on the much approved Murrumbidgee style will be held. No invitation cards will be issued, but several dusky kings and queens will be 'at home' during the day. Few of them possess any aboriginal weapons. They visited the Aquarium on Friday, and announced it 'budgery' [good].[27]

---

24 'Aboriginal Corroboree', *Australian Star*, 30 January 1888, 8. A nobbler is slang for a measure of spirits.

25 'Corroboree at Bondi', *Daily Telegraph*, 4 February 1888, 5.

26 'Cricket', *Maitland Mercury and Hunter River General Advertiser*, 17 March 1888, 8.

27 'Aboriginal Corroboree', *Australian Star*, 30 January 1888, 8.

Other reports insisted upon the performers' 'authenticity', including one writer who assured readers that they are all 'Queensland aboriginals, and not as is supposed by some, white men and women disfigured for the occasion'.[28]

Whatever expectations had been built by the press coverage, the 1888 performances were, by all accounts, a success. The first 'corroboree' attracted an audience of around 2,000–3,000, which apparently increased to 6,000–7,000 for the second.[29] When the Wild Australia Show arrived to perform at the same venue five years later, an appetite for Aboriginal corroborees and spectacle was still strong. For its opening performance, the Show was reported to have attracted a 10,000-strong audience.[30] With those crowds, its summer season in Sydney looked promising indeed.

As entertainment, Aboriginal corroborees at the Bondi Aquarium were a precursor to the Wild Australia Show, but there are other overlaps too. In all cases, a large gathering of Aboriginal people from regional areas to perform for metropolitan audiences invariably provoked settler anxiety. During a debate about funding for the New South Wales Aborigines Protection Board (NSW APB) in Parliament in mid-1888, Aboriginal performances at Bondi were recalled. As one parliamentarian opined:

> There was a gathering of blacks on the occasion of the opening of the Bondi Aquarium, and the people who saw them about the streets of the city must have regretted that they had been brought here for such a purpose.[31]

Similarly, a reminiscence recorded many years later about the 1888 celebrations recalled the controversy as vividly as the spectacle:

> [The] corroboree item did not last long on the bill of fare. Many of the young Aboriginals were brought before the court for over indulgence of alcohol, and were sent back to the bush.[32]

But had the government not paid them for their services in 'nobbler' (i.e. whisky or spirits)?

---

28 'Amusements', *Sydney Morning Herald*, 3 February 1888, 8.
29 'Corroboree at Bondi', *Daily Telegraph*, 4 February 1888, 5; *Freeman's Journal*, 4 February 1888, 10.
30 '"Wild Australia" Entertainment'.
31 'Aborigines Protection Board', NSW Parliament, Hansard, 27 June 1888, 5879.
32 Gilchrist in Wuhrer, *A Short History of Bondi Aquarium*, 10.

When the Wild Australia Show arrived in the last week of 1892, that earlier episode had still not quite faded from memory, and continued to be invoked. Official correspondence in response to the Wild Australia Show's arrival referred expressly to 'a previous occasion [when] a number of aborigines were brought to Sydney by speculators and turned adrift without the means to enable them to return to their homes'.[33] It was the alleged 'turning adrift'—the apparent absence of supervision and control as much as the supposed unseemly spectacle of Aboriginal people in the city's streets—that spooked the authorities. Indeed, the spectre of Aboriginal people 'on the loose' in the city, and powerful tropes about 'natives' being out of place in urban areas, had contributed directly to the NSW APB's foundation in the early 1880s.[34] The NSW APB emerged from an effort to remove Aboriginal people camping at the government boatsheds at Circular Quay. A decade later, the board was still shutting down camps. In 1891, it had closed two Aboriginal camps not far from the Bondi Aquarium—one at the Randwick Toll Bar and the other at Moore Park.[35] And it was preoccupied with trying to keep a check on activities at the La Perouse Aboriginal settlement on Botany Bay, around which a tourist precinct and pleasure grounds were growing.[36] (Indeed, it is not inconceivable that some Aboriginal people from La Perouse saw the Wild Australia Show at Bondi.) As this indicates, the New South Wales Government's position was that Aboriginal people from other places were not welcome in the city. Aboriginal people who actually came from the Sydney region and were custodians for the Country were hardly welcome there either.

And so, for the month, while the troupe was successfully performing at the Bondi Pleasure Grounds and elsewhere in Sydney, attracting audiences to twice-daily performances, the NSW APB was expending effort and resources to try to close it down and to return the performers from where they came. This miserly official view was at odds with the Wild Australia Show's popular appeal, as well as the enjoyment and rewards the performers themselves experienced as they flexed their performative muscles (as will be shown). With hindsight, it is clear that the government's meddling

---

33   Secretary, Aborigines Protection Board, to colonial secretary, 14 January 1893, SRNSW, 93/1422.

34   For studies on Aboriginality and urban spaces in colonial contexts, see: P. Edmonds, *Urbanizing Frontiers: Indigenous Peoples and Settlers in 19th-Century Pacific Rim Cities* (Vancouver: University of British Columbia Press, 2010), doi.org/10.59962/9780774816236; Coll Thrush, *Native Seattle: Histories from the Crossing-Over Place* (Seattle: University of Washington Press, 2007).

35   NSW APB Minutes, 5 March 1891, SRNSW, 4/7108 and 7 July 1892, SRNSW, 4/7110.

36   M. Nugent, *Botany Bay: Where Histories Meet* (Sydney: Allen & Unwin, 2005); P. Irish, *Hidden in Plain View: The Aboriginal People of Coastal Sydney* (Sydney: NewSouth Books, 2017).

would contribute to the beginning of the end for the Wild Australia Show enterprise. But that was still to come. For now, the troupe had a week of shows to put on—two a day, weather permitting. Through both written and visual representations of those performances, we are granted further glimpses and insights into the performers' lives and experiences during the Sydney season.

By the seaside

During its time in Sydney, the Wild Australia Show troupe was accommodated in a couple of cottages near the pleasure grounds where they performed.[37] These were owned by Alfred Wyburd, the Bondi Aquarium's proprietor. Thirty or so people housed in two small seaside cottages would have been quite a different experience from the St Lucia camp in Brisbane (see Chapter 7). However, like St Lucia, the Bondi area, with its ocean beaches and scrubby heaths, was at that time only sparsely settled.

The extensive grounds of the Bondi Aquarium seem to have provided the performers with room to move, both literally and metaphorically. Reports of initial performances suggest that the performers stuck fairly closely to the repertoire that had been drilled in Brisbane (described in detail in Chapter 7). They performed the same dances, gave the same demonstrations of skills and acted the same historical drama. Yet, no two live performances are ever the same. They are always ephemeral, shaped by context, setting, atmosphere, and audience size and response as much as by the players themselves. And so, while superficially, the repertoire given in Sydney remained true to its Brisbane beginnings, the conditions under which it was performed subtly altered it.

A series of photographs of troupe members at the Bondi Aquarium gives a sense of the performance space that the seaside venue provided (see Figures 7.6, 8.1 and 8.2). In Sydney, the troupe attracted the attention of Charles Kerry, owner of one of the largest photographic studios in the city at the time.[38] On at least one occasion, perhaps more, a photographer from the studio travelled out to the Bondi Aquarium to take pictures of the troupe

---

37   'Aborigines Protection Board. Aborigines at Bondi', *Evening News*, 6 January 1893, 2.
38   For details about the creation of the Wild Australia Show's photographs, see: M. Aird and P. Memmott, 'Photographic Identification of the Troupe Members of the Wild Australia Show', *Memoirs of the Queensland Museum—Culture* 12 (June 2021): 8–13, doi.org/10.17082/j.2205-3239.12.1.2021.2021-02.

members performing their dances and drama. (Other Kerry photographs of the Wild Australia Show troupe are portraits taken in a studio.) Only a few of the Kerry photographs are taken inside the pavilion with the performers on the stage in front of the painted backdrop (see Figures 7.6 and 8.3). Most in the series are taken outside on the beach (see Figures 8.1 and 8.2). Perhaps seeking a naturalistic setting with plenty of natural light, unimpeded by crowds and away from built structures (such as the switchback railway that generally dominated views of the pleasure grounds), the photographer must have persuaded the performers to go through their routine on the sand with waves pounding in the background. The result is a quite unique set of photographs.

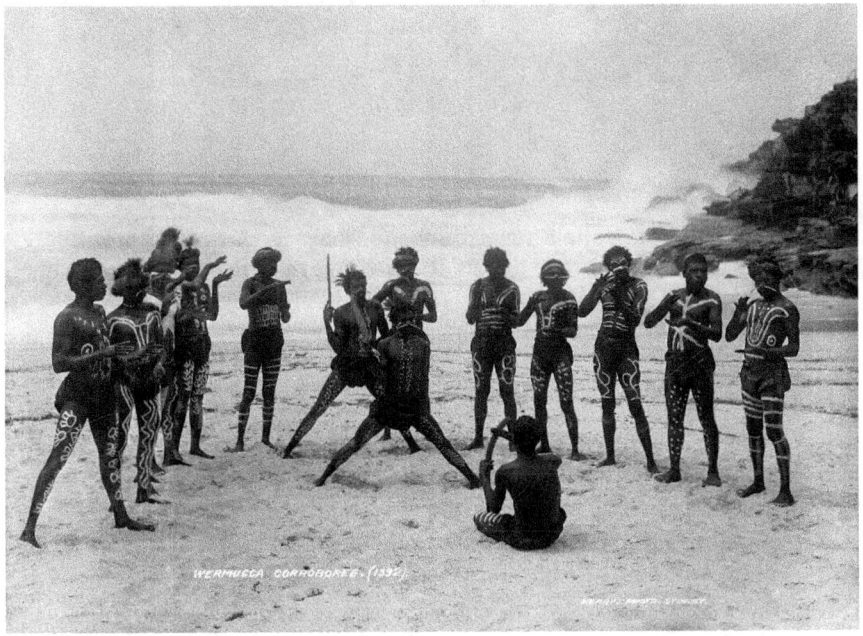

Figure 8.1: Wild Australia Show troupe members performing a dance on Tamarama Beach during its season at the Bondi Aquarium in Sydney in either December 1892 or January 1893

Source: Powerhouse Museum. Gift of Australian Consolidated Press under the Taxation Incentives of the Arts Scheme, 1985. Photographer: Kerry and Co., Sydney. Object no. 85/1284-660.

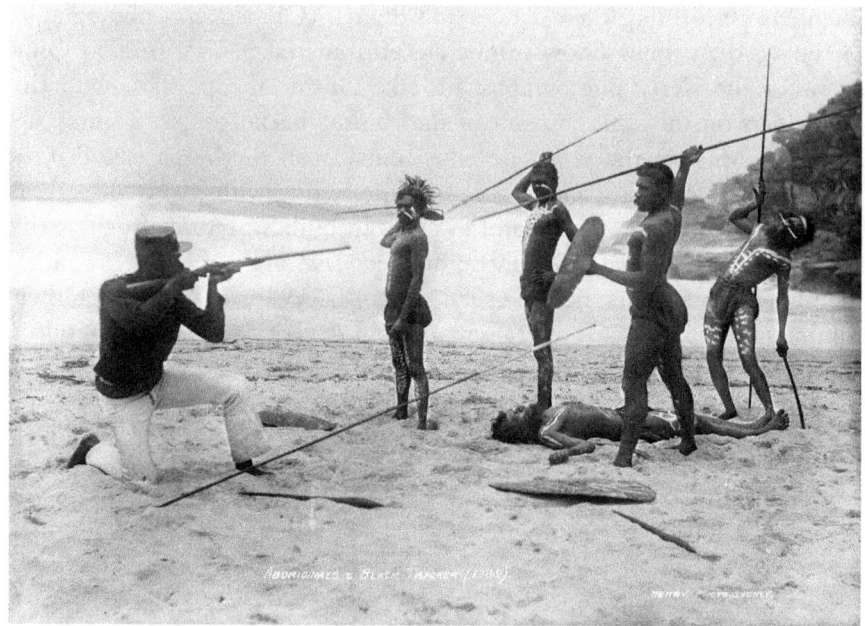

Figure 8.2: Wild Australia Show troupe members performing a frontier tableau on Tamarama Beach during its season at the Bondi Aquarium in Sydney in either December 1892 or January 1893

Source: Powerhouse Museum. Gift of Australian Consolidated Press under the Taxation Incentives of the Arts Scheme, 1985. Photographer: Kerry and Co., Sydney. Object no. 85/1284-658.

This valuable visual record helps in the work of reconstructing and re-viewing the dances that were a central component of the Show. By their very nature, the photographs provide details and perspectives missing from written accounts. Although stills, the photographs nevertheless give a sense of the arrangement and movement of bodies in space. The churned-up sand under the performers' feet suggests plenty of movement as the beach temporarily became a dance arena and stomping ground. There is something more stilted about the photographs taken in the pavilion, as the dancers stand on a hard surface in front of a painted scene. Perhaps the photographer had sensed that lack of verve before deciding to go outside.

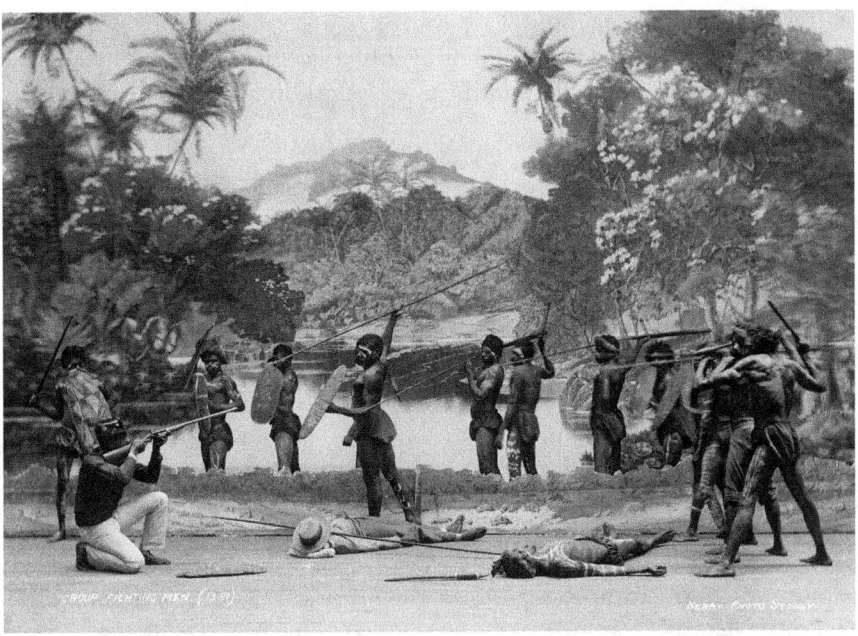

Figure 8.3: Members of Wild Australia Show troupe performing historical tableau of Native Police shooting on stage in Sydney in either December 1892 or January 1893

Source: Powerhouse Museum. Gift of Australian Consolidated Press under the Taxation Incentives of the Arts Scheme, 1985. Photographer: Kerry and Co., Sydney. Object no. 85/1284-657.

Three photographs within the series taken on the beach show 15 male performers, including Yamurra but not the three men from Thursday Island, doing the 'cockatoo dance', also referred to as the 'Wermugga corroboree' (see Figure 8.1). In each, the same songman sits cross-legged on the sand, clapping two boomerangs together. One image shows the dancers arrayed closely in a line, all with their legs wide apart, their ankles overlapping each other, and their hands either held behind their backs or resting on their thighs. The dancers orient in slightly different directions, moving their torsos. In a second image, perhaps the next in the sequence, two dancers have broken away from the line and occupy the central space between the songman and the company. With their straight legs spread wide apart, they each hold a boomerang or club aloft and appear to move in formation, one dancer following behind the other. The ensemble watches on, all clapping hands to keep the beat. A third image, possibly the final in the sequence, shows just one man in the central dance space and the songman still seated at the front. The remaining 13 performers are arranged in a semicircle behind the principal dancer, imitating his movements. With their usual wide-legged stance, they all hold their arms aloft, in a gesture that seems to suggest the dance's climax.

The vibrant colours—the red and yellow ochre on rainforest shields or the lurid colour of bird feathers in hair ornaments—that were part of the spectacle are not captured in the monochrome or sepia images. Nevertheless, they document the ways in which the performers were painted up, all with distinct individual designs; the types of ornaments, including headdresses, they wore; and the objects, such as shields, boomerangs and clubs, that they used. Visual images convey specificity and particularity that descriptions in press reports, which typically resorted to stock phrases such as 'gaudily decorated', 'wild gesticulation', 'extraordinary movements' and 'almost childish delight', fail to convey.[39]

Two further photographs in this small series document another key component in the troupe's repertoire: the historical tableau (see Chapter 7) that was typically performed as the Show's finale. One image depicts opposing small parties of 'warriors' facing off and two injured men, perhaps already dead, lying prone in the sand. One man prepares to deliver a final blow with his club to one of the victims. The other photograph is of the retributions for the killings, and includes a member of the Native Police, uniformed and crouching on one knee, training his firearm at the culprits (see Figure 8.2). If these two scenes made up the drama as played on the beach, then it had become an all-Aboriginal drama. There was no settler or swagman in sight.

Within the Kerry photographs, there is a single photograph of the three Kaurareg men standing together, one wearing a dance mask,[40] looking confidently at the camera. And another of the entire ensemble, except the women, probably taken post-performance. Offered for sale, either singly or as a set, before too long, the photographs of the Wild Australia Show performers on Tamarama Beach would soon get jumbled up with the many hundreds of images of other Aboriginal people and Torres Strait Islanders in the Kerry Studios' vast collections and archives (see Chapter 11). They would

---

39   '"Wild Australia" at Bondi Aquarium', *Clarence and Richmond Examiner*, 7 January 1893, 2.

40   '"Wild Australia" Entertainment': 'A devil dance by a couple of Desert men (Central Australia) aroused considerable interest. So, too, did a weird mask dance, in which the performer used a gorgeous mask made of tortoise shell, cockatoo feathers, beads, fine grass, &c. The mask stands about ?ft height, and is valued at from £10 to £15.'

be numbered out of sequence, wrongly captioned and separated from each other, and the details of the day and reasons they were taken, and/or of the story and biographies of the performers, would be lost in the process. Before long, the photographs would become dislodged from the Wild Australia Show, circulating instead as generic images of unidentified representatives of an imprecise place.

While it is not clear if the beach was the usual stage on which the troupe performed for paying customers, various reports do refer to a village on the lawn and the performance being held both indoors and outdoors, and in the daytime and the night-time. As a *Sydney Morning Herald* reviewer explained:

> The first part of the performance yesterday afternoon was given in the main hall of the pavilion, and included the Churrumboola war dance, the Werrmugga (Cockatoo) [corroboree], Prince of Wales Island dance, young men's [corroboree], and the lighting of fires by means of fire-sticks. From the main hall the blacks proceeded to the lawn and represented a native village with myalls at work, and showed their wonderful skills in throwing boomerangs and spears, following this up with nulla-nulla fighting, ducoons [?] throwing, archery practice, &c. In the evening the performance was given wholly on the lawn.[41]

The night-time performance sounded impressive. As one article noted:

> The performance in the evening, which took place on the lawn, which was brilliantly illuminated with the electric light and at intervals with Greek fire, was even a more remarkable one than that in the afternoon, the 'warriors' under the strange conditions of the weird illuminations offering a singularly savage spectacle. A devil dance by a desert man from Central Australia, in which a hideous mask is worn, was full of uncanny suggestions.[42]

Thus, the Bondi Aquarium, with its extensive grounds, diverse attractions, extended opening hours and electricity, allowed the repertoire and program to develop. If reviews are a faithful guide, it became even more spectacular. The larger open space suited the skills demonstrations better than a small stage and also allowed for some elaboration of the historical drama. Not only

---

41   Ibid.
42   'Wild Australia', *Evening News*, 29 December 1892, 2.

did the 'warriors' murder the swagman, but they also burnt his hut to the ground.[43] Pyrotechnics added to the spectacle and in ways that apparently made 'the audience shudder'.[44]

The move outside also meant that the performers—and audiences— were released from Meston's accompanying monologue. Inside, Meston performed as white expert and orator giving a 'descriptive lecture'.[45] Outside, there was scope for the performances—and, thus, the performers—to speak for themselves and to command their own show. And, perhaps, it was this gradual assumption of greater creative control that prompted the Kaurareg to propose an addition to the repertoire. On 31 December 1892, after almost a week of performances, a change in the program was announced:

> a fight will take place between an aboriginal and a shark. 'Dagum,'
> a Prince of Wales Islander, undertakes to fight the man-eating shark
> 11ft. in length, and the contest will take place in the seal pond.[46]

In the end, this addition to the program was prevented from going ahead, but perhaps the intimation it would was enough to increase custom. Similarly, press notices and advertisements reveal how Meston was also making himself part of the spectacle:

> Especial interest was centred in a realistic contest between
> Mr. Meston and a Mary River black (i.e. Yamurra), who engaged
> in a duel with paddymelon sticks and war boomerangs—a set-to
> attended with no little danger, as the combatants were in evidence
> earnest, and a chance blow from one of the weapons might have had
> serious results. Mr. Meston also demonstrated his ability to throw
> the boomerang.[47]

However, the outside, seaside venue had some downsides as well, not least the weather. One report noted that: 'To some extent the performance was interfered with, as the boisterousness of the wind rendered the boomerang throwing, with any degree of precision, a matter of absolute impossibility.'[48] Another noted the problem of 'heavy rains [that] interfered with the

43 Ibid.
44 Ibid.
45 'Bondi Aquarium', *Sydney Morning Herald*, 2 January 1893, 9.
46 'During the Week', *Sydney Morning Herald*, 31 December 1892, 10.
47 'Bondi Aquarium', *Sydney Morning Herald*, 16 January 1893, 6.
48 Ibid.

arrangements made'.[49] While the Show went on despite these obstacles, it was clear that further adjustments would need to be made for it to be a going concern.

Second week in Sydney: Performing at the School of Arts

In January 1893, it was announced that a completely new venue had been added to the troupe's schedule. An arrangement had been entered into with the owner of another troupe, the Walshe Family Circus (aka Walshe Novelty Company), for the Wild Australia Show to perform on its bill each night at the School of Arts in the city.[50] This was, on the whole, warmly received:

> The amalgamation of Walshe's Novelty Company and Mr. Meston's Aboriginals at the School of Arts results in an entertainment which has a stronger claim to public support than that of mere variety.[51]

More than entertaining, it also apparently provided 'object lessons in history',[52] and had 'a certain amount of value from an ethnological point of view'.[53] These snippets contain a clue as to why the amalgamation of two quite divergent shows was attempted at all: variety acts like the Walshe Novelty Company were struggling to survive and, as shown, the Wild Australia Show was also already facing challenges. Their respective proprietors clearly saw an advantage in joining forces. The economic downturn of the 1890s was starting to bite. Clearly, too, the night-time shows at the Bondi Aquarium were not sustainable. The lighting and pyrotechnics involved were costly. Margins were tight. As Caroline Ford notes in her discussion of Sydney's seaside pleasure grounds, the Bondi Aquarium and other privately owned coastal leisure precincts were always economically precarious and constantly on the brink of collapse.[54] They could struggle to attract audiences to their out-of-the-way locations.

---

49   '"Wild Australia" Entertainment'.
50   'School of Arts', *Sydney Morning Herald*, 7 January 1893, 10.
51   'Amusements', *Daily Telegraph*, 7 January 1893, 5.
52   Ibid.
53   'School of Arts', *Sydney Morning Herald*, 7 January 1893, 10.
54   Ford, 'A Summer Fling'.

Not surprisingly, then, the arrangement was presented primarily as a convenience for audiences. After opening night at the School of Arts, the *Evening News* reported:

> Since the commencement of the holidays [Wild Australia Shows] have been showing with success at Bondi Aquarium. There were naturally many people who desired to see the exhibition, but could not conveniently arrange for a visit to Bondi. This being recognised by Mr. Wyburd [proprietor of Bondi Aquarium] and Mr. Meston, an arrangement was effected with Mr Ralph Walshe by which the aborigines might be introduced into his variety performance. It may be pointed out, however, that the afternoon entertainments are still being held at the aquarium grounds.[55]

Rather than audiences travelling, it was the troupe who would be transported to the city nightly. With this new arrangement in place, the Wild Australia Show's three o'clock afternoon slot at the Bondi Aquarium continued, and its evening show was performed in the city. The troupe's usual workload of appearing twice a day did not change.[56]

At the School of Arts, the Walshe Company was the opening act, performing its various singing and burlesque numbers, followed, after the interval, by a condensed version of the Wild Australia Show adapted for a squeezed space. As one review noted: 'The small stage space necessarily involved the curtailment of the programme, it being impossible, of course, to display the powers of the blacks in boomerang and spear throwing.'[57] Demonstrations of skills were dropped, giving way to the dances and the drama. Putting a positive spin on the cramped conditions, another journalist claimed it 'showed to advantage the specially painted scenery, and the judicious use of the limelight produced that exceedingly pleasant effect which is frequently achieved by collaboration of art and nature'.[58] An item in the *Daily Telegraph* explained that during an hour's entertainment:

> There were war dances, a 'devil dance' by two Central Australians, dances peculiar to the Prince of Wales Islanders, [corroborees] of various kinds, firemaking, and a number of what might be called dramatic sketches, in which some of the aboriginals showed quite a histrionic aptitude.[59]

---

55 'Wild Australia', *Evening News*, 6 January 1893, 3.
56 '"Wild Australia" at the School of Arts', *Daily Telegraph*, 6 January 1893, 6.
57 'Wild Australia', *Evening News*, 6 January 1893, 3.
58 '"Wild Australia" at the School of Arts'.
59 Ibid.

The two dances singled out for special mention in the press report were also the subjects selected for studio photographs. As already noted, the Kerry photographic studio had created images of ensemble dances being performed on the sands at Tamarama. It added to these a series of photographs taken in its studio. Located at 808 George Street, the Kerry photographic studio was just a short walk from the School of Arts at 275 Pitt Street. It is not inconceivable, then, that the performers visited the studio while performing in the city and that the images were offered for sale during their show.

One of the studio photographs is of the three Wakaya men, showing them wearing the conical headdress that was used for the so-called 'devil dance' (see Figure 8.4a). With two sitting and one standing, they are arranged in a triangular shape that mimics the headdress worn by one of them. The men's faces are covered with tufts of white wool, which is likely a substitute for feathers.

Other studio photographs are of the three male Kaurareg (Prince of Wales Island) performers. In one image, Dugum sits with one knee raised, looking directly at the camera. He wears a headdress (a white dhari or dari of the kind now featured on the Torres Strait Islander flag), has a fibrous 'apron' over his shorts and holds a bow and arrow in one hand. In another, which only shows him from waist up, he has feather ornaments tucked into armbands and wears a different headdress. Another photograph in this series shows one of the Kaurareg men in profile, sitting on the ground, wearing an elaborate mask with a protruding jaw (see Figure 8.4b). When made into a postcard, the mask was wrongly captioned as a 'devil mask'. As Chantal Knowles notes:

> The title on the postcard is erroneous, since no [Torres Strait Islands] mask is described as a devil's mask in any other context. It was no doubt designed to excite interest, peddling an embellished exotic image of other cultures to a wide audience.[60]

The mistake originated with the Wild Australia Show program of dances, which typically included a 'devil dance' performed by the Wakaya. From performance to photograph to postcard, that descriptor was loosely used and transposed from one group to another without much concern for geographical or cultural precision (see Chapter 11 for more discussion of this theme).

---

60 C. Knowles, 'Unmasking the Torres Strait: Objects and Relationships', in *Ancestors, Artefacts, Empire: Indigenous Australia in British and Irish Museums*, ed. G. Sculthorpe, M. Nugent and H. Morphy (London: British Museum, 2021), 203.

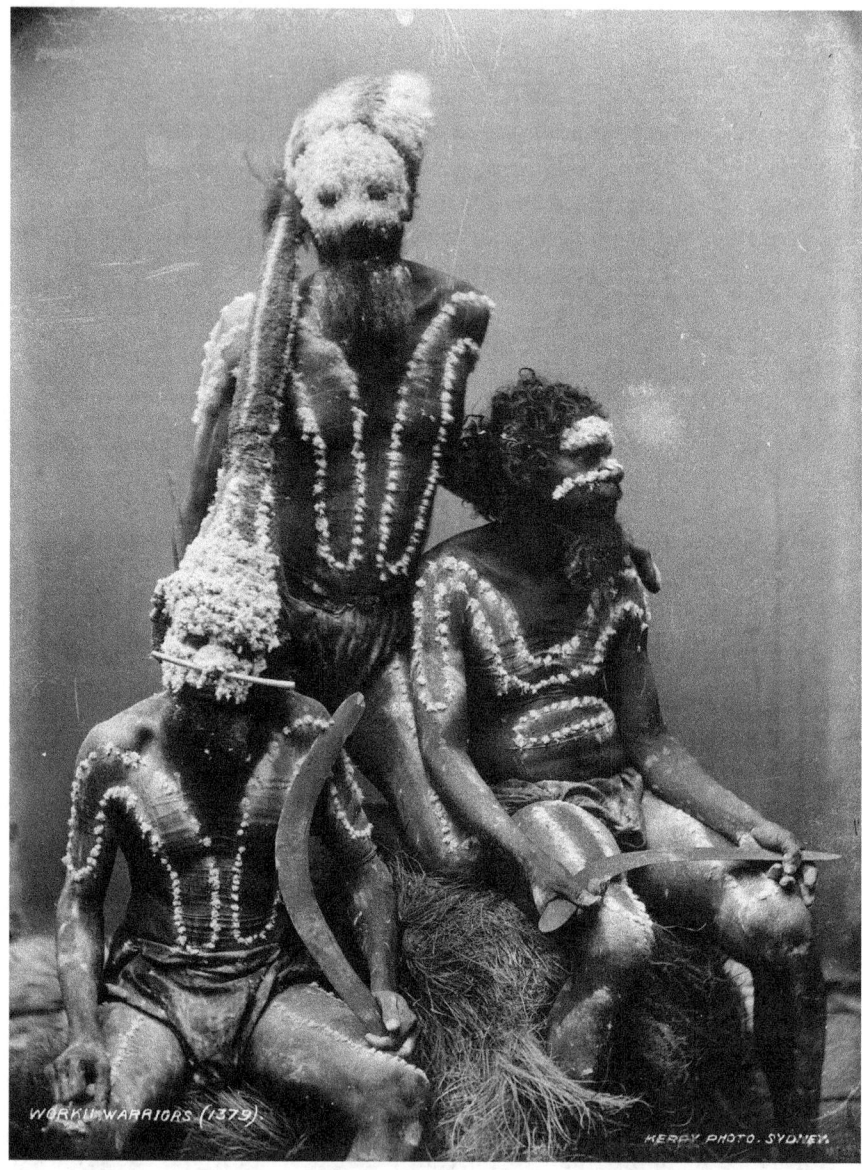

Figure 8.4a: Wakaya men—Narimbu (left), Kudajarnd (centre), Dangakura (right)—photographed in Kerry Studio, Sydney, January 1893

Source: Powerhouse Museum. Gift of Australian Consolidated Press under the Taxation Incentives of the Arts Scheme, 1985. Photographer: Kerry and Co., Sydney. Photographic negative 85/1284-2821.

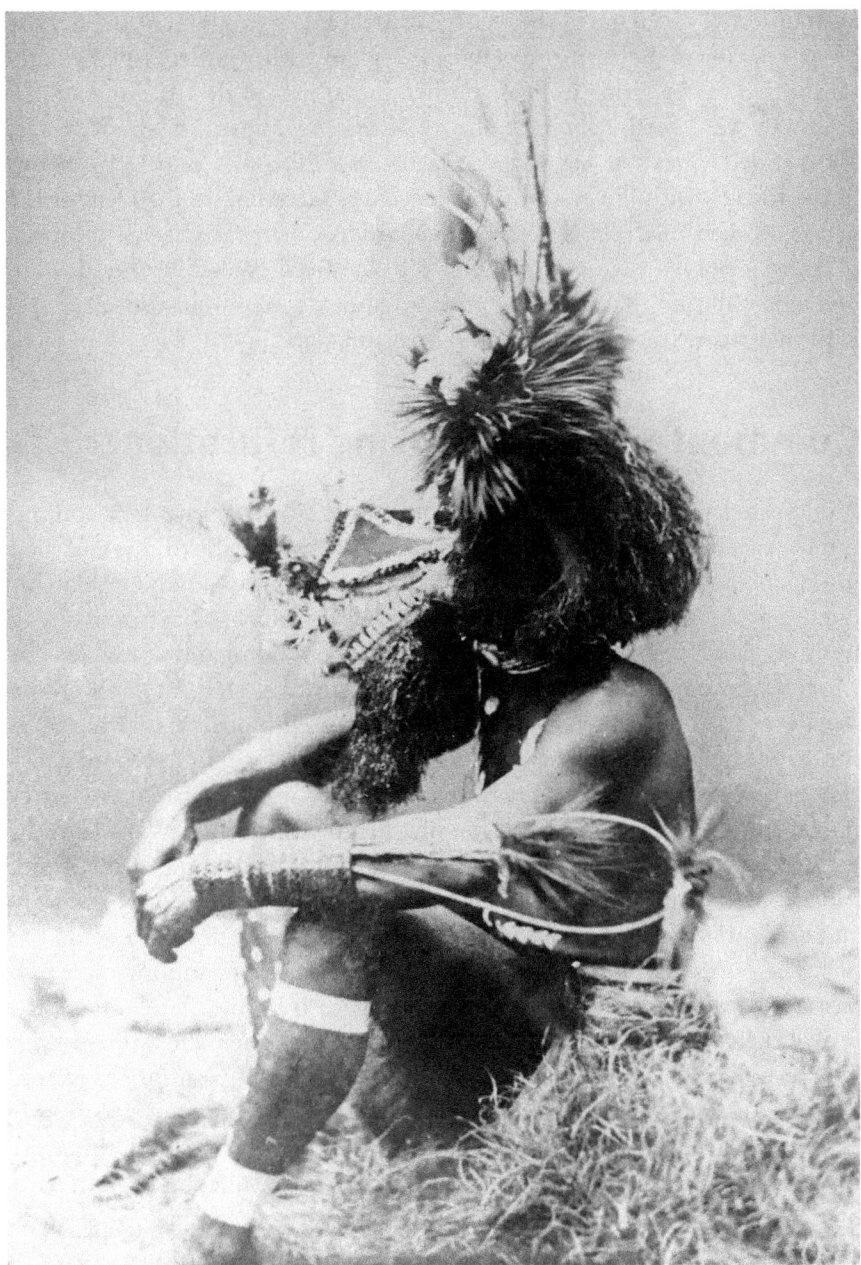

Figure 8.4b: Kaurareg man, Dugum, wearing dance mask, photographed in Kerry Studio, Sydney, January 1893

Source: Powerhouse Museum. Gift of Australian Consolidated Press under the Taxation Incentives of the Arts Scheme, 1985. Photographer: Kerry and Co., Sydney. Object no. 85/1284-638.

In addition to the dances, the Wild Australia Show program at the School of Arts retained the historical tableau, replete with murder, violence and retribution. One writer suggested that the scene of the tracking of the swagman was 'worthy the best efforts of the melodramatic school'.[61] The Show ended with what was described as an assemblage of '"the black demons of the forest", with illustrations of vengeance, according to the ideas of the savage, and so on'.[62] This description borders on the burlesque, creating, perhaps, a point of connection with the Walshe show before the interval, one report noting that 'Messrs Crawford and Mooney were also successful with their eccentric negro songs and acrobatic dancing'.[63]

Commentary, criticism and refutation

As indicated, the Wild Australia Show generated much commentary, and this was the case in Sydney also. During its season in Sydney, the troupe and their managers garnered column inches of copy in the press—and considerable interest in other quarters as well. A good deal of it was paid publicity—positive, largely descriptive reviews, with copy probably provided by Meston (the journalist), Purcell, Browne (also an 'old pressman') or Webster. Whatever its source, certain themes were repeated, not least of which was the degree of 'contact' the performers had had with Europeans. 'Contact'—also glossed as 'civilisation' or 'contamination'—was a constant matter of public concern. For instance, in the first lengthy review the Wild Australia Show received in the Sydney press a few days after its opening at the Bondi Aquarium, as many words were given to explaining the troupe's history and credentials as to describing and evaluating its repertoire. Presented as being of particular appeal to those with an interest in 'the manners and customs of the Australian aboriginals as practiced prior to ... contact', the review stressed that the performers themselves were men and women 'who had never been brought into contact with the whites'.[64] Contrary to fact, as the chapters on recruitment show, this is how the company was persistently portrayed in the Sydney press. Even if some had been living with 'the white man' for a while, the troupe nevertheless was heralded as coming from parts of the continent understood as frontiers, yet to be completely 'settled', and thus seen with city eyes through lenses of savagery, primitiveness and

---

61 '"Wild Australia" at the School of Arts'.
62 Ibid.
63 'School of Arts', *Sydney Morning Herald*, 7 January 1893, 10.
64 '"Wild Australia" Entertainment'.

lawlessness. The Wild Australia Show in Sydney brought this imagined distant frontier closer—and this in turn fed metropolitan discussions about what should happen in such remote regions, particularly how they might be developed, and how to 'manage' and 'govern' Aboriginal people, like those represented in the troupe, in the process.[65]

In Sydney, the commentary around the Wild Australia Show had another edge that had been largely absent from the Brisbane press coverage a month or so earlier. This concerned Aboriginal mobility and visibility. Being a widely publicised travelling spectacle, the Wild Australia Show provoked a minor panic in government circles about both. What was this group of Aboriginal people from Queensland's northern regions doing, travelling from colony to colony? Under whose authority? Why had the Queensland Government allowed it?

Almost as soon as the troupe stepped off the ship in Sydney, the NSW APB got itself involved. This particular institution of colonial governance of Aboriginal people was only a decade old, and it had emerged quite explicitly to deal with what was seen as the problem of Aboriginal people 'congregating' in Sydney.[66] Throughout the 1880s, the NSW APB pursued policies and practices of forceable removal and containment, creating a network of small reserves across the colony for Aboriginal people's exclusive use.[67] While Aboriginal people interpreted them as a form of compensation for dispossession and as acknowledgement of their (former) status as sovereigns, the authorities regarded them more as depots for rations, as segregation sites, and as havens for the old and dying.[68] The assumption remained that the Aboriginal population in New South Wales was dying out.

The Wild Australia Show troupe's arrival in Sydney coincided with the NSW APB's efforts to institute restrictions on Aboriginal people's freedom of movement across the colony, and, in particular, to stop them from coming into Sydney. The minutes of an APB meeting in 1891 noted that 'it is very undesirable for Aborigines to come to Sydney at all'.[69] When the

65   See: T. Rowse, *Indigenous and Other Australians since 1901* (Sydney: NewSouth Publishing, 2017).
66   See: J. Mitchell and A. Curthoys, 'How Different Was Victoria', in *Settler Colonial Governance in Nineteenth-Century Victoria*, ed. L. Boucher and L. Russell (Canberra: ANU Press, 2015), 190–2, doi.org/10.22459/SCGNCV.04.2015.
67   See: H. Goodall, *Invasion to Embassy: Land in Aboriginal Politics in New South Wales, 1770–1972* (St Leonards: Allen & Unwin, 1996).
68   See: R. Egan, *Power and Dysfunction: The New South Wales Board for the Protection of Aborigines 1883–1940* (Canberra: ANU Press, 2021), doi.org/10.22459/PD.2021.
69   NSW Aborigines Protection Board Minutes, 5 March 1891, SRNSW, 4/7108.

Wild Australia Show troupe arrived in Sydney in late 1892, it was stepping into a context in which the visible presence of groups of Aboriginal people was not only not welcome, but also was actively resisted.

The NSW APB took immediate action by putting the Wild Australia Show troupe under surveillance. It sent local police, its usual agents, to inquire into and report on the troupe's activities and plans while in Sydney. That enquiry is how we know the troupe members were staying in cottages in Tamarama. Sergeant Sherwood was dispatched to look into the matter, later reporting that 'the aborigines referred to numbered 32 in all, and were quartered in some cottages in Delview-street, close to the aquarium'.[70] Citing the mysterious number of 32 members, he must have taken the size of the troupe on faith rather than conducted his own headcount. By then, as we showed in the previous chapter, it only numbered 27. Sherwood reported to his superiors that they were 'under the control and in the charge of Messrs. A. Meston, J. Webster, and B. Purcell'.[71] Only Webster and Purcell were at home when the policeman called, and they offered the following in response to his queries:

> they were making a tour of this colony and Victoria previous to going to England and America. For this purpose they had to obtain the sanction of the Colonial Secretary of Queensland, who required them to enter into a bond and give a guarantee for the aborigines' safe return to their native colony … and the troupe had an engagement in Melbourne for the 26th instant.[72]

Upon receiving the policeman's report (a copy of which has not been located), the NSW APB 'decided to ask the superintendent of police in the Waverley district to keep the aborigines under close observation while they were in Sydney and to report when they left'.[73] Meston et al. were on notice.

The NSW APB probed Purcell and Webster's claim that they were acting under the sanction of the Queensland Government. This initiated a government-to-government correspondence that sought to clarify the authority and conditions under which the Wild Australia Show troupe was travelling. Purcell and Webster's version of events was not quite accurate, and Meston's public assertions that he was operating with the Queensland Government's permission were soon to be contradicted by that colony's

---

70   'Aborigines' Protection Board. The Aborigines at Bondi', *Evening News*, 6 January 1893, 2.
71   Ibid.
72   Ibid.
73   Ibid.

colonial secretary.[74] The Queensland Government eventually conceded that it had not provided permission (since it had not been asked); however, initially, it did not see this as an issue. Only the badgering of its New South Wales counterparts pressed it to take a stand on the matter.

With this trouble brewing in the background, Meston went on the (charm) offensive. He attended a meeting of the NSW APB on 19 January 1893, where he no doubt soothed worried brows and made undertakings to sort things out.[75] However, by this time, the situation was already losing urgency since the troupe would be leaving Sydney within a few days. Nevertheless, Meston did respond to the bad publicity he had received, mainly via the NSW APB, since arriving in Sydney. Using his journalistic skills and contacts, in early January he published a long article, presented as an interview with a 'reporter', seeking to correct the impression 'that the "Wild Australia" Show … is merely an indiscriminate collection of aboriginals gathered anyhow, having no proper supervision, and run purely as speculation'.[76] By implication, these were the kinds of accusations that the NSW APB was making. While Meston did not deny it was 'a speculation', he rejected that it was only motivated by money making and was not well managed. Neither would he tolerate assertions that it was 'merely … indiscriminate', which implied that it lacked ethnographic and scientific substance.[77]

Meston used the opportunity to praise the performers' credentials and prowess, and to outline his views on how Aboriginal people should be treated, particularly those in north Queensland from where the troupe members hailed. To make his arguments, Meston relied on a convention of dividing Australia into 'north' and 'south' and distinguishing between Aboriginal people who were, as Meston put it, 'contaminated by civilisation' (i.e. those in the southern colonies) and those, represented by the troupe, 'from the wild tribes of the west and north of Queensland' who were 'free from the vices of civilisation'.[78] The picture Meston painted of Aboriginal people in the 'southern' portion of Queensland was one of gradual and inevitable extinction, a fate that Aboriginal people in New South Wales were deemed to face. 'The once powerful tribe of the Darling Downs', Meston claimed,

---

74   Telegram, chief secretary, Queensland, to chief secretary, NSW, 31 January 1893, SRNSW.

75   'Aborigines Protection Board', *Sydney Morning Herald*, 21 January 1893, 10.

76   '"Wild Australia", Some Facts about the Natives, Aboriginals in Queensland—A Dying Race', *Daily Telegraph*, 9 January 1893, 4.

77   Ibid.

78   Ibid.

'would be represented by no more than 50'.[79] He predicted that 'as things are now, the next hundred years will see the last Australian black', indicating that, like many others at that time, he subscribed to the doctrine of a dying race—but only for people already brought into 'contact'.[80] The greatest threat to Aboriginal people was, he believed, 'civilisation': 'They don't take to civilisation at all', he asserted.[81] But he believed that the course of history as it had already unfurled in the 'south' could be redirected in the 'north', where Aboriginal people were numerous, physically strong, religiously active (i.e. performing sacred rites and possessing a 'priesthood' of sorts) and still, in a sense, autonomous and sovereign.[82] And he strongly believed that their autonomy could be preserved, so long as a large reserve—or reserves—were set aside for them where no whites could interfere and where they would have time 'for the blending of the elements of civilisation with their own mode of existence, so that the transition from barbarian might be gradual and effective, and not sudden and fatal'.[83] It was a fantasy in so many ways, but the creation of big reserves was an approach to protective governance that the Queensland Government would pursue across the twentieth century, and this had been one of Meston's key recommendations when he had been commissioned to prepare proposals for governing Aboriginal people.[84] His role in instituting such reserves, and the forcible removal of Aboriginal people to them, is why his name is still so despised among Aboriginal people, families and communities across Queensland today.

While Meston was working hard to put on a good face, behind the scenes at the Wild Australia Show the picture was less than pretty. The business, always precarious, was already beginning to fall apart; the maverick Meston was having to fight fires on various fronts. At the same time, as he was attempting to appease the NSW APB, he was trying to keep his creditors onside while also pressing friends and relatives for further financial support. Later accounts produced once the tour was over make it clear that in Sydney the viability of the troupe was already hanging in the balance. But Melbourne, the next stop on the troupe's itinerary, was seen as a chance to

79   Ibid.
80   Ibid.
81   Ibid.
82   Ibid.
83   Ibid.
84   See: J. McKay and P. Memmott, 'Staged Savagery: Archibald Meston and His Indigenous Exhibits', *Aboriginal History* 40 (2016): 181–203, doi.org/10.22459/AH.40.2016.07; P. Memmott and J. Richards, '"Where Is the Aboriginal Act?" Archibald Meston and the Emergence of Aboriginal Policy in Queensland', *Memoirs of the Queensland Museum—Culture* 12 (June 2021): 123–46, doi.org/10.17082/j.2205-3239. 12.1.2021.2021-05.

save it. Certainly, if all went well there, there was money to be made, since Meston had entered into a lucrative contract to perform at the Australian Natives' Association Fete in Melbourne on 26 January 1893. So, almost a month to the day since arriving, the troupe and their minders were again on the move going southwards—and into a headwind of trouble.

Nevertheless, in many ways, the summer season in Sydney was a success. Wherever it played, the Wild Australia Show had attracted good crowds; it had received positive (if not necessarily entirely independent) reviews; it had generated a rich photographic archive; and it had, it seems, been an enjoyable and formative experience for the performers as they stretched their creative muscles. However, with constant performances both day and night, and living under the shadow of surveillance in probably less than satisfactory accommodation, the troupe members must have been experiencing fatigue tinged with homesickness as they departed for Melbourne. Although free of the NSW APB's oversight once they crossed the border, they would not find much support when they needed it from colonial Victoria's equivalent.

9

Moving on to Melbourne

Lindy Allen

The Wild Australia Show troupe arrived in Melbourne on Wednesday, 25 January 1893, on board the passenger and cargo steamer SS *Warimoo* that docked around noon at Railway Pier (now Station Pier), Sandridge (now Port Melbourne).[1] Purcell later reported to Queensland Colonial Secretary Horace Tozer that the troupe had 'left [Sydney] per S.S. "Warimoo" … in [the] charge of R. Brown Business Manager for Melbourne, myself on the 24th January overland [and] Mr Meston arrived Melbourne 26th January'.[2] Robert Browne, as discussed in Chapter 8, was Meston's friend and secretary of the Queensland Press Club. Meston had booked the troupe to perform the following day as one of the major attractions of the Foundation Day Fete—the Fourth Annual Fete of the Australian Natives' Association (ANA).[3] The ANA fete was part of a campaign to have 26 January, the day in 1788 when Governor Phillip had planted the British flag at Sydney Cove, as a national day:

---

1   Readers are advised that some quotations contain terms and phrases that are no longer in common use, and that are likely to be considered racist and to cause offence. That is not our intention. These terms and phrases are retained within quotations from archival material for the purpose of demonstrating historical ideas and attitudes only. *Argus*, 26 January 1893, 4.

2   B. H. Purcell to Colonial Secretary's Office, Queensland, Colonial Secretary's Office, Inwards Correspondence, QSA ITM847483, 1893/847.

3   The Australian Natives' Association was founded in Melbourne on 24 April 1871 and was originally known as the Native Victorian Society. It was a society devoted to white people born in the Australian colonies.

> The ANA fete, to be held in the Exhibition building and grounds,
> offers a unique attraction in the appearance of a band of Australian
> aborigines from the northern tribes of Australia. It is a somewhat
> singular circumstance that while American Indians have been brought
> to the chief Australian towns to illustrate phases of American wild
> life, the Australian black of whose manners and customs Australian
> whites are almost equally ignorant, has not received much attention
> as a source of amusement and instruction. The blacks will engage in
> mimic combats and go through some of the remarkable ceremonies
> and corroborees which are a part of their life.[4]

The 'American Indians' refers to the Wild America Show that had arrived
in Melbourne in 1890 and had variously toured between there and Sydney
before disbanding in 1893.[5] In an overview of theatre performances in
Brisbane, Sydney and Melbourne in early January 1893, the *Melbourne
Punch* column, 'Theatre Gossip', drew attention to the potential of the Wild
Australia Show to rival the Wild America Show, observing that the latter 'is
not to have it all its own way for they now have in Brisbane Meston's "Wild
Australia" troupe of aboriginals ... a novel show and well worth witnessing'.[6]

The troupe was to perform in the quadrangle of the Exhibition Building
(now the Royal Exhibition Building)[7] and demonstrate boomerang and
spear throwing in the arena—a venue for various spectacles including bicycle
races, athletics, wood chopping competition and other sports, together with
'brass bands, gymnasts & acrobats, a children's procession, Punch and Judy
show, swings, merry-go-rounds'.[8] It commanded top billing in advertising
for the opening of the ANA fete, as the following advertisement shows:

> A Unique, Sensational, and Interesting Display by WILD
> ABORIGINALS, Selected chiefly from the Wild Tribes of North
> Queensland ... A Collection of over 3000 Weapons and Ethnological
> Specimens. Every phase of Aboriginal Life as seen by the Pioneers

---

4   'Foundation Day', *Argus*, 25 January 1893, 6.
5   In December 1890, William Frank 'Doc' Carver arrived in Melbourne with the 'Wild America
Show'. It opened at the Friendly Societies Gardens later that month and included a 'genuine Indian village'.
However, economic depression saw the 'Wild America Show' disbanded in 1893. See: Stage Whispers,
'When Cowboys and Indians Ran Wild on Australian Stages', March/April 2016, www.stagewhispers.com.
au/history/cowboys-indians-australian-stages.
6   'Theatrical Gossip', *Melbourne Punch*, 5 January 1893, 7.
7   The Exhibition Building was constructed for the Melbourne International Exhibition (1880–81)
and was the venue for the Centennial International Exhibition (1888–89).
8   'Foundation Day. The Australian Native Association Fete', *Age*, 26 January 1893, 6.

of Australia. Combats, Boorool Ceremonies, Camp Life, Peace and War Corroborees, Death Scenes, &c. Most Astonishing and Exciting Scenes ever witnessed on the World's Stage.[9]

However, the inclusion of the Wild Australia Show in the ANA program also attracted criticism and comment in the press:

In celebrating the 'national holiday' of Australia at the Melbourne Exhibition to-day, there is a touch of irony in the fact that the committee of the Australian Natives' Association partly rely on the dispossessed aboriginals of the soil to make their role a success.[10]

The inherent colonial contradiction between 'national possession' and 'Indigenous dispossession' was to be a consistent theme in editorial coverage of the Wild Australia Show throughout its entire tour. It was there from the outset, when Meston's initial proposal for Chicago was to highlight Queensland's natural resources and thus its attractiveness to migrants while also exhibiting Aboriginal and Torres Strait Islander people whose future would be further threatened by the intensive settlement that Meston was promoting.

The *Herald* (Melbourne) newspaper printed the most comprehensive overview of the troupe's anticipated performance at the fete on the day of their arrival in Melbourne, and its descriptions indicate that the program would not deviate much at all from what had been on offer in both Brisbane and Sydney in the months and weeks preceding. The same copy was being used almost word for word:

The indoor performance begins with a representation of camp life, introducing a war dance, in the background in a beautiful scene showing the Bellenden-Ker Range with the Mulgrave River at its foot. On the stage will be a camp scene, and gunyahs at either side, in which gins recline; a kangaroo and a cassowary will form the rest of the audience. Dancers painted, feathered and armed then rush on in an effected manner. They form a circle, maintaining a dance and hand clapping to a rhythmical chant, after which some of them, by rubbing sticks in the palms of their hands, produce a good fire. The corroborees they will give during their six performances at the Exhibition will be the Werrmugga, Rengwinna, Walklinga and the Rah Min, besides others of equal interest.[11]

---

9   'Great Annual Meeting Day for All Australians', *Argus*, 26 January 1893, 8.
10   'Foundation Day. The Australian Native Association Fete'.
11   'The Wild Aboriginals Their First Appearance in Melbourne', *Herald*, 25 January 1893, 2.

As with much of the coverage, Meston's name was given prominence in this report (and perhaps had been penned by Meston himself), since part of the attraction relied on the biography (however embellished) of the 'frontiersmen' who had encountered Aboriginal people 'in the wild' (also exaggerated) and brought them to metropolitan audiences for education and edification:

> Mr Meston, who has spent so much of his life among the wildest and perhaps most powerful of all the Australian tribes, will be in charge of the troupe to-morrow and following nights, when they appear in the Exhibition Building in connection with the A.N.A. fete.[12]

In the Melbourne press, a good deal of focus was also given to the 'magnificent collections' that were part of the Wild Australia Show, and which Purcell and Meston still intended taking overseas:

> Some idea may be gained of the entertainment that is given by them from the following. In the first place there is a magnificent collection of nearly 3000 weapons and ethnological specimens. Among these is a 12ft gore-tipped spear with which one of the aboriginals, a six foot man, had given a death thrust to a European who sought to carry off his gin.[13]

This, too, was old copy (see Chapter 7 for previous descriptions of the collection).

While the Show began indoors in the quadrangle with the camp scene, fire making and the program of dances, the skills demonstrations (boomerang throwing, etc.) were taken outside to the arena, as had been the practice in Sydney at the Bondi Aquarium and in Brisbane at the showground. These two parts of the repertoire, which had initially been performed together when the Show opened in Brisbane, had increasingly become separated. This demonstrates the ways in which the Show was constantly modified and tailored depending on the venues available:

> The Melbourne public, as a rule, can form very little idea of the peculiarities of boomerang throwing, but on Saturday afternoon next they will have the opportunity of witnessing the wonderful flights of this ingenious weapon of the blacks.

---

12 Ibid.
13 Ibid.

In Melbourne, the historical drama that typically provided the finale in the stage show had also found a new spot in the program as the venue allowed for certain dramatic qualities to be finessed:

> Under the electric light in the quadrangle of the Exhibition they will give a tableaux representing the murder of a swagman by a native and shooting of the criminal by a black tracker.

Attracting audiences relied upon conveying a sense of rarity, and this tactic was used in Melbourne as elsewhere:

> Owing to the numerous engagements that Mr Meston is already called upon to fulfil, the troupe will appear for the first time to-morrow and will only continue their performance every night up to 1st February. A special display will be given on Saturday afternoon.[14]

Probably unaware of the anticipation that was building thanks to Meston's savvy with the media, the troupe disembarked onto Railway Pier in the early afternoon on 25 January 1893. From there, they most likely boarded the steam train that would take them directly to the city.[15] This short journey, probably seated in second class, would have been a welcome relief from the two-night ocean passage from Sydney. The train first crossed the mile-long remnant of a great saltwater lagoon (now Lagoon Reserve in Port Melbourne), then the wetlands that stretched along the southern bank of the Yarra River, both of which would have been teeming with birdlife. As the train approached Sandridge Bridge and pulled into Flinders Street Station, 'Marvellous Melbourne' would have loomed large. At that time, Melbourne was the second largest city in the British Empire (after London), its extraordinary wealth a result of the gold rushes of the 1850s and 1860s that triggered a land and building boom in the 1880s; within a decade, the city's population rose to close to half a million people. However, the economic depression of the 1890s had hit Victoria (and Melbourne in particular) the hardest of all the Australian colonies. Reaching its peak by early 1893, it would have serious implications for the success of Meston's commercial venture with the Wild Australia Show.[16]

---

14 Ibid.
15 A direct service from Station Pier to Flinders Street Station ran every half hour.
16 Most banks and friendly societies curtailed or ceased trading, investors faced financial ruin, and unemployment was endemic across the city. See: B. Fitz-Gibbon and M. Gizycki, 'The 1890s Depression', Reserve Bank of Australia, 2001, www.rba.gov.au/publications/rdp/2001/2001-07/1890s-depression.html.

Brabazon Purcell had travelled overland from Sydney, a practice adopted since Brisbane, probably in order to transport the large painted backdrop and the huge collection of artefacts and other props and paraphernalia used in the Wild Australia Show. Meston was yet to arrive when the troupe disembarked in Melbourne; no one would have anticipated that a week later he would abandon the troupe and return to Sydney, nor that the Wild Australia Show's scheduled itinerary of a few weeks would extend to four months. In Melbourne, the troupe was accommodated in Fitzroy on the northeast edge of the central business district and adjacent to Carlton Gardens, where the Exhibition Building was located.[17] They had little more than 24 hours to ready themselves to perform.

Big crowds attended the opening day, which was a public holiday, and, over the following days, attendance grew to around 50,000 people:

> [The] anniversary of what is termed Foundation day was yesterday celebrated by the members of the Australian Natives' Association by a grand fete at the Exhibition building and grounds. The gathering was the largest ever witnessed on any similar occasion.[18]

While the troupe was promoted as the 'most prominent and novel feature of this event',[19] their opening performance attracted negative reviews:

> Not the least remarkable feature of the day's doings was the performance of the Queensland blacks, whose appearance produced the liveliest interest. They were described in the bills as 'Wild Aborigines', but the poor creatures seemed objects of sympathy and commiseration rather than of dread, as they listlessly shambled along urging their way through the crowds of sightseers. They came, some armed with spears and others with boomerangs, with which they give exhibitions of their skill.[20]

17   Fitzroy was reached by cable tram from Flinders Street Station. See: F. A. Hagenauer, general inspector of Aborigines, Board of Protection for Aborigines (Victoria), to Senior Inspector Jesse, Police Station, Fitzroy, 28 February 1893, refers to the troupe 'Presiding in Fitzroy', NAA, Letter Books, B329, Roll 9.

18   'Foundation Day. The Australian Natives' Association Fete. Immense Gathering at the Exhibition Building', *Age*, 27 January 1893, 6.

19   'Foundation Day. The A.N.A. Fete', *Weekly Times*, 4 February 1893, 22.

20   'Foundation Day. The Australian Natives' Association Fete. Immense Gathering at the Exhibition Building'.

This report suggests that, in Melbourne, the shine of touring was beginning to wear off and taking a toll on the performers. They had not stopped working since they opened in Brisbane in early December and, indeed, had been in rehearsal for some time before then. The workload—and the travelling—was demanding.

Afternoon performances in the arena had been well promoted in the press, as discussed above, in the week prior to the fete opening, and these more than the other components of the Wild Australia Show were anticipated as being of the greatest interest to Melbourne audiences. Much was riding on them:

> But the real interest centres in the boomerang throwing and spear competition, in which the men take an almost childish delight. The precision with which the spears are thrown at a target bespeaks strength of arm and quickness of eye, whilst the dexterity with which these dangerous weapons are avoided or caught by the warriors on their shields must be seen to be believed.[21]

The reference to 'childish delight', although infantilising, might also be read as suggesting, however faintly, the point at which the performers' enjoyment and pleasure came to the fore. Yet audiences were disappointed with what they perceived as lacklustre demonstrations, which may, perhaps, be unsurprising given how little time the troupe had to recover from its journey before it had a scheduled afternoon and evening performance on the first day, a single performance on the following day, and an afternoon and evening performance again on Saturday.

This is how one Melbourne journalist recounted the story of the increasingly marginal enterprise:

> A short time ago 26 Queensland blacks were induced to form a travelling company, go south, and give an exhibition of wild life in the far north. In the theatrical jargon, the 'ghost' refused to walk almost from the start. The chief question at present uppermost among colonists is not how to support autochthones, but how to support themselves. Again—to fall back once more on the expressive *argot* of the stage—the display was a 'frost' from the beginning. It consisted of spear-throwing, boomerang-hurling, dancing, stalking, painting on the nude, tracking, and various other illustrations of native life. I[n] spite of all they had to show, these talented people failed to

---

21   'Australian National Fete', *Leader*, 21 January 1893, 42.

draw. The few whites who did attend expressed their surprise, not that the newcomers failed to make a living in Victoria, but that they managed to make a living anywhere.[22]

This conveys a sense that the times were not right, as the economic downturn started to bite, and settlers were preoccupied with their own futures, rather than the admitted talents of representatives of the continent's original inhabitants, who, in Victoria, were surviving in very small numbers. As historian James Boyce and others have shown, the Victorian frontier had been quick and brutal, and population demise radical. By the 1890s, Victoria's *Aborigines Protection Act 1886*, and its amendment, the *Aborigines Act 1890*, would see the consolidation and removal of those designated 'Aboriginal natives' onto a handful of government stations and reserves, and the vacated land given over to pastoral interests. The 1886 Act, described as the most coercive since the settlement of the colony, required Aboriginal people of mixed descent to gain a licence from the Board for the Protection of Aborigines (BPA) to reside with their families on the stations and reserves, and the amended legislation determined their removal from these.[23] This meant that such people had to support themselves and participate in the settler economy, which suited the board whose membership was 'politically conservative and closely associated with squatting interests [and] critical of the humanitarians' policy of supporting Aboriginal communities on segregated reserves overseen by missionaries'.[24]

Given this context of draconian and assimilationist legislation aimed at Victorian Aboriginal people, interest in an ethnographic exhibition was slight. Many people were seemingly indifferent towards Aboriginal people and their plight. However, at least one journalist sought to assess the troupe through a lens of actual frontier violence. How dangerous were the men who threw the spears? Adopting the second person 'you' to place the reader in a life and death situation, he suggested that this was no mere 'academic' display: it was a demonstration of threat—a warning—for those still engaged in conflict on Queensland's frontiers. The reader—and, hence, the audience—was encouraged to focus not only on the skill but also on the implication of the skill for settlers:

---

22 'Meston's Blacks', *Western Star and Roma Advertiser*, 18 March 1893, 3.
23 R. Broome, *Aboriginal Victorians: A History since 1800* (Crows Nest: Allen & Unwin, 2005), 185.
24 B. Attwood, *Rights for Aborigines* (Crows Nest: Allen & Unwin, 2003), 13.

Judging from the throwing at a target we should conclude that the danger lies in having a flight of heavy spears aimed at you. For at 25 to 30 yards, only about one-third of the spears hit a target 5ft wide: those that did hit hit very hard, and would have gone through a man's body. Had you only one black firing at you you would be able to avoid shots. When you hear of white men being killed it is when attacked by a mob. The light spear-throwing at 40 yards seemed agreeable sport, and it was easy for the combatants to avoid being struck. The waddy-throwing at the same distance, where the combats took the form of duels, was similar. Apparently one black could not hit another except by accident.[25]

Despite these various performances and demonstrations, the viability of the Wild Australia Show was hanging by a thread. Behind the scenes, contractual disputes were brewing, and the ANA Metropolitan Committee, the organisers of the fete, cancelled the troupe's evening performance on the last day. Purcell immediately reported this turn of events to Queensland Colonial Secretary Horace Tozer. Purcell reported that, after three days, the committee:

> or rather their secretary Mr T. W. Heider refused to carry on the show as Mr Meston had no agreement and had not fulfilled his contract namely—that in making arrangements he had no specified number of aboriginals but was advertising 32 aboriginals, 3000 curios for months and on those grounds the money owing was not paid.[26]

In other words, Meston had not fulfilled his contractual conditions, since there were not 32 in the troupe nor 3,000 curios. This was a terrible blow for the troupe.

---

25 'Mr Meston's Queensland Blacks', *Australasian*, 4 February 1893, 23.

26 B. H. Purcell to colonial secretary, 21 July 1893, Colonial Secretary's Office, Inwards Correspondence, QSA ITM847483, 1893/8474. With a gap in the ANA's archives for 1893, any specific contractual conditions or arrangements for the Wild Australia Show cannot be confirmed. The Australian Unity Library Collections hold the ANA Archives and advised that: 'The Metropolitan Committee ... underwent a restructure between the 1892 Fete and the 1894 Fete ... [which] may have been caused by the controversy which surrounded the running of an Art Union at the Fetes. So even the broader [ANA] Board reports ... [have] nothing about the 1893 Fete.' See: Beryl Armstrong, Australian Unity Library Collections, to Michelle Stevenson, Museums Victoria, 26 May 2017 [pers. comm]. The art union lottery conducted at the fete was deemed unlawful and there was an investigation and subsequently a summons was issued to committee officials. The lottery 'was exposed by an undercover policeman on 26 January 1893' ('The A.N.A. Art Union: The Promoters Summoned', *Age*, 17 March 1893 5), and a report on the outcome of court proceedings stated 'the summons was issued on the information of Senior Constable Gleeson ... [and a]fter a short consultation a fine of 10s with 2s costs was imposed' ('The A.NA. Art Union Promoters Fined 10s Each', *Age*, 28 March 1893, 7).

Stranded in Melbourne

As a result of the contractual difficulties with the ANA, the relationship between Meston and Purcell deteriorated dramatically. A few days following the ANA's cancellation of the troupe's final performance, Meston fled, returning to Sydney and leaving finances for the troupe critically short. Purcell would again reach out to Colonial Secretary Tozer explaining the circumstances:

> Meston agreed to see the boys well cared for—having obtained £50 in Sydney from the [Australian Natives'] Association and last Wednesday week instead of doing so or keeping any of his appointments he left by the mail train for Sydney leaving the 27 blacks starving on my hands without money or even tobacco … not having any money I myself have succeeded in carrying them on up to this present sooner than let them starve and may yet make satisfactory arrangements for the completion of the tour.[27]

In further correspondence with Queensland's under colonial secretary, Parry Okeden, Purcell maligned Meston's character and his lack of ongoing commitment to the joint venture:

> Meston's conduct both here and in Sydney towards the unfortunate blacks is denounced in very strong terms—that a man of his stamp who professes to be such a friend to the aboriginals should be a member of the Aborigines Board of Queensland or even a J.P. is a standing disgrace and I trust the Government will deal with him a prompt and effective manner. I have seen the Native Police Officers … work but even they were human compared to Meston … The only reason I can see why Meston cleared [out] was to try and evade payments as he was promised writs and also because he found that the blacks were likely to be stranded so in his usual style he took care of himself and left.[28]

Soon, the debacle was being covered in the press with regular commentary on the unfolding events in Melbourne:

---

27   B. H. Purcell to colonial secretary, Colonial Secretary's Office, 24 February 1893, QSA ITM847483, 1893/6869.

28   B. H. Purcell to colonial secretary, Colonial Secretary's Office, Inwards Correspondence, QSA ITM847483, 1893/12837.

Trouble seems to have arisen in connection with the troupe of twenty-seven blackfellows who appeared at the A.N.A. fete. In the first instance, they were badly managed. It could not have been a politic proceeding to cart them through the streets on two drays, as though they were black sheep. Then, again, the show at the Exhibition was badly arranged. Thousands of those who were present in the afternoon were dissatisfied, and did not fail to say so both openly and loudly. Afterwards business troubles arose between the blackfellows' managers and the A.N.A. committee [and] till now the representatives of the Northern Queensland tribes with the extraordinary names are literally and verbally stranded.[29]

A newspaper in Rockhampton was among a number in Queensland reporting the escalating situation:

At Melbourne no better encouragement was received, and now telegrams have appeared in the southern newspapers telling us Mr. Meston has deserted his troupe, and left them to shift for themselves. This they were unable to do, and they fell into the hands of the Victorian Mission to the Aboriginals. For pity's sake they could not be let starve, while the Mission had no funds to devote to the maintenance of aboriginals from a strange colony.[30]

With all this public attention, and his monumental fall from grace, Meston sought to plead his own cause to Tozer. Writing from Sydney in March 1893, Meston sought to place the problems at his erstwhile partner's feet rather than to take any or all responsibility for the mess:

I bitterly grieve to be compelled to say that disaster has overtaken my enterprise with the aboriginals. I need not here relate my troubles with Purcell nor his treachery to me since I gave him a third share and placed the blacks absolutely under his control. Ill luck of all kinds has followed me from the start finishing a month ago in Melbourne with a gross breach of agreement by the 'Australian Natives Association' whereby I only received £150 out of £550 due. This left me in Melbourne without a shilling and I returned to Sydney to civilization to raise more capital but my friends would

---

29 'Our Melbourne Letter, Friday', *Ovens and Murray Advertiser*, 18 February 1893, 3. No information has come to light regarding the journalist's comment that the troupe were carted 'through the streets on two drays'.
30 'Current Notes', *Capricornia*, 18 March 1893, 19.

not invest a shilling unless Purcell went out. I left Purcell with £200 worth of scenery weapons and curios [?] to either to go with some other partner or sell the properties and send the blacks home.[31]

Meston had composed his version of events, which included a combination of bad luck and poor choice in business partner, and he repeated it whenever he got the chance. In June, as the fallout continued, he gave the same explanation to Parry Okeden, stating again that he had left Purcell with the means to secure funds to return the troupe to Queensland, although, given the economic downturn, it is unclear what market value stage scenery or Aboriginal artefacts would have had at that time:

> Through an unfortunate choice of partner with whom it was impossible for me to continue I left him in Melbourne free of all debts, with the complete scenery and weapons which cost me over [£]300 ... I had to do this for the sake of the blacks. Purcell was either to sell the outfit and return the blacks or continue the tour and make what he could. The blacks were all brought down by him and were at all times under his entire control. My share was providing the total cost, including Purcell's board and expenses.[32]

Here, Meston seeks to pull a swifty and shift responsibility to Purcell, describing his role as little more than a silent partner. This is not borne out by the way in which his name was prominent during the troupe's Brisbane and Sydney seasons when they were often referred to as 'Meston's troupe' or 'Meston's Wild Australia'. Soon Meston's name would be dropped from all publicity.

For his part, Purcell had been aware that Meston had secured funds in Sydney to support the Wild Australia Show tour to Melbourne, and apprised Tozer of the fact that:

> before leaving Sydney Mr Meston was again in a borrowing humour getting £30 from Alfred Shaw, £40 from Mr Lucas the former gentleman's then partner, and wiring to Melbourne got an advance of £50 from the Australian Natives Association.[33]

---

31   A. Meston to colonial secretary, 12 June 1893, Colonial Secretary's Office, Inwards Correspondence, QSA ITM847483, 1893/6869.

32   Ibid.

33   B. H. Purcell to colonial secretary, 21 July 1893, Colonial Secretary's Office, Inwards Correspondence, QSA ITM847483, 1893/8474.

Purcell went on to outline further borrowings by Meston from individuals in Melbourne. The Wild Australia Show, it seems, was heavily in debt, making the success of performances ever more critical:

> On Wednesday 2nd February 1893 about 11 am I saw Mr Meston and arranged to meet him to see what we were to do with the blacks, and while walking up Collins Street about 5 pm with I. [J?] R. Webster met Alfred Shaw of Sydney [nephew of Mrs Meston] who for the first time told us that Mr Meston had bolted to Sydney on the advice of his solicitors Messrs. Taylor Russell and Renwick on whom I called next day and found out that Shaw told us the truth. Before leaving Mr Meston called on Mr Cosgrove of Messrs. Dalgety and Co. Melbourne and borrowed £10 to keep the blacks going which he never repaid up to the time of my leaving although threatened with a warrant. Never heard from Meston after his desertion. A few days after that the Australian Natives Association paid Alfred Shaw £30 for money Meston borrowed. Taylor Russell and Renwick £5 50 shillings Meston's advices. I. [J?] R. Webster and self £14 each.[34]

In a libel and malicious prosecution case in the Supreme Court of Queensland, which was brought against Meston by Purcell late in 1893, Purcell reported that:

> the day before defendant [Meston] left Melbourne witness [Purcell] and he had a conversation about affairs and asked defendant about a clearing up of accounts. At that time threats had been made to put the blacks out of their lodgings.[35]

Purcell used his payment from the ANA committee to pay the 'expenses of blacks and R. Brown Business Manager',[36] but a further complication arose when 'about 4 days [later] I. [J?] R. Webster Treasurer bolted leaving blacks virtually on my hands'.[37]

This disastrous situation weighed heavily on the performers, who were increasingly left without provision and with little certainty about their immediate future. They had been engaged to tour the world but were now struggling to get beyond Melbourne. Returning the troupe to Queensland was not possible without securing further funds. Despite the pressure that

---

34 Ibid.
35 'Supreme Court … Purcell v. Meston', *Brisbane Courier*, 22 November 1893, 7.
36 B. H. Purcell to colonial secretary, 21 July 1893, Colonial Secretary's Office, Inwards Correspondence, QSA ITM847483, 1893/8474.
37 Ibid.

the Sydney authorities applied, the Queensland Government continued to take no responsibility for the performers, a fact that was widely reported in the press, particularly in Queensland. The *Cairns Post* reported that:

> no official action has been taken for the purpose of bringing Meston's stranded blackfellows from Melbourne to Queensland. It now transpires no agreement has been entered into for their return as was generally understood.[38]

Other Queensland newspapers similarly questioned arrangements brokered (or not brokered) between Meston and the colonial government for the Wild Australia Show to tour to New South Wales and Victoria:[39]

> A few months ago when it was given out that these aboriginals were about to make a tour of the world, it was generally understood that Mr A. Meston had entered into some agreement with the Government authorities to safely return the blacks to their homes at some future time. It now appears, however, that no such agreement exists, and in fact could not exist, as no law is in force to prevent the aboriginals of the colony from being taken beyond its bounds. About a month ago a communication was received by the Colonial Secretary from the New South Wales Government on the subject, and Mr Tozer, replied that no agreement had been entered into for the return of the blacks. So far no official action had been taken for the purpose of bringing the stranded blackfellows from Melbourne to Queensland.[40]

Holding out in Sydney, where he was desperately seeking to sell a collection of artefacts to the Australian Museum to raise some funds, Meston provided his own defence in an article in the *Bulletin*, repudiating Purcell's assertion that Meston was 'solely responsible for the stranding in Melbourne without means of the Queensland aboriginal troupe collected for the Chicago Fair'. The *Bulletin* quoted Meston as saying:

> Mr Purcell is posing in Melbourne as a much-injured person who has lost everything by the speculation. The weakness of this complaint lies embedded in the simple fact that the total cost of collecting the blacks, and weapons, and purchasing scenery and outfit was borne by me alone, and represents an expenditure of over £1000.[41]

---

38 'Meston's Blacks', *Cairns Post*, 3 March 1893, 2.
39 Adelaide was also originally included in the tour.
40 'The "Wild Australia" Show Stranded in Melbourne', *Brisbane Courier*, 30 March 1893, 5.
41 'Sundry Shows', *Bulletin*, 25 March 1893, 6.

Meston also attributed blame to the ANA committee, describing them as 'pirates' who 'broke their engagement with me, and only paid £150 under compulsion, out of the £550 that was due'. However, Purcell was Meston's main target. According to his version of how events unfolded:

> I left Purcell with the whole outfit, worth £250 (I had paid £130 for the scenery alone) and no liability whatever, and remained personally responsible for all the debts in Sydney and Brisbane. I came out of the concern without a shilling. He would neither sell out, or go out and leave the blacks in other hands, and as there was no prospect whatever of our working amicably together I legally transferred all to him, or some buyer he professed to have secured two months ago, and made the best of an exceedingly bad bargain. To ask me to accept the responsibility of his own failures since he stated on his own account displays much coolness.[42]

The journalist, clearly sympathetic to Meston's position, concluded that:

> this business is a most unfortunate one. Mr Meston cannot thus quite get rid of his moral responsibilities to the unhappy blacks. However, it is but fair to say that he feels the position most acutely and is understood to be doing his best to remedy matters as far as possible.[43]

By now, the public spectacle of Meston's scandalous behaviour, covered in detail in the newspapers, was the show to watch more so than the troupe's onstage performances.

In correspondence with Okeden, Meston once again defended himself and accused Purcell of being solely responsible for the troupe's demise in Melbourne:

> From day to day he was negotiating with some prospective partner, made another engagement with the Exhibition people and finally has been stranded in Melbourne, after having either disposed of the properties or they have been disposed of by some one else … It is bitter enough God knows for me to have expended every shilling I could raise, over a thousand pounds and 16 months of my time to hear of the blacks being placed in their present position through the action of a partner whom I could neither work with nor get rid of. I am powerless to do anything having expended all I had and even left my family short of funds.[44]

---

42   Ibid.
43   Ibid.
44   A. Meston to colonial secretary, 12 June 1893, Colonial Secretary's Office, Inwards Correspondence, QSA ITM847483, 1893/6869.

Meston continued in strong emotional terms, saying that he would cover any further costs for the return of the troupe members when he was able to in the future,[45] which of course never eventuated. But Meston's proposal that Purcell sell the backdrop and 'curios' was unrealistic, even though that was the path he was pursuing to raise urgent funds. Back in Sydney, Meston quickly entered into negotiations with the Australian Museum for the sale of a collection of artefacts, possibly from among the Wild Australia Show's 'curios' or from his own private collection (see Chapter 7), seeking £100 'on behalf of [William] Miller Esq. Hensen Street Summerhill',[46] his brother-in-law, to whom he presumably also owed money. In time, the Australian Museum would purchase over 400 items from Meston.

The troupe in Melbourne without Meston

Purcell was committed to the Wild Australia Show continuing as a going concern and to the plan for it to travel to England and then onto Chicago. He secured clothing, hats and boots for the performers from friends in Melbourne, borrowed money from family, and sought more bookings for the Show. He also successfully leveraged support from Melbourne's scientific establishment, ingratiating himself when he stepped in as a replacement for Meston to deliver a lecture to the Royal Geographical Society of Australasia (Victorian Branch) at the Athenaeum on Friday, 3 February 1893.[47] The meeting was chaired by the society's president, internationally respected botanist Baron Ferdinand von Mueller:

> A lecture on the aborigines of tropical Australia was delivered by Mr. B. H. Purcell at the Athenaeum, last night, to the members of the Royal Geographical Society. The lecturer took the place of Mr. Meston, who was detained in Sydney. He said that although the Queensland blacks were looked on as a low and lazy race, there was really something in their customs and institutions to be proud of ... Mr. Purcell then introduced several of the natives lately exhibited in

---

45   Ibid.
46   'Australian Museum Purchase Schedule 1893', 10, Australian Museum Archives. See also: S. Price, L. Allen and C. Knowles, '"The (Not-So) Sacred Ibis": Archibald Meston, The Colonial Collector, and the Queensland Museum', *Memoirs of the Queensland Museum—Culture 12* (June 2021): 73–121, doi. org/10.17082/j.2205-3239.12.1.2021.2021-04.
47   Joseph Bradshaw was also a member of the Victorian Branch of the Royal Geographical Society at this time.

Melbourne, including the Royal family of Prince of Wales Island. One of the party gave an illustration of the aboriginal method of producing fire by frictional contact of two sticks.

A Vote of thanks was moved by the President, Baron von Mueller, seconded by Mr. A. C. Macdonald, and carried with acclamation.[48]

The renowned ethnologist Alfred Howitt, a member of the society, was in the audience that day. Meston later wrote to Howitt, maligning Purcell and dismissing any perceived expertise on Purcell's part. 'After manifold troubles', Meston wrote:

> tossing on the strong seas through 3 or 4 months ... I am at last composed enough to write to you and express my earnest regret for being deprived of a chance to spend an hour or two with you on our favourite subject. Doubtless Purcell has said many unkind things of me. Ah well had I never seen him I would have been at least a couple of thousand pounds better [and] been saved a heap of misery that no money could represent. You were doubtless amused at his lectures. Twelve months ago he was profoundly ignorant of Australian ethnography and what he knows is from my lectures, and the works of Curr, Brough Smyth & Dawson loaned from me ... many of his statements as I am doubtless conjectured were pure fiction. He is a shameless liar.[49]

Pituri was one of the topics covered by Purcell in the lecture, reprising the talks he had given earlier. This was a subject on which he could speak from personal experience, as discussed in Chapter 7, and also a topic of interest to Howitt. In 1861, Howitt had led the Contingent Exploring Party to the border region of Queensland and New South Wales in search of survivors of the Burke and Wills Expedition. At the expedition's Coopers Creek camp, they located John King, who had survived for seven months stranded in the desert, easing his hunger by using pituri. Howitt returned to Melbourne with the samples of the plant, which he gave to von Mueller, who renamed it *Duboisia hopwoodii*.[50]

In his book *The Native Tribes of South-East Australia*, Howitt wrote about a Prince of Wales Island man 'whom I once met'. He explained:

---

48   'The Aboriginals of Australia', *Age*, 4 February 1893, 9.

49   A. Meston to A. W. Howitt, 23 May 1893, Alfred Howitt Collection, Museums Victoria, XM259.

50   M. Letnic and L. Keogh, 'Pituri Country', in *Desert Channels: The Impulse to Conserve*, ed. L. Robin, C. Dickman and M. Martin (Collingwood: CSIRO Publishing, 2011), 61–80.

> It was, that his tribesmen are accustomed to migrate periodically in their sea-going canoes, according to the prevalent winds, either southwards along the coast of Queensland, or northwards to the further islands of Torres Strait, or even to the mainland of New Guinea.[51]

There is no evidence that Howitt travelled to the Torres Strait, and it is highly unlikely that any other Prince of Wales Islanders travelled to Victoria around this time, and so his commentary most likely referred to the Kaurareg leader, Gida, a member of the Wild Australia Show. Howitt also observed that:

> I was much struck, when comparing some men from Prince of Wales Island with other men from the Cloncurry River, on the mainland, by the marked Papuan character of the former, and the marked Australian character of the latter. The intermixture through friendly intercourse between the Kaurarega of Prince of Wales Island and the Gudang of Cape York is well known.[52]

Given that the troupe included men from the Cloncurry region, and since we know that Howitt attended the Royal Geographical Society lecture, this commentary very likely drew upon a personal observation Howitt made of the performers. How else could he have compared a Torres Strait Islander with Aboriginal people of the Cloncurry region?

The photographer J. W. Lindt was another member of the Royal Geographical Society who was also likely present at the lecture.[53] The affirmation of such an eminent member of Melbourne society would have been important in Purcell's pursuit of further appearances for the Wild Australia Show. As discussed elsewhere (see Chapter 11), Lindt made photographic portraits of troupe members in the weeks following the lecture and personally presented Purcell with an album of 52 albumen prints (see Figures 9.1 and 9.2 for examples). A dedication to Purcell is inscribed in Lindt's hand inside the album. This album is now held in the collections of the British Museum.[54]

---

51   Howitt, *The Native Tribes of South-East Australia* (Canberra: Aboriginal Studies Press, 1996, fasc. 1904), 11.

52   Ibid., 29.

53   See: V. Frost, 'John William Lindt (1845–1926)', *Australian Dictionary of Biography*, National Centre of Biography, The Australian National University, published first in hardcopy 1974, adb.anu.edu.au/biography/lindt-john-william-4023/text6385.

54   The album was donated to the British Museum by Purcell in 1893 and is registered in the museum's collections as: Oc,A8.1-Oc,A8.52 Album of 52 Albumen Prints. The following is inscribed on the third page in pencil—'presented to Brab. H Purcell Esq. M.R.S.S. by J.W. Lindt Esq. FRGS Melbourne 27 March 1893'. At least four enlargements of the portraits by Lindt survive in the collections of the National Gallery of Australia (2005.576, 93.450, 93.449) and Museums Victoria (XP22731).

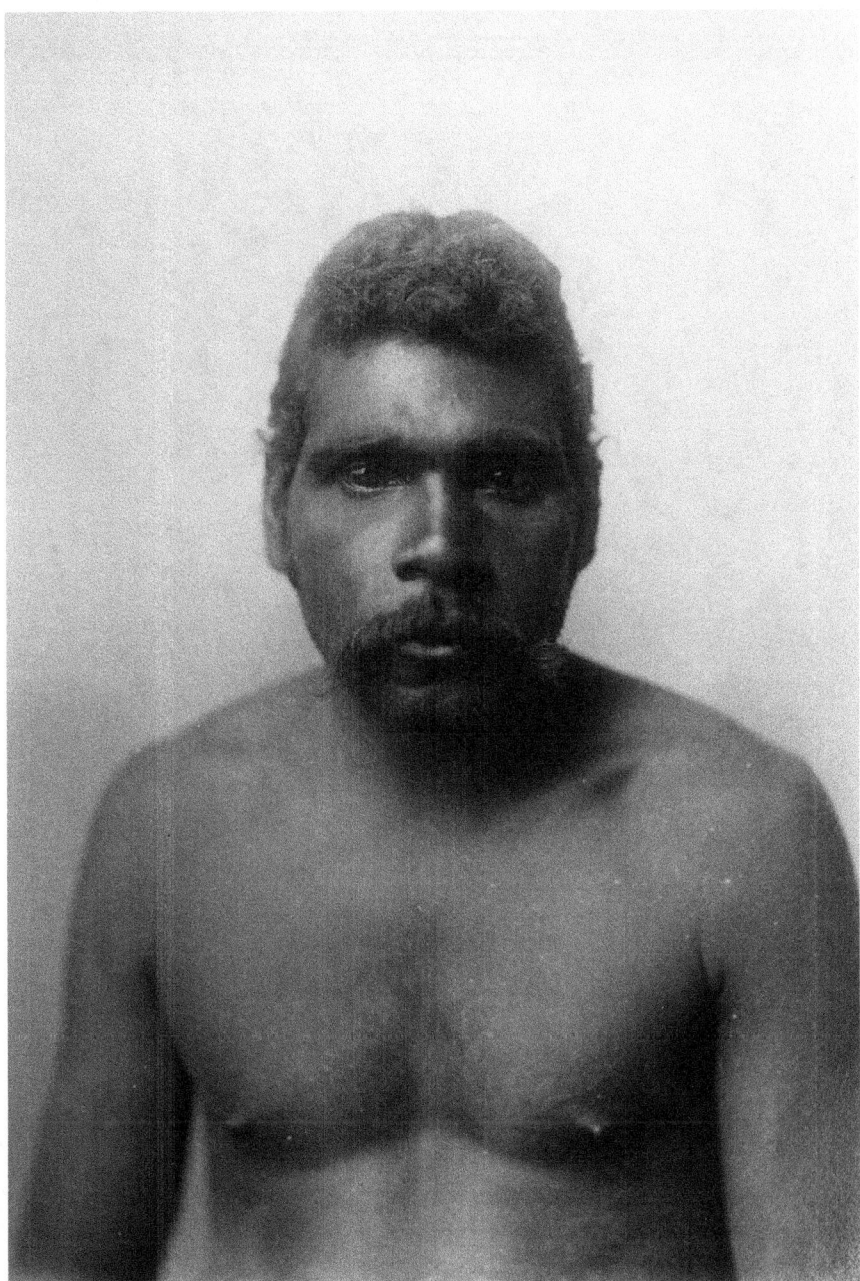

Figure 9.1: Yamurra photographed by J. W. Lindt in Melbourne, early 1893

Source: The Trustees of the British Museum. Shared under a Creative Commons Attribution-NonCommercial-ShareAlike 4.0 International (CC BY-NC-SA 4.0) licence.

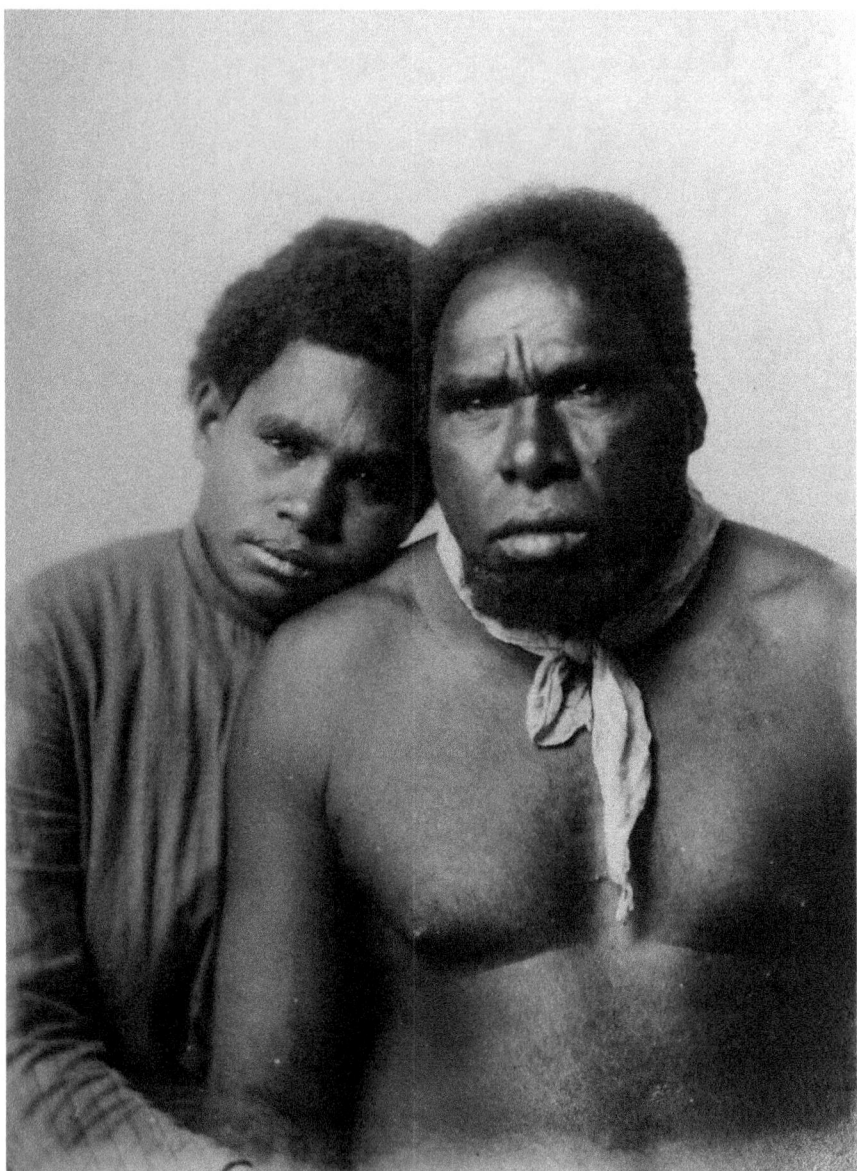

Figure 9.2: Kemaliya and Gida (originally captioned Camaleea and Geedah) photographed by J. W. Lindt in Melbourne, early 1893

Source: The Trustees of the British Museum. Shared under a Creative Commons Attribution-NonCommercial-ShareAlike 4.0 International (CC BY-NC-SA 4.0) licence.

Lindt's portraits of the Wild Australia Show performers are noticeably different from the images that the Kerry Studio had created in Sydney just months earlier. As discussed later in Chapter 11, some of Lindt's photographs have had an especially long afterlife, particularly the sympathetic portrait of 'Kudajarnd' and his partner, which Lindt would later produce as an enlargement together with at least two other portraits (see Figure 11.5).[55]

Both Lindt and Howitt were likely also present at a second address that Purcell gave to the Royal Geographical Society. On 15 February 1893, Purcell was once more speaking on 'micka' (the practice of subincision). The three Wakaya men who accompanied him were no doubt there as living exhibits of this customary practice undertaken during high-level men's ceremonies. The audience included 70 men who were the 'leading medical and scientific' contingent of the society's membership as well as 'other medical and professional gentlemen'.[56]

While the troupe remained in Melbourne, hoping to be able to generate the means to continue its tour, Purcell worked diligently to make new bookings. However, it was a few weeks before the troupe would perform again. In the interim, their circumstances became quite dire and were brought to the attention of Victoria's BPA. At the same time, renewed calls for their return appeared in the Queensland press:

> At a meeting of the Aborigines' Protection Board today a letter was received from [Police] Superintendent Sadler, stating that twenty-six Queensland aboriginals brought here by Mr A. Meston as a performing company had been left without means of support. The inspector pointed out that the board was prohibited by Act of Parliament from incurring expense in providing for blacks from another colony. He had, however, arranged for their keep for forty-eight hours. It was stated that two of Mr Meston's partners were still in Melbourne though Mr Meston himself had gone to Sydney, and it was considered probable that arrangements might be made with these gentlemen for the transport of the aboriginals back to Queensland.[57]

---

55 See: British Museum, [photographic print], www.britishmuseum.org/collection/object/EA_Oc-A8-1.
56 Editor, 'Sturt's Terrible Rite', *Royal Geographical Society of Australasia Transactions* (Victorian Branch) 11 (1894): 4.
57 'The Wild Aust Show', *Queenslander*, 11 March 1893, 4. See also: 'The Wild Australia Show Stranded in Melbourne', *Courier*, 3 March 1893, 5.

This attention had been prompted by Kabi Kabi man Yamurra (see Figure 9.1) making a complaint to the local police in Fitzroy, asserting that the troupe had been left for three days without food. Months later, Yamurra, who seems to have remained loyal to Meston despite him abandoning the troupe, would recount his experiences in Melbourne:

> He asserts the company were, when in Melbourne, left in a house for three days without anything to eat, and it was only by appealing to the police that he obtained bread for himself and for the others. Mr Meston gave Yamurra three pairs of trousers and five shirts, and served the other aboriginal actors in like manner, besides supplying them liberally with tobacco, but after Mr Meston's departure nothing but tobacco found its way to the descendants of aboriginal royalty … On being closely questioned Yamurra said he had only two complaints to make regarding Mr Purcell's treatment of the company. First that he left them for three days in Melbourne without food, and secondly that he failed to provide them with clothing. For Mr Meston, Yamurra professes the greatest regard and affection.[58]

As will be remembered from previous chapters, Yamurra had joined the tour at Meston's invitation. The relationship between Purcell and Yamurra was always strained, since he was always seen as Meston's man or friend. It is worth wondering whether Meston had left Yamurra with the troupe in Melbourne as his 'agent'.

For his part, once the tour was over, the only troupe member Purcell was critical of was Yamurra. When he eventually returned to Brisbane, Purcell told a journalist that all the performers bar one—namely, Yamurra—had been easy to work with. In a letter to a Queensland newspaper, Meston's 'business manager', Robert Browne, questioned the veracity of Yamurra's complaints after the tour had ended:

> A few days subsequent to Mr. Meston's exodus from Victoria, Mr. Purcell, the natives, and myself were stranded through lack of supplies. Some time elapsed before funds could be raised to carry on the show, and during this interval, upon two occasions only, the boys' breakfast was not forthcoming. Every means was taken to secure them, under the most trying circumstances, their meals regularly—even to the length of handing the caterer Mr Purcell's watch as security, which I did myself, and so satisfied were the police

---

58 'Wild Australia', *Queenslander*, 22 July 1893, 18. The *Aborigines Act 1890* gave the board control of the lives of Aboriginal people on missions, reserves and stations across the colony of Victoria. These powers did not extend to Aboriginal people from outside of Victoria.

on this score that they took no steps to interfere when each omission was brought by Yamurra under their notice. Nearly all Yamurra's other statements are equally inaccurate.[59]

The secretary of the Victorian BPA, Rev. Friedrich Hagenauer, responded to the original inquiry from Senior Inspector Jesse at the Fitzroy Police Station by pointing out that 'it was not a matter for this Board to deal with'.[60] He suggested that:

the Police Department should endeavor to have them returned to their home as soon as can be done either by the parties who brought them here and got well paid for it, or by the shipping company, who carried them as passengers.[61]

Purcell was aware that Meston had sent a negative report about him to the Victorian BPA:

It has also come to my knowledge that Mr Meston has accused me of chaining and kidnapping the western blacks, the report going to the Victorian Aborigines Society who were very indifferent regarding his treatment of the blacks and who appear to me to be on a par with the rest of these Societies in the colonies, simply salary drawers and experimentor of the purist type, Mr Meston's accusations are simply too absurd to even listen to … I again refer to my previous letter on this unfortunate matter of Mr Meston's desertion of the troupe and saddling me with responsibilities and worries connected there with for months but I can only say that were I placed in a similar position again I would act as I have done in keeping the natives from being arrested in Sydney and Melbourne as vagrants.[62]

The lives of Aboriginal people in Victoria were tightly controlled by the BPA, which had been established in 1869. However, as this correspondence shows, the BPA expressed no desire to assume responsibility for the troupe. The BPA regulated where Victorian Aboriginal people could reside, and it was responsible for the provision of clothing and food on government stations and reserves in the colony—but its jurisdiction did not extend to Aboriginal people from outside of Victoria.[63]

---

59   'Meston's Black Troupe', *Brisbane Courier*, 26 July 1893, 3.
60   H. A. Hagenauer to Senior Inspector Jesse, Fitzroy Police Station, 18 February 1893, NAA, Letter Books B329, Roll 11 (digitised).
61   Ibid.
62   B. H. Purcell to colonial secretary, 21 July 1893, Colonial Secretary's Office, Inwards Correspondence, QSA ITM847483, 1893/8474.
63   Broome, *Aboriginal Victorians*.

Since it was clear that little government assistance would be forthcoming, Purcell secured a booking for the Wild Australia Show at the Third Grand National Baby Show in Melbourne, which opened at the Exhibition Building on 16 February. When Meston noted that Purcell had sought 'another engagement with the Exhibition people' in his correspondence with Parry Okeden discussed above, the 'Exhibition people' were the commissioners of the Exhibition Buildings, not the ANA. The *Age* reported:

> The arrangements for the exhibition appear exceedingly satisfactory. A military band was in attendance during the afternoon ... In the quadrangle the wild aborigines, as they are facetiously designated, displayed their skill in handling their warlike native weapons of offence and defence, while an admirable and varied programme, was gone through with a good deal of applause. The Show will be open to-day, and will not close on Saturday until a late hour in the evening.[64]

For the first time, the baby show entrants included a young Aboriginal boy. Sensationalised in the press, the copy revealed the patronising and denigrating attitudes towards Aboriginal people that prevailed in Victoria:

> Jack Friday, aged 3 years and 6 months, together with his father and mother, occupied a place of honor apart from the vulgar crowd. The simple child of nature was fashionably attired in tan shoes, white socks, and a little white sleeveless frock, with bows of pink ribbon on the shoulders. He is the only pure bred picaninny in Victoria (so his father [Jack Friday] says), and he desists from chewing a stick of barley sugar to survey for a moment the jostling crowds that throng round his raised dais. Little Jack was born at Warrnambool, but his present residence is Coranderrk Station, where his brothers and sisters live, and where he himself will grow to dusky manhood in due course.[65]

The presence of this family would not have gone unnoticed by the Wild Australia Show troupe, which performed on each of the three days of the baby show at 3.30 pm and in the Concert Hall on the last evening.[66] According to an advertisement in the *Herald*:

---

64   'The Baby Show', *Age* (Melbourne), 17 February 1893, 6.
65   Ibid.
66   Ibid.

Notwithstanding the enormous expense involved in this great
exposition the directors have also arranged with the whole
of the troupe of
WILD ABORIGINALS
From the Far Interior,
The SPINIFEX DESERT,
And Northern Parts of Queensland.
These Representatives of
A FAST DYING RACE
Will give
In the QUADRANGLE
THIS (THURSDAY) AFTERNOON,
COMMENCING at 3.30 p.m.,
A
UNIQUE, WEIRD and HIGHLY
FANTASTIC EXHIBITION of
BOOMERANG THROWING,
AERIAL FLIGHT of SPEARS,
THROWING SPEARS at DISTANCE,
GRAND CORROBOREE,
TREE CLIMBING,
TARGET PRACTICE,
SPEAR FIGHT
&c, &c, &c.[67]

An unfortunate incident on the second day attracted press attention,
but there were no adverse consequences:

> During the afternoon a troupe of Queensland aboriginals gave
> an interesting entertainment with spears and boomerangs in the
> Exhibition grounds. By an unfortunate accident, however, one of
> the spears, when thrown, rebounded from the asphalt path and
> struck a visitor named Thomas French about the foot. The weapon
> pierced the ankle, and the sufferer was taken to Melbourne Hospital,
> where his injury was dressed, and proved not to be serious.[68]

---

67 'The Great National Baby Boom', *Herald* (Melbourne), 16 February 1893, 2.
68 'The Baby Show', *Argus* (Melbourne), 17 February 1893, 6.

Two weeks later, on 6 March, the Wild Australia Show opened to good reviews at the Rotunda Hall on Bourke Street—one of four state-of-the-art cycloramas in Melbourne:[69]

> The floor of the hall had been utilised for the establishment of a native camp, and the gins in their gunyahs with the usual accompaniments of war-like weapons and domestic implements presented quite a realistic appearance, much appreciated by all who witnessed the scene. The corroborees and other numbers by the members of the troupe were well received.[70]

What seemed to be missing from the Melbourne performances was the historical drama, perhaps suggesting that it had been included at Meston's insistence and was not much relished by the performers themselves. They gave an afternoon matinee and evening performance on weekdays, with Purcell delivering 'private Lectures for Gentlemen Only at the Conclusion of the evening performance'.[71] According to one report:

> what excited the most interest was the exhaustive lecture by Mr. B. H. Purcell, for gentlemen only, in which he gave his audience a graphic description of the history and details of that curious custom practised amongst the tribes of Central Australia known as Sturt's Terrible Rite. The entertainment will be repeated every afternoon and evening during the current week, but the lecture will only be delivered after the night performance.[72]

While the Wild Australia Show attracted good audiences and reviews at the Rotunda Hall, the troupe was only booked for a limited period:

> The interesting entertainment of the troupe of northern aboriginals at the Rotunda Hall, Bourke street, has drawn good houses during the current week, and the afternoon matinees for ladies and children have been especially well supported ... The troupe ... are announced

---

69   The first cyclorama at Eastern Hill (now Victoria Parade, Fitzroy) featured a scene of 'The Eureka Stockade', and 'Jerusalem at the Time of the Crucifixion' was installed for Easter 1893. The second cyclorama was built in Collins Street (situated immediately behind the Rotunda Hall) and had a scene of the 'Siege of Paris'. A small cyclorama was included in the Exhibition Building complex and featured a scene of Melbourne in the 1840s. See: S. Ryan, 'Cycloramas in Melbourne', State Library of Victoria, 14 April 2014, blogs.slv.vic.gov.au/such-was-life/cycloramas-in-melbourne/.

70   'Amusements', *Age*, 9 March 1893, 6.

71   'Theatres, Entertainment. Other Shows', *Herald* (Melbourne), 13 March 1893, 3.

72   'Amusements', *Age* (Melbourne), 9 March 1893, 6.

elsewhere to give four entertainments to-day for the benefit of the visitors to the metropolis. They will close their season at the end of the week, and proceed to tour the provinces.[73]

On 21 April, the troupe appeared in a procession through Melbourne's central business district celebrating the achievement of an eight-hour day:

> Punctually at 10 o'clock the Fitzroy Military Band moved off amidst cheers along Victoria Street towards Elizabeth-street ... Altogether 44 distinct societies and 11 bands took part in the procession ... Th[e] latter post was occupied yesterday, strangely enough, by pioneers of another sort—the 'wild aborigines from Central Australia' concluding this procession.[74]

The troupe's presence in the procession was positively reported:

> The unofficial part of the show was to the crowd its most interesting feature—this was a group of the North Australian blacks, as nearly naked as the autumn weather and the surrounding circumstances would permit. They were painted for battle, and each carried a spear—a novel and grotesque sight even to the majority of Australians, with the weals and scars from flint knives, which are a black's idea of personal beauty, showing on the shoulders and the muscles of the back.[75]

A regional newspaper suggested that Purcell was seeking engagements for the troupe beyond Melbourne: 'The secretary reported as to various novelties he had secured for the [annual Bendigo Easter] Fair ... [and] was endeavouring to arrange for a visit of the Queensland blacks and other troupe'.[76] That arrangement did not eventuate, but the troupe's booking at the Rotunda Hall was extended at least twice, taking it up until mid-May when they would eventually depart Melbourne. 'The wild blacks from north Queensland gave their performance on Saturday afternoon in the Rotunda Hall, Bourke street', one report noted: 'Their season is rapidly drawing to a close, and the troupe will take its departure in about 10 days for Sydney, where they are under engagement to Sir George Rignold.'[77] On 22 May 1893, the Wild Australia Show members embarked on a steamer bound for Sydney.

---

73 'Amusements', *Age* (Melbourne), 17 March 1893, 5.

74 'Eight Hours Day. Yesterday's Celebrations', *Age* (Melbourne), 22 April 1893, 10.

75 'The Eight Hours Demonstration. A Fine Display', *Argus* (Melbourne), 22 April 1893, 15.

76 'Bendigo Easter Fair', *Bendigo Independent*, 25 February 1893, 2.

77 'Theatres and other Amusements', *Herald* (Melbourne), 8 May 1893, 3.

Conclusion

The Wild Australia Show's five months in Melbourne, commencing in late January and finishing in late May 1893, were challenging and tumultuous. Yet, despite initial mixed reviews of the troupe's performances and press coverage of their dire situation, they ended up having an unexpectedly extended season of performances there. A baby show, a workers' procession and a long run at the Rotunda Hall in Bourke Street proved their popularity with the Melbourne public during remarkably hard times.[78] What began as a disaster when the ANA's contract was not honoured and Meston abandoned them was partly redeemed through the combined efforts of Purcell, Yamurra and the other performers. Nevertheless, the troupe would continue under the shadow of growing hostility between Purcell and Meston. Earlier plans to take the Wild Australia Show overseas, or even to Adelaide, had long since faded, and pressure was mounting for the tour to be abandoned altogether and troupe members returned home. It is difficult to discern what the performers themselves wanted, but perhaps they too were tiring of the whole shebang. Things had not turned out exactly as they were promised. No doubt the cold climes of Melbourne and the approaching winter played some part in their decision to leave and return to Sydney.

Rather than pressing on to Queensland, the ever-resourceful Purcell had secured at least one booking back in Sydney—the troupe was engaged to perform in the play *It Is Never Too Late to Mend*, which was to open at Her Majesty's Theatre on Saturday, 27 May. The steamer was due to arrive a few days beforehand.[79] However, as they travelled north, Purcell was still awaiting a reply regarding permission for the troupe to perform. He still nursed hope for its wider success, and the performers, too, might have looked forward to performing again in Sydney after their initial successful season there. How the troupe's second Sydney season actually panned out is the subject of the following chapter.

---

78   As mentioned earlier in the chapter, the impact of the 1890s depression would see the Wild America Show close in Melbourne in 1893 and, within a year, Lindt would also close his studio at the 'Paris end' of Collins Street due to a lack of wealthy clientele seeking his services. See: Frost, 'John William Lindt (1845–1926)'.

79   The *Arawatta* was the only vessel listed as departing for Sydney around this time. It left on Saturday 20 May 1893 with 54 passengers in saloon and 61 in steerage ('Shipping Intelligence', *Age*, 23 May 1893, 4). The troupe was most likely numbered among the latter.

10

Return to Sydney and then home

Paul Memmott and Maria Nugent

A return visit to Sydney was not part of the original plan for the Wild Australia Show. Its projected itinerary had been of forward movement, not backtracking; it was supposed to go from city to city, and country to country, until it slowly wended its way to Chicago in time for the opening of the 1893 World's Fair. If all had gone to plan in Melbourne, it was either intending to head to Adelaide and then possibly Albany before travelling onto Europe. Or, alternatively, to Hobart, then New Zealand and then onwards. Its tour dates were never set in stone. One booking was enough to get it from place to place, but each stop along the way would depend on making good in each of the cities in which it performed. The loss of income from the ANA fete contract, coupled with the ongoing meddling of government authorities, not to mention the fact that the Chicago Exposition organisers had announced it was imposing a hefty bond to ensure that performers would be returned home, meant that the Show's original ambitions were severely curtailed. It had completed a three-city tour—Brisbane, Sydney and Melbourne. From then on, its choices were primarily about keeping body and soul together. The troupe would work for subsistence and survival, rather than fame and fortune. Going back to Sydney was a means to this end. They were by now a professional troupe of performers who could still draw a crowd, and who seemed prepared, at least, to keep going on the stage. It could not have been coercion, or at least not completely, as Purcell did not appear to have wielded that kind of power over the performers. Perhaps hunger was motivation enough, but maybe there were other factors as well, including that the troupe members saw themselves as professional performers. There's evidence, too, to suggest that others saw them this way as well.

May 1893: Return of the troupe to Sydney

It was not until 22 May 1893, as Melbourne began to grow cold, bookings began to dry up and an offer in Sydney materialised, that the troupe secured passage back to Sydney. Upon arrival, the performers went straight to work. They had been contracted by theatre impresario George Rignold to perform in the play *It Is Never Too Late to Mend* at Her Majesty's Theatre, which was then located on the corner of Pitt and Market streets. The theatre had been established in 1887, and Rignold was the lessee in 1893.[1] The play was based on an 1856 novel by English writer Charles Reade. According to Mary Poovey, it was this, his third novel, that 'had catapulted Reade to fame', and his novels continued to have strong 'sales … in the British colonies' into the late decades of the century.[2]

Opening night was 27 May 1893. The troupe had a few days after its arrival back in Sydney to rehearse. This preparation—as much as their well-honed theatrical skills—paid off. The play was well received, and the troupe's part in it was routinely singled out for positive comment, as this snippet shows:

> taking it all in all, the acting, the mounting, the introduction of novel effects in the matter of genuine aborigines, and all other details which form part and portion of the ensemble, Saturday night's representation was such as to merit very high praise, and to command admiration in all who can appreciate a play which at the same time points a very wholesome moral and supplies material for an evening's relaxation and amusement.[3]

---

1   Readers are advised that some quotations contain terms and phrases that are no longer in common use, and that are likely to be considered racist and to cause offence. That is not our intention. These terms and phrases are retained within quotations from archival material for the purpose of demonstrating historical ideas and attitudes only. R. Thorne, 'Sydney's Lost Theatres', *Dictionary of Sydney*, 2016, dictionary ofsydney.org/entry/sydneys_lost_theatres. See also: 'Supreme Court', *Brisbane Courier*, 22 November 1893, 7.

2   M. Poovey, 'Forgotten Writers, Neglected Histories: Charles Reade and the Nineteenth-Century Transformation of the British Literary Field', *ELH* 71, no. 2 (2004): 434, 435, doi.org/10.1353/elh. 2004.0029.

3   'Stage, Song and Show', *Australian Star* (Sydney), 29 May 1893, 3.

The play had an Australian colonial rural setting, and the drama revolved around a theft, with the perpetrator ending up in prison, becoming repentant and then reconciling with his victim: a classic story of temptation, fall and redemption. The script included a typical role for an Aboriginal character in the guise of a loyal Jackey, but this part was not played by one of the Wild Australia Show troupe. Rather:

> Mr. Tolano, who at first had a tendency to local dialect, made tremendous fun as the faithful blackfellow, Jackey, one of the most wonderful of his strange performances being the heating of a saucepan of soup without the aid of fire.[4]

The Wild Australia Show was engaged for dramatic effect and to add a touch of 'realism' to this (imagined) Australian frontier story. Troupe members were limited to non-speaking roles. They also performed variations of the dances, demonstrations and drama for which they had become widely known and much praised. With their inclusion, the play was modified to incorporate an attack on a bush dwelling, allowing the troupe to draw from their well-practised repertoire:

> Reference has already been made to the remarkable doings of the Queensland aborigines in the bush scenes, and without attempting to describe the weird wonders of the attack on the hut, the whizzing of flame-tipped spears, the strange dances, the fire lighting by means of friction, and the many other things that these people bring to us from the wilderness, we may say that this portion of the performance evoked the wildest enthusiasm, and in each instance the curtain had to be raised several times.[5]

The troupe's contributions to the staging of the play, which were also featured in advertising posters, were favourably reviewed by another Sydney theatre critic:

> The great Australian scene in the third set should certainly be seen by everyone who appreciates effect and realism. Nothing more striking has ever been witnessed in this city. The Queensland aboriginals are wild looking fellows, and their dances are weird, but they appear to know their way about the stage, and get through their business like old stage hands. The burning of the hut is particularly well done. If this scene could only be put on in London, it is safe to say business would be enormous.[6]

---

4   Ibid.
5   Ibid.
6   'Footlight Flashes. Important Revivals', *Referee* (Sydney), 7 June 1893, 7.

Even Archibald Meston, who had increasingly distanced himself from the Wild Australia Show, mildly praised the troupe's performance during its return to Sydney. He wrote to Under Colonial Secretary Parry Okeden in Brisbane, saying:

> After a tour in Victoria he [Purcell] returned to Sydney and is now exhibiting the blacks there at Her Majesty's [Theatre]. By all accounts he has done well with them.[7]

The play led to further invitations. Attending a performance were the daughters of the governor of New South Wales, Lord Duff. They were so delighted with the play that they encouraged their parents to attend a future performance. As a result, the troupe was soon afterwards invited to perform in the grounds of Government House.[8]

June and July 1893

After their season with Rignold's play had closed, the troupe would spend June and most of July 1893 in Sydney. They were accommodated in the City Stables from 5 June to 15 July (a total of five weeks) and there provided with provisions.[9] The City Stables were located at 97 Castlereagh Street, between King and Market streets, and were owned by Thomas Hassall, a member of parliament. We know from an invoice sent from the New South Wales authorities to the Queensland Government for accommodation and keep of the troupe that negotiations had been with E. S. Rowe, so we surmise that he was leasing the stables from Hassall. (Hassall had, in fact, auctioned all his horses and carriages in October 1892, some seven months earlier.)[10]

This location put the troupe right in the centre of Sydney, a spot they would have been familiar with after their run at the School of Arts in January. There was a hotel nearby where Purcell may have stayed, and the proximity

---

7   A. Meston to colonial secretary, 12 June 1893, Colonial Secretary's Office, Inwards Correspondence, QSA ITM847483, 1893/6869.

8   'Australian Aborigines at Government House', *Goulburn Herald*, 23 June 1893, 4; 'Lost Race to Entertain the Governor', *National Advocate* (Bathurst), 23 June 1893, 3.

9   Detective Greaves to inspector general of police, NSW, Colonial Secretary's Office, Inwards Correspondence, QSA ITM847483, 1893/7643.

10   Rowe had been connected to the stables since 1888, and buggies were still being hired out there by the firm of Emanuel and Co. Our hypothesis is that Purcell's previous career as a stock and station agent and horse trader had generated past collegial relationships with Hassall and/or Rowe, and that he was able to secure this accommodation option at a modest fee and at short notice, once the troupe got news of its theatre contract.

of Hyde Park might have provided respite for the troupe from the busy street environment of horses and carriages. We presume they were sleeping in the stables on straw and that they would have had a coal-fuelled brazier or burner, around which to warm themselves, cook meat and yarn about the bustle of the city and memories of home. The nocturnal sounds and smells of horses would have been familiar to those in the troupe with pastoral or police experience.

A couple of days before taking up residence in the stables, Purcell had given another public lecture. On or about 3 June, he spoke on the topic of message sticks with various exaggerated embellishments, using an example of a Wakaya message stick for illustration.[11] It had been obtained by Purcell in the vicinity of Lake Nash during his first reconnaissance in late 1891 (see Chapter 3) and was one of many Wild Australia Show artefacts that Meston sold in Sydney for personal gain.[12] Meston sold it to Andrew Barton Paterson, better known by the pseudonym 'Banjo Paterson', the poet and popular author who wrote 'Waltzing Matilda' and 'The Man from Snowy River'. Paterson, in turn, sold it, or passed it, to Andrew Lang Esquire, who presented it to the Pitt Rivers Museum in Oxford.[13]

Following his lecture on message sticks, Purcell was invited to deliver a lecture to the Royal Geographical Society of New South Wales on the, by now, well-rehearsed topic of subincision. One report noted that:

> Mr Purcell, who was received with applause said when he came back from Melbourne the other day his friend, Mr. Crummer, asked him particularly to lecture on 'Sturt's terrible rite, circumcision and the moral and social laws of the blacks'.

As in Melbourne, the audience for this lecture were said to be largely 'medical and scientific men'. As well as having some members of the Wild Australia Show on the stage with him, Purcell showed lantern slides of portraits of other troupe members.[14]

---

11   'Aboriginal Writing', *Australasian*, 3 June 1893, 45.
12   '"Wild Australia". Purcell v. Meston. Libel Action', *Telegraph*, 24 November 1893, 5.
13   See: 'A Message Stick Held in the Pitt Rivers Museum', Piers Kelly, ed., *The Australian Message Stick Data Base* (beta version), amsd.clld.org/contributions/PRM1893_32_1#4/-20.32/137.46. See also: Pitt Rivers Museum Collections, Object Reference [1893.32.1]: 'Message stick with diagonal incisions and a narrow waist with a strip of textile tied round it. The stick and part of the textile are covered in ochre. [?]'T' and [?]'7' and an upwards arrow are incised on the stick', databases.prm.ox.ac.uk/fmi/webd/objects_online (site discontinued).
14   'Our Australian Blacks', *Australian Star*, 1 July 1893, 8.

During the lecture, Purcell talked on many topics, including Kaurareg knowledge of winds (northwest wind 'koukee' is the time of dugong and turtle hunting); a technique of catching fish by hand in specially placed hollow logs to create preferred habitats for particular species; the love of men for their spouses; knife duelling between two men when one is aggrieved by the interest of the other in his wife (presumably based on Wakaya duelling custom); socially sanctioned punishments of men but particularly women for adultery; the equally grievous crime of selfishness; and details on practices of male initiation, circumcision and subincision. Troupe members also provided a fire-making demonstration on stage.[15] Some of these topics seem intriguingly intimate and tender, and so perhaps the content was born from living in close proximity with Aboriginal couples and families over many months.

In addition to commenting on message sticks, Purcell also described a pair of feathered shoes (or kadaitja) that he had procured when in Lake Nash in 1891 or 1892. A Sydney newspaper carried a story on them on 1 July 1893:

> NATIVE SHOE INDUSTRY—A peculiar evidence of native industry was received by Mr. B. Purcell, whose recent lecture on the aborigines of Australia at the Royal Geographical Society's meeting was so much appreciated by local ethnologists, from the neighbourhood of Alice Springs (S.A.). The curio is in the shape of a pair of shoes worn by the native warrior when on a tour of destruction against some hostile tribe. The shoes are composed of a mixture of blood and emu feathers for the soles, and a net of human hair twine for the uppers. The soles are 'straights', and have neither heels nor toes, so that the impressions left on the ground by the wearer are merely oblong dents that give no indication as to the direction travelled, and thus are a great value in leaving practically no tracks for the avenging warriors to follow up. In the native dialect of the district the articles are termed kady-tcha, and they are a rarity even among the aboriginals.[16]

Interestingly, five months later, just before Christmas 1893, Purcell would publish a fictitious story of a kadaitja titled 'Only a Pair of Boots' in the *Queenslander*. The story commences with a violent attack by Aboriginal warriors on a frontier homestead from the perspective of a visiting white man (Purcell's own character). An exaggerated description of a traditional duel

---

15   Ibid.
16   'Native Shoe Industry', *Daily Telegraph*, 1 July 1893, 9.

follows between one of the strong leaders of the Aboriginal attack and one of the Aboriginal workers named 'Silver' who was loyal to a local pastoralist. The contest in the story involves a sequence of exchanges between the two Aboriginal men using, in turn, spears, boomerangs, fighting sticks ('nullas'), tomahawks and lastly 'flint' knives. Silver wins the fight, but his adversary's brother comes back to kill the victor's spouse. So, Silver takes his revenge by wearing his 'kadaitja' shoes.[17] The story had resonances with the historical tableau that the troupe performed.

Throughout this period, and as had been his practice in Melbourne, Purcell was making valiant efforts to keep the tour afloat until a way to return home could be secured. One assignment was to pose for photographs in a natural bush setting for the renowned Sydney photographer Henry King (see Figure 10.1). The photographs show a banksia woodland setting, and although the location is not recorded, it likely was either at Botany (in the Joseph Banks Pleasure Grounds) on the north side of Botany Bay, or at Kurnell directly across from Botany on the southern side of Botany Bay. Or perhaps, the location was around the troupe's old haunt at the Bondi Aquarium and Pleasure Grounds.

Since its return to Sydney, interest in and concern about the fate of the troupe members on the part of the Queensland Government—initiated months earlier at the behest of the New South Wales Government—was intensifying. The troupe had forces working against it that it had little power to control or avoid. Throughout this period, Meston had not tired of discrediting Purcell at every opportunity or of putting obstacles in the way of plans to continue with the tour. In a letter to Queensland's colonial secretary, Horace Tozer, and under secretary, Parry Okeden, Meston wrote:

> Purcell may be contemplating leaving Sydney on a tour of the world if he can find another friend ass enough to find money for the cost. *This ought not to be allowed.* He ought to be compelled to return the blacks as I left him with sufficient to do that and he must have made a good deal since. He is in no way kind or careful of them, a fact they themselves will all emphatically endorse. I would have returned them from Melbourne only Purcell's action and ill luck left me without a shilling.[18]

17 B. H. Purcell, 'Only a Pair of Boots', *Queenslander*, 23 December 1893, 1222.
18 A. Meston to colonial secretary, 12 June 1893, Colonial Secretary's Office, Inwards Correspondence, QSA ITM847483, 1893/6869 (original emphasis).

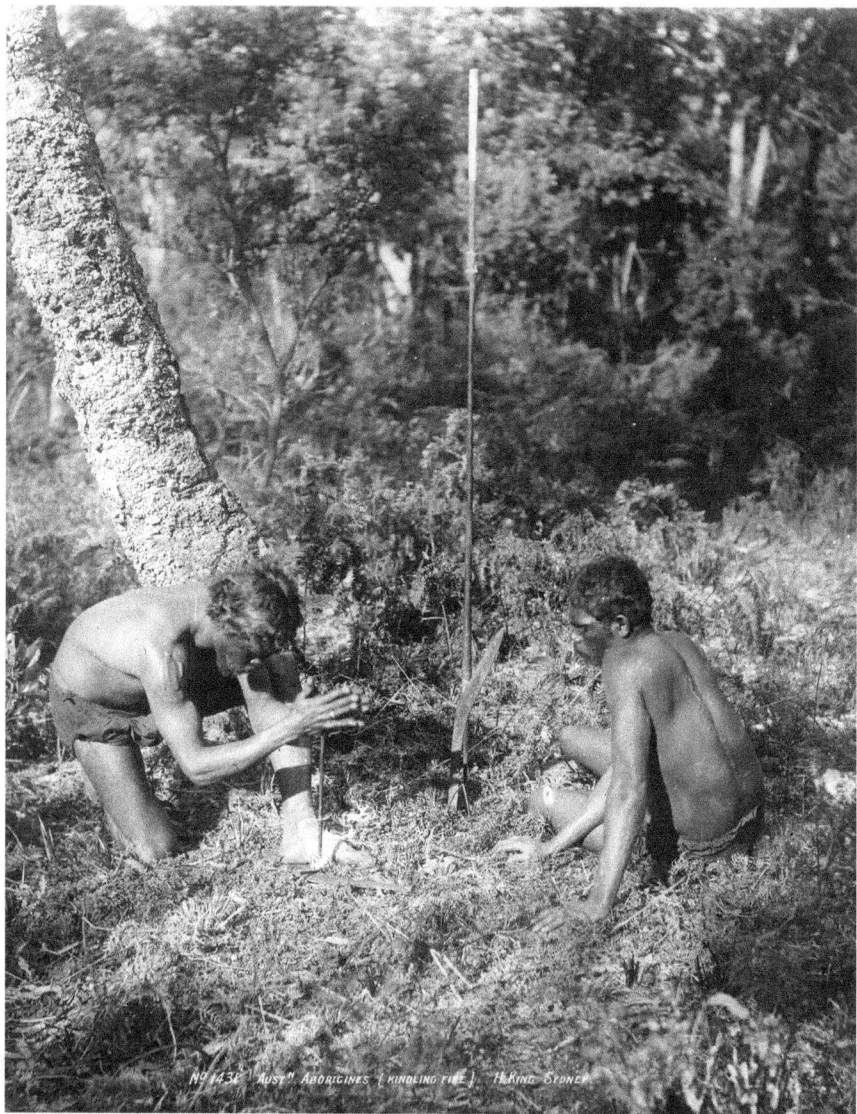

Figure 10.1: Two troupe members from the Wild Australia Show—Kalaringa (kneeling on left) and Werdbura (seated on right)—possibly at Botany Bay in mid-1893 on the troupe's return visit to Sydney

Source: Powerhouse Museum. Gift of Australian Consolidated Press under the Taxation Incentives for the Arts Scheme, 1985. Photographer: Henry King [attributed]. Object no. 85/1285-1178.

The competitiveness between the two former business partners was on display for all to see. Added to this was the pressure that the New South Wales Aborigines Protection Board (NSW APB) was again applying to its Queensland counterparts. On the letter cited above, Tozer wrote in the margins the following note (not all of which is legible):

> Let Mr [?] Douglas see this reply … See Mr Purcell's present address be discovered and then write him stating that the original intention of taking these blacks to Chicago having been abandoned arrangements satisfactory to this Department would at once be made for permission to help [?] them out of Queensland and unless such are made the Government will … [?] that the aboriginals be returned as promised to the places from which they were taken … Part of the bargain was that … under the personal care of Mr Meston as that gentleman is now in … and … having severed his connections with the enterprise or project it is all the more necessary that Mr Purcell should negotiate with the Government for an enlargement [?] of the permission under which these blacks were allowed to leave the colony H. T. 20/06/93.[19]

Thus, it is clear that by late June 1893, the Queensland Government's position on the matter was for the troupe members to be returned home rather than to embark on a world tour. The only matter of disagreement between the two colonial governments was who would foot the bill for the troupe's upkeep and repatriation. Rations for the troupe had been authorised by the New South Wales Government, but the Queensland Government was not yet showing signs that it would pay up. A George R. Dibbs in the New South Wales Chief Secretary's Office wired Tozer in early July 1893 asking whether his government would pay for the 'keep' and transport of the troupe back to Brisbane—an amount totalling £65. Dibbs wrote:

> This Government [i.e. New South Wales] is not responsible for them coming here but the unfortunate creatures cannot be allowed to perish because these persons who brought them have gone away and left them.[20]

Clarifying the matter, Okeden wrote to the principal under secretary of the New South Wales Government, advising that:

---

19 Ibid.

20 Telegram, Chief Secretary Dibbs, NSW, to 'The Honorable, The Prime Minister of Queensland, Brisbane' [under colonial secretary], Colonial Secretary's Office, Inwards Correspondence, QSA ITM 847483, 1893/7755.

Meston and Purcell took twenty-seven (27) aboriginals and Meston has returned to Queensland. Purcell who gives his address as 'Royal Geographical Society Sydney' wires that 'the blacks are stranded'. Will you kindly cause them to be returned here by steamer making the best arrangements you can in the circumstances? This Government will repay any necessary expense incurred and will, when the blacks arrive send them to their homes. Please advise by telegraph when they are coming.[21]

The matter then was settled, and preparations for the troupe to return got underway, but not before Meston had Purcell arrested on a warrant a week later (11 July) at the New South Wales Colonial Secretary's Office. The alleged offence was stealing £50 from him on 19 September 1892. Purcell appeared at the Central Police Court before Captain Fisher, but owing to some technicality, the case was dismissed.[22]

13 July 1893: Return of the troupe to Queensland

The troupe was eventually provided with 'deck passages' on the SS *Wodonga* to Brisbane. They left Sydney on 13 July 1893 and arrived in Brisbane the following day, but short one member. It was later reported that:

The Prince of Wales Islander remaining in Sydney asked me specially to be allowed to remain, he speaks good English and is engaged by a gentleman who is very kind to him and his wage is 5 [shillings] per week and board.[23]

The Islander to remain behind must have been either Bula or Dugum. Dugum probably had the best English since he had been a native policeman. Here again, we see that some members of the troupe were acting on their own account and making their own choices, however constrained these might have been under the circumstances. It seems feasible that the gentleman employer was one of the actors or theatrical managers of the Reade play; however, whatever the situation, it did not work out. A week later, the

21 Ibid.
22 'Notes and News', *Gympie Times and Mary River Mining Gazette*, 18 July 1893, 2; '"Wild Australia" Show. Arrest of B. H. Purcell', *Week*, 21 July 1893, 19; 'Supreme Court', *Brisbane Courier*, 22 November 1893, 7.
23 B. H. Purcell to colonial secretary, 21 July 1893, Colonial Secretary's Office, Inwards Correspondence, QSA ITM847483, 1893/8474.

young Islander was on another steamer bound for home. A telegram was sent from the Roma Street Police Station in Brisbane to the Queensland Police Commissioner's Office on 26 July, not more than a fortnight after the others had left Sydney, advising that 'the Aboriginal Black Boy' who had remained in Sydney had been sent by Howard Smith's steamship *Peregrine* on 25 July and was due to arrive at Townsville on 28 July, and thence to be transferred on to the SS *Aramac* for Thursday Island.[24]

Purcell's passage home was more eventful still. Having only been arrested a few days earlier in Sydney, he was immediately arrested again upon his arrival in Brisbane. This time, it was at the Prince Consort Hotel in Fortitude Valley by a detective named Herders, who placed him in the Brisbane watch house. The following day, Purcell was brought to court, where he was remanded until 20 July.[25] Upon appearing in court on 21 July, the charge was dismissed.[26] Coincidentally, the troupe departed from Brisbane the next day, but Purcell did not travel with them, and it is not clear if he had an opportunity to farewell them.

Running parallel to his efforts to have Purcell charged, Meston was busy trying to further sully the man's name. When accusations began to be made that force and coercion had been used to recruit troupe members, Meston pointed the finger at Purcell. Perhaps emboldened to speak out by the public debacle that the Wild Australia Show had become, Mr Coghlan, the manager of Glenormiston Station when Purcell was on his recruitment drive, wrote to the government about what he had witnessed (see Chapter 3), claiming that violence had indeed been used. The accusation was directed at Meston as much as Purcell; however, in his usual fashion, Meston sought to abrogate all responsibility, informing Tozer that he had given Purcell 'express instructions by letter and wire to bring no blacks under any circumstances without their own consent'.[27] Worried about the fallout, Meston desperately did not want Coghlan's accusations to stick.[28] But Tozer rejected Meston's demands for either official silence or an enquiry and pressed ahead with the repatriation of the troupe members:

---

24 Senior Sergeant P. Higgins to W. Finucane, Queensland Police Commissioner's Office, about an Aboriginal man travelling by steamship from Brisbane to Thursday Island between 25 and 30 July 1893, Roma Street Police Station, Brisbane, 26 July 1893.

25 'Supreme Court', *Brisbane Courier*, 22 November 1893, 7; '"Wild Australia Show". Arrest of B. H. Purcell'.

26 'Supreme Court', *Brisbane Courier*, 22 November 1893, 7.

27 A. Meston to colonial secretary, 18 July 1893, Colonial Secretary's Office, Inwards Correspondence, QSA ITM847483, 1893/8366.

28 Ibid.

> I do not feel inclined to detain these blacks from their homes whilst Messrs. Meston and Purcell are settling their disputes. If as stated they were kidnapped or taken away by force it is all the more reason for their speedy return to their homes without occasioning to them the delay which this enquiry would necessitate.[29]

On 22 July 1893, a Brisbane journalist wrote in the *Queenslander* that the Aboriginal troupe members were resuming their voyage to their 'homes in the North', leaving on the steamer *Wodonga*, and that they would be landed at either Cooktown, Thursday Island or Normanton, where the police would take charge of them and 'see that they reach their own tribes'.[30] Although one newspaper report had indicated that the Wakaya contingent would disembark in Townsville, other evidence suggests that they travelled to Normanton. Perhaps they wanted to remain with the troupe for as long as possible.

The 5 Wakaya and the 16 people from the Gulf region arrived in Normanton on about 31 July 1893. A police telegram indicates that the 5 Wakaya then travelled to Burketown (possibly by coach). Of the 16 Gulf region people, 11 (9 men, 2 women) travelled by train (described as a 'tram') to Croydon, and 5 remained behind in Normanton.[31] Upon their return to Thursday Island, the arrival of Gida and his party was reported thus:

> A Police telegram confirmed that four Prince of Wales Islanders (two men, one woman, one boy) returned to Thursday Island where Sub Inspector Savage was instructed to send them on to their home village or camp.[32]

A week later, as already noted, the other Kaurareg man would arrive back, his extended Sydney stay over.

It is not clear how Yamurra from the Mary River travelled back from Brisbane to his Country, but a journalist who briefly interviewed him explained that he was mightily happy to be home:

---

29   Ibid.
30   'The "Wild Australia" Show', *Brisbane Courier*, 17 July 1983, 6.
31   Inspector D. Graham to Queensland Police Commissioner's Office, re troupe members reaching Normanton, Commissioner of Police Ref 07262, 31 July 1893.
32   W. Finucane to sub-inspector Savage, Thursday Island, advising of return of four Prince of Wales Islanders, Queensland Police Commissioner's Office, Brisbane, 22 July 1893.

He [Yamurra] expressed himself as intensely glad to get back to Queensland, and stated that he had never been warm since he left our shores. 'Sydney and Melbourne great big places', he said 'but cold—my word'. He had plenty of fun everywhere, and until the moment Mr Meston left the show stated that he had had a 'budgery [good] time altogether'.[33]

Purcell, too, was in a reflexive mood when he was later interviewed by a journalist: 'They worked hard', he said, 'were honest, straightforward, obedient, sober and steady, with the one exception that of Bob or Yammara [Yamurra] Meston's pet from the Mary River'. Purcell's bad relations with Meston extended to his so-called 'pet'. Purcell went on: 'He I had arrested several times for drunkenness and disorderly conduct.'[34] Purcell, it seems, never really warmed to or reconciled with Yamurra, and the feeling was, by all accounts, mutual. Whatever the reason, they were forever engaged in a tug of war for power over—or, perhaps, the affection and respect of—the troupe.

July 1893: Recriminations in court

With the performers returned home, Meston and Purcell, once business partners who shared a vision, lost little time in dragging each other through the courts in hopes of retrieving their investments as much as their reputations.[35] The *Bulletin*, which had closely followed the Wild Australia Show saga—but not the show itself—reported, in predictably racist language, that 'there threatens to be yet some ugly work between Meston and Purcell, the two late partners in those myall niggers'.[36] After Meston had again accused Purcell of stealing £50 from him (see above),[37] Purcell launched a counterclaim, accusing Meston of 'false imprisonment, malicious prosecution, and slander'.[38]

---

33 'Wild Australia', *Queenslander*, 22 July 1893, 180.
34 B. H. Purcell to colonial secretary, 21 July 1893, Colonial Secretary's Office, Inwards Correspondence, QSA ITM847483, 1893/8474.
35 'The "Wild Australia" Show. Return of the Aborigines. A Police Court Case. One of the Blacks Interviewed', *Brisbane Courier*, 17 July 1893, 6.
36 'At Poverty Point', *Bulletin*, 29 July 1893, 18.
37 'The "Wild Australia" Show. Return of the Aborigines. A Police Court Case. One of the Blacks Interviewed'.
38 'At Poverty Point', *Bulletin*, 5 August 1893, 7.

The feud between Meston and Purcell continued unabated. It was, for a time, the only show in town. Each initiated civil legal action against the other, culminating in court proceedings during November 1893. Purcell claimed £1,500 in damages from Meston for 'injury to his character and reputation' and for false arrest. Meston, in turn, seeking a claim of £2,000, accused Purcell of injuring 'his credit, reputation, and character'.[39] The court found that Meston's charges were 'not proved' because he had failed to give Purcell written instructions before the troupe members were recruited.[40] Purcell, however, was awarded £50 damages—a minor victory—though, in 1896, an unpaid debt of Meston's to Purcell of £111 (presumably £50 plus interest) was listed in Meston's second insolvency, suggesting he never actually paid him.[41]

Yet there was one positive outcome from the various court cases: they created a quite detailed account of the Wild Australia Show scheme and its tour, as the court cases demanded information about who did what, when, why and how. The Wild Australia Show was written into the records, and a valuable archive was created. Indeed, it is on those court documents and summaries that we have often relied to reconstruct the story of the Wild Australia Show here.

What happened after the Show still eludes us. Once the 27 troupe members had returned to their regions, very little more is known about them, and hardly any memory of them has survived over the last 130 years—four generations or so. Only occasionally is some passing reference made in surviving records. For instance, the government resident on Thursday Island was to write the following just a couple of years after the tour was over:

> On the Prince of Wales Group the number of natives is gradually diminishing; they will soon die out altogether. The civilization of Thursday Island kills them off by its contact; meanwhile Misgidda, commonly known as 'Tarbucket', presides over about sixty natives, the remnant of a once powerful and numerous tribe. Misgidda and his wife, together with Doogoom and Bulla, joined the troupe of aboriginals who were taken to Brisbane, Sydney and Melbourne by

39   'Wild Australia', *Telegraph* (Brisbane), 23 November 1893, 2.
40   'Supreme Court', *Brisbane Courier*, 24 November 1893, 2.
41   'At Poverty Point', *Bulletin*, 2 December 1893, 7; Audit Liquidation File, MESTON, Archibald, QSA ITM1615768.

Messrs. Purcell and Meston. They returned to Thursday Island after their adventurous tour, and are now living at Prince of Wales Island none the worse, to all appearance, for their southern experiences.[42]

As we explain in the following chapter, the post-tour archival pickings are slim. The performers who toured left the stage and dropped from view. Yet, in other ways, the Wild Australia Show lives on with diverse, long-lasting and unpredictable legacies. Its various afterlives are traced in 'Act III: Enduring'.

---

42   J. Douglas, 'Report of the Government Resident at Thursday Island for 1892–3', *Queensland Votes and Proceedings*, vol. 2 (Brisbane: James C. Beal, Government Printer, 1894), 907–22.

ACT III
ENDURING

11

Afterlives: Biography, image, performance, memory

Chantal Knowles, Michael Aird, Jonathan Richards
and Maria Nugent

Although the Wild Australia Show tour came to an end sooner than expected, and the ambition to tour internationally was abandoned, the troupe experienced much, both highs and lows, in the nine or so months that they were on the road together and far away from home. A paradoxical situation emerged in the immediate aftermath of the Show's demise. On the one hand, the Aboriginal men and women who had comprised the Wild Australia Show troupe largely dropped from public view, apart from one or two exceptions. They returned to their lives in their home regions, the details of which went largely unrecorded. Curiously, they seem not to have been remembered in visible or lasting ways within their communities and families. Certainly, our efforts to tap into enduring memories of the Wild Australia Show performers have not met with much success. This is not to say that the men and women were completely forgotten; instead, it is to underscore, again, that their tenure with the Wild Australia Show tour was not the only or most significant part of their complete lives. On the other hand, while the actual men and women of the Wild Australia Show were slipping from public view, their photographed images, created in Brisbane, Sydney and Melbourne by the leading photographers and studios of the day, were circulating widely, including making their way overseas to places that had momentarily been dreamed of as destinations for the troupe itself. These images have rarely, if ever, not been in public view and circulation, but they were hardly ever properly documented as depicting the Wild Australia

Show nor were the individuals in them (correctly) named. They quickly became generic images representing a category of people or activity rather than the occupation and identity of the person/people photographed. That situation has now been reversed. Over the last decade or so, the photographs themselves have become the key source for unlocking the story of the Wild Australia Show and of histories of Aboriginal performance more broadly.

Biographies: The afterlives of the Wild Australia Show performers

In 1932, the *Age* newspaper in Melbourne published excerpts from an interview with a woman named Blanche Lewis. Under the heading, 'An Old Actress, Bright Memories', Lewis reminisced about her time as a performer during the late nineteenth and early twentieth centuries.[1] In 1893, along with her husband Albert Norman, she had appeared in George Rignold's *It Is Never Too Late to Mend* in Sydney, the play in which the Wild Australia Show troupe had also performed during its second stint in Sydney (see Chapter 10). Lewis recalled that during the play's run, her husband had become friendly with Gida (who she called 'King Tarbucket', a derogatory name he had acquired on Thursday Island).[2] When the Wild Australia Show troupe returned to Queensland soon afterwards, 'we lost sight of them', she said[3]—a phenomenon that we have also experienced when trying to trace the performers after the Show was over.

Blanche Lewis and her husband formed their own touring company, the Norman-Lewis Co., described by one chronicler as a 'vehicle for [Lewis's] original dramas'.[4] By May 1894, the company was wending its way through Queensland, travelling out west and far north, including to Thursday Island, where it played to a 'large audience composed of Malays, Kanakas, and pearl divers' who apparently expressed some dissatisfaction at the short length

---

1   Readers are advised that some quotations contain terms and phrases that are no longer in common use, and that are likely to be considered racist and to cause offence. That is not our intention. These terms and phrases are retained within quotations from archival material for the purpose of demonstrating historical ideas and attitudes only. E. H., 'An Old Actress. Bright Memories', *Age* (Melbourne), 31 December 1932, 5.

2   P. Memmott, J. Richards and J. Kane, 'A Man of the "Wild" Queensland Frontier: King Gida of the Kaurareg', *Memoirs of the Queensland Museum—Culture* 12 (June 2021): 29, doi.org/10.17082/j.2205-3239.12.1.2021.2021-03.

3   E. H., 'An Old Actress'.

4   For details about the Blanche Lewis and the Norman-Lewis company, see: Australian Variety Theatre Archive, 'Blanch Lewis', ozvta.com/practitioners-other-a-l/2/.

of the show (it was an hour long).[5] To appease the audience, the players quickly added some ad hoc recitals, which were well received. Yet it was not the experience of performing on Thursday Island that Blanche Lewis fondly recalled in her old age. Rather, with undimmed delight, she remembered how their old friend Gida, when hearing they were on the island, sent them 'an offering of numerous green coconuts'.[6]

We know of only one other account describing a post-tour encounter with one of the Wild Australia Show performers. It also took place in 1894, the year after the Show's tour had ended, and it too was published as a memory decades later. The reported encounter happened when 'Chip', the teller of the story, was with a mate on 'the eastern shore of the Gulf of Carpentaria'. There, he met a local Aboriginal man whom he described as tall, armed with 'spears, womerah and shield', and looking 'real myall'. Initially doubting the man would understand English, Chip was surprised when, in reply to his greeting, the man answered: 'Good day; been to the theatre lately?' Upon further enquiry, it transpired that the man 'had accompanied Meston to Sydney'. Quizzed about his view of cities, the Aboriginal man replied that 'town life was "no good to him", and [he] had found "simple life best for blackfellow"'.[7] It is not clear from the report which troupe member this was, as Chip did not name him, perhaps because he never learnt the man's name or, more likely, because he failed to remember it.

Devoid of much detail and only belatedly recalled, these curious snippets are suggestive of the ways in which the lives and fates of the Wild Australia Show troupe members fell from public view once the show was over. This happened quite quickly after they had returned to their homes. Indeed, the post-show lives of the performers have left as faint an imprint in the archives as their lives before they signed up to the Wild Australia Show. This is true

---

5   E. H., 'An Old Actress'. A report in *Gympie Times and Mary River Mining Gazette* (18 October 1894) notes that the Norman-Lewis Dramatic Company had been in Queensland since May, and 'have since been touring the north and west, going as far as Thursday Island and Croydon in one direction, and Hughenden and Winton in another'. (In Croydon they might have run into other former performers of the Wild Australia Show.) A report in *Table Talk*, Melbourne, on 6 July 1894 noted that: 'The Norman-Lewis Company at latest dates were at Croydon (Queensland), from thence they go to Thursday Island.' A later report in the *Mercury* (Hobart) on 2 March 1905 noted that: 'East Lynne, most doleful of melodrama, was once upon a time played at Thursday Island by the Norman Lewis Company under the most mirth-provoking surroundings. It was put up as a last resource as a farewell piece.'
6   *Mercury* (Hobart), 2 March 1905, 8.
7   Chip, 'A Meston Memory', *Richmond River Herald and Northern Districts Advertiser*, 13 July 1923, 6. It is also possible that the encounter never happened and that 'Chip' imagined this scene, which is heavy with familiar tropes about surprising encounters between white adventurers and Indigenous people on remote beaches.

for all the performers except Gida who, because of his various dealings with a steady stream of anthropologists, missionaries and government officials flowing into Thursday Island and the Torres Strait, appears reasonably regularly in written records.[8] The result is that we see only a partial view of their entire biographies—the portions when they were, momentarily, public property.[9]

If, post-tour, the erstwhile performers quickly dropped out of sight, the same cannot be said for the photographic portraits and other images of them created while the tour was underway, which earlier chapters have touched on when describing their experiences within the three main cities in which they performed. Troupe members were photographed regularly and extensively by the major metropolitan photographic studios of the day. They were photographed in poses in studios (see Figures 8.4a–b, 9.1, 9.2 and 11.5), out in the open performing historical tableaux (see Figures 7.3 and 8.2) and indoors on a stage (see Figures 7.6 and 8.3). These photographs of individual performers, pictured both singly and in pairs or small groups, have remained in view and in circulation—although the people 'captured' in them have rarely been correctly identified as Wild Australia Show troupe members, representing yet another kind of erasure of their lives, experiences and work histories. Even today, it is still possible to stumble across a photograph of one of the Wild Australia Show performers without learning that the person in the image once performed to audiences in Australia's east coast capital cities, or learning their name. Like many historical photographs created by studios, these images have been recycled for purposes beyond their original intention. Although the Wild Australia Show photographs still implicitly carry traces of the histories and practices of exhibiting Aboriginal people for public consumption—since, in whatever format they circulate, and however they are captioned, their purpose is exhibition and consumption—the *actual* history of the *actual* performance that was the *actual* context and condition for creating the photographs in the first place is invariably obscured or erased. Reassembling the archive of Wild Australia Show photographs and documenting each photograph's own 'afterlife' has been at the heart of the larger project to reconstruct the history

---

8   Memmott, Richards and Kane, 'A Man of the "Wild" Queensland Frontier', 44–7. See also: P. Memmott, 'Gida (c. 1849–1899)', *Australian Dictionary of Biography*, National Centre of Biography, The Australian National University, published online 2022, adb.anu.edu.au/biography/gida-31121/text38497.
9   See: A. Curthoys, S. Konishi and A. Ludewig, *The Lives and Legacies of a Carceral Island: A Biographical History of Wadjemup/Rottnest Island* (London: Routledge, 2023), 13, doi.org/10.4324/9781003254843.

of the Wild Australia Show.[10] Further, the republication of the photographs with their historical and biographical details restored has inspired other creative projects on Aboriginal performers and performance.

Photographs and portraits: The Wild Australia Show visual archive

More than 150 unique photographs of the Wild Australia Show troupe members, comprising studio portraits, theatre tableaux and open-air shots, are known to exist.[11] Since the time of their creation, they have been reproduced, reframed and recirculated. They exist in many forms,[12] including negatives, contact sheets, prints and postcards.[13] And they have been transformed in multiple ways: as high-quality printed photographs for purchase, as lantern slides for lectures and teaching, as mass-produced postcards for sale, and so on. A handful of individual images have also been turned, variously, into paintings, a sculpture, book illustrations and street art. Others have been reprinted and re-captioned in magazines and newspapers, and sometimes included in museum and art exhibitions both in Australia and overseas. Many of the Wild Australia Show photographs were acquired by public repositories where they have been documented, catalogued, archived, conserved, stored and digitised. This subsequent 'curation' of the Wild Australia Show photographs creates new meanings, connections and values.[14]

---

10   M. Aird and P. Memmott, 'Photographic Identification of the Troupe Members of the Wild Australia Show', *Memoirs of the Queensland Museum—Culture* 12 (June 2021): 7–26, doi.org/10.17082/j.2205-3239.12.1.2021.2021-02.

11   This number is a baseline. It has been arrived at through Michael Aird's detailed listings of individual photographs and numerous formats and repositories. The number is likely to grow. As not all photographers have been identified, there may be other unattributed Wild Australia Show photographs circulating.

12   E. Edwards, 'Objects of Affect: Photography beyond the Image', *Annual Review of Anthropology* 41 (October 2012): 225, doi.org/10.1146/annurev-anthro-092611-145708. Edwards lists the following: 'contact prints, enlargements, postcards, lantern slides, or transparencies for example. They exist as professional formats, snapshots, art works, or the products of bazaar and street photographers. They are glossy or matte, black and white, coloured or hand-tinted.'

13   Edwards, 'Objects of Affect', provides a valuable summary and discussion of many key scholars and works in this field, including J. Hevia's 'photography complex' model. See: J. L. Hevia, 'The Photography Complex: Exposing Boxer-Era China (1900–1901)', in *Photographies East: The Camera and Its Histories in East and Southeast Asia*, ed. R. C. Morris (Durham: Duke University Press, 2009), doi.org/10.1215/9780822391821-004.

14   For an example of how an anthropological archive is constructed, see: C. Morton, 'Photography and the Comparative Method: The Construction of an Anthropological Archive', *Journal of the Royal Anthropological Institute* 18, no. 2 (June 2012): 369–96, doi.org/10.1111/j.1467-9655.2012.01748.x.

Today, Wild Australia Show photographs can be sourced from more than 20 institutions in four countries across three continents.[15] This includes the British Museum in London and the Metropolitan Museum of Art in New York, as well as state libraries and galleries in Brisbane, Sydney and Melbourne. They are well represented in collections of university museums and archives. These institutions acquired the images based on their priorities at the time; for most, creating 'representative collections' was a key selection criterion. The collection of Wild Australia Show images at the University of Sydney, for example, was originally acquired for teaching purposes—but not necessarily about the Show itself. The collection of portraits, many of them showing naked torsos in addition to full-frontal or profiled faces, lent themselves to the visual examination of physiology and body markings.

Any image can be categorised (and re-categorised) by certain criteria, such as content (e.g. generic 'Aborigines'), technique (e.g. wet plate) or association (e.g. social history or biography). The large collection in the Museum of Applied Arts and Science, Sydney (also known as the Powerhouse Museum), for instance, came into the institution as part of an extensive private collection from a commercial source encompassing the output of leading Sydney studio photographers of the nineteenth and twentieth centuries. Such capaciousness speaks to diverse themes (e.g. photographic technology, commerce, consumption). Meanwhile, the incidental individual photographs scattered within them possess the power to elicit and illuminate varied emotions, histories and perspectives. Within these larger photographic archives, the Wild Australia Show photographs are dispersed, mixed up by the studios that created them even before entering a public repository.

In addition to their place in extensive public collections, copies of Wild Australia Show photographs (and postcards) are also held privately—sought, collected, swapped and reproduced by private collectors and vendors.

---

15 Repositories include Queensland Museum, Brisbane; Queensland Art Gallery and Gallery of Modern Art (QAGOMA), Brisbane; Museum of Applied Arts and Sciences, Sydney; World Museum, Vienna; Ipswich Art Gallery, Ipswich, Queensland; Art Gallery of New South Wales, Sydney; Museums Victoria, Melbourne; Metropolitan Museum of Art, New York; Natural History Museum, Washington; British Museum, London; State Library of Queensland, Brisbane; State Library of Victoria, Melbourne; State Library of New South Wales, Sydney; National Library of Australia, Canberra; Wellcome Library Collection, London; State Archives and Records Authority, New South Wales; Royal Anthropological Institute, London; Royal Geographical Society, London; Macleay Museum (now Chau Chak Wing Museum), University of Sydney, Sydney; University of Queensland Anthropology Museum, Brisbane; Peabody Museum, Harvard University; Pitt Rivers Museum, University of Oxford; Museum of Archaeology and Anthropology, University of Cambridge.

For example, a small selection of historical postcards carrying Wild Australia Show photographs (although not necessarily captioned as such) are always available for sale on eBay, and original postcards and photographs transformed into copy prints are likewise readily available through print-on-demand from online retailers like e-seller 'russtygold'. That they are still found for sale within antiquarian and second-hand markets underscores the enduring currency of the Wild Australia Show photographs.[16]

Paradoxically, it is the ubiquity and mutability of the photographs that keeps the Wild Australia Show troupe members in view even as they also work to erase them. From the outset, the photographed performers were routinely misnamed or unnamed. And as their individual photographs were inserted into generic sets of images of 'Aborigines', they quickly became detached from the Wild Australia Show. Likewise, their biographies as touring performers dropped from view. Once embodied exhibitors of their own distinct cultures, as photographed 'subjects', they were turned into dislocated examples of pan-Aboriginality.

This process has recently been reversed, and it is the surviving, if still widely dispersed, photographs that have enabled the history of the Wild Australian Show and its troupe to be written. Some years ago, photographer, photographic historian and curator Michael Aird began reassembling the Wild Australia Show photographic archive and tracing its many and varied surrogates across time and place. With a forensic eye that can spot a Wild Australia Show troupe member in uncaptioned or incorrectly labelled and described images, he increased the number of Wild Australia Show images and surrogates, producing an impressively large visual resource. Working with anthropologist and architecture historian Paul Memmott, who was also led to the Wild Australia Show via an intriguing image, Aird compared the photographs with newspaper and other historical reports to identify the individuals who made up the troupe. By this means, eventually, all the men and women of the Wild Australia Show had their names restored to them, laying the groundwork for more expansive histories of the Wild Australia Show to be told.[17]

16   On 16 April 2023, an eBay search for 'postcard aborigin* Kerry' listed 71 postcards of which 13 were Wild Australia Show photographs produced by Kerry's studios. Sellers came from Australia, France and the United Kingdom, and prices ranged from NZD26.99 to NZD210.00 (excluding postage).
17   See: Aird and Memmott, 'Photographic Identification of the Troupe Members of the Wild Australia Show', 7–26.

In time, the number of photographs and reproductions grew sufficiently large to inspire an exhibition. Curated by Michael Aird, Mandana Mapar and Paul Memmott, *Wild Australia* (the exhibition) opened at the University of Queensland Anthropology Museum in 2015.[18] A visual history of the Wild Australia Show, the exhibition introduced new audiences to a little-known history while also renewing Aird's and Memmott's commitment to finding out more about the Show and its performers. The swiftly assembled exhibition revealed that the many photographs created during the Wild Australia Show's short existence—and primarily for publicity and commercial reasons—were essential resources for reclaiming the Show's lost history. That exhibition was inspirational, provoking wider and further engagements with the Wild Australia Show, including this book.

Making images

The Wild Australia Show troupe was photographed by at least four photographers,[19] three of whom have been definitively identified. In Sydney, Charles Henry Kerry (1857–1928) photographed the troupe in early 1893 (see Chapter 8); Henry King (1855–1923), another Sydney photographer, did the same on the troupe's return to Sydney a few months later (see Chapter 10). John William Lindt (1845–1926) took a series of portraits when the troupe was in Melbourne (see Chapter 9). Uncertainty remains about the photographer or photographers who created images in Brisbane, although some were likely the work of William John Stark ([?]–1914).[20] Unlike the other three, Stark did not have a studio; rather, he styled himself as 'The Wandering Photographer', and likely sold negatives and prints to studios for commercial use.

---

18   M. Aird, M. Mapar and P. Memmott, *Wild Australia: Meston's Wild Australia Show 1892–1893* (St Lucia: University of Queensland Anthropology Museum, 2015).

19   In addition to the studio photographs, the Brisbane photographs include a lantern slide held in the collection of the Queensland Museum (EH5719). Another glass lantern slide of the same image is held in the private collection of Nicolas Peterson. A series of other outdoor scenes are most likely attributable to William Stark, but might include at least one other photographer.

20   Best known as Will Stark, he briefly had a studio with Ellis Sutton (rough) but by 1885 was on the road and styling himself as 'The Wandering Photographer'. See: Picture Ipswich, 'Trademark of Will Stark, Wandering Photographer, 1890', Ipswich Libraries, www.pictureipswich.com.au/nodes/view/82. Michael Aird identifies Stark as the most likely photographer of the Brisbane images, but that identification is not proven beyond doubt. Other possible photographers are Paul Poulson and Albert Lomar. See: Aird and Memmott, 'Photographic Identification of the Troupe Members of the Wild Australia Show', 12.

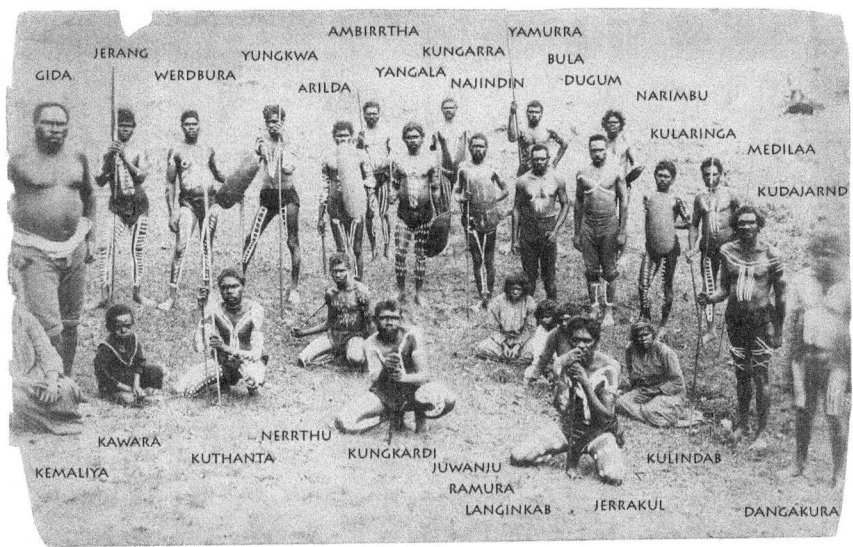

Figure 11.1: Wild Australia Show troupe photographed at Chelmer Reach on the Brisbane River during the Queensland Press Club's Annual Picnic in November 1892

Notes: An overlay of each performer's name was prepared by Michael Aird and Paul Memmott based on comprehensive visual and historical research. The photograph was used in the Wild Australia exhibition at the University of Queensland Anthropology Museum in 2015.

Source: Michael Graham-Stewart (photograph); Michael Aird and Paul Memmott (overlay of names).

Among all the photographs taken, it was one created in Brisbane before the troupe held its first paid public show that was the key to unlocking the troupe's story. One of two photographs taken on 12 November 1892 on the banks of the Brisbane River at Chelmer Reach, it shows the entire troupe together, including the five women (although Gida's wife is only partly in the frame) and one child, and is the only photograph to do so (see Figure 7.4). An annotated version of the photograph, with each person's name, sourced from newspaper and other records and established by comparing body markings and facial features, written on a copy of the photograph by hand, took centre stage at the *Wild Australia Show* exhibition at the University of Queensland in 2015 (see Figure 11.1). Inscribing the image in this way had the striking effect of transforming a group of anonymous individuals into a professional troupe of identified and named performers. Somewhat ironically, this significant photograph was not created for wide circulation or for publicity purposes and sale. The performers are wearing everyday clothes—they are not dressed as they would be for their future stage shows. They stand as a group, not stilted in a studio or caught in mid-performance. Rather, the photograph has the quality of a snap, perhaps taken opportunistically as a memento and record of a unique event.

The only other photograph within the extensive visual archive of the Wild Australia Show troupe that could also be described as a snap is one taken at the Bondi Aquarium in Sydney. It is of Narimbu and Dangakura and has a joyful and relaxed quality about it (see Figure 11.2). They are wearing everyday clothes (trousers but no shirts), laughing for the camera, with the switchback rail ride behind them. The pair appear more like visitors to the pleasure grounds, consuming its attractions, than an exhibit that punters had paid to see. The only clues that they are performers are the traces of ochre on their bodies and the firesticks they hold in their hands. The photograph provides a rare glimpse of life beyond the strictures and demands of studio poses and choreographed and staged performances. It takes us behind the curtain. A whole other perspective spills out from this moment, caught—perhaps unexpectedly and opportunistically—on film. Like the group shot in Brisbane, it seems that this photograph, too, was not made available for sale or chosen to grace a postcard. It is an archival estray.

By contrast, the studio-produced photographs were composed, catalogued and circulated. Kerry's photographs, for example, entered the market immediately: they were assembled into prospectus sheets and displayed in his studio's front windows and along the walls of the first-floor reception area. Prints of these grouped photographs, each image carrying a short caption, were distributed to institutions and learned societies as catalogues and contact sheets from which to order. The grouped photographs were organised by themes, rather than by event, place or person. They were typically captioned according to region (e.g. Queensland or western New South Wales), subject (e.g. 'a lubra', a pejorative term for an Aboriginal woman, but rarely, if ever, with a personal name) and/or activity (e.g. hunting, tracking). Through these commercial processes, the Wild Australia Show became mixed with other images grouped by the same imposed category and soon lost their actual details and particularity. None of the captions made explicit reference to the Wild Australia Show or to any staged and professional performance. Rather, people and staged scenes of and from the Wild Australia Show were presented as though they came from 'real life'.

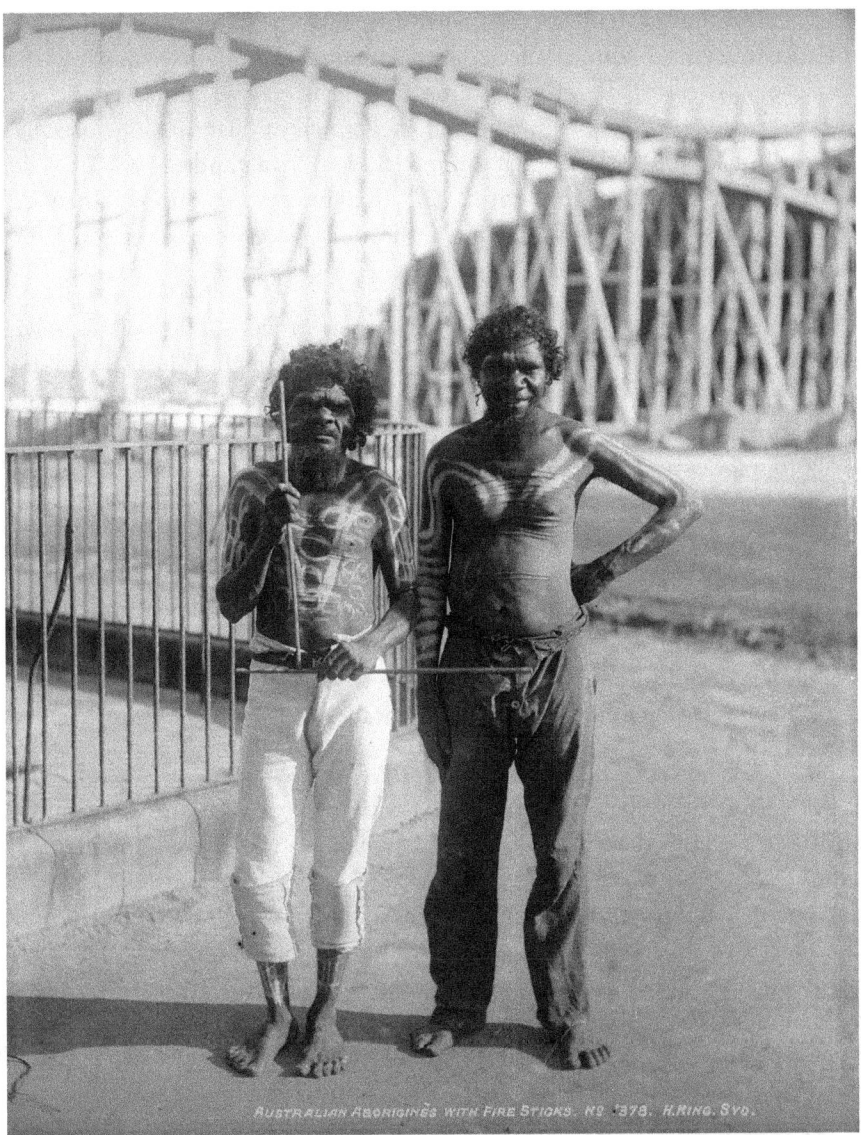

Figure 11.2: Narimbu and Dangakura at the Bondi Aquarium pictured in front of the Switchback Railway in either December 1892 or January 1893

Source: Powerhouse Museum. Gift of Australian Consolidated Press under the Taxation Incentives for the Arts Scheme, 1985. Photographer: Henry King [attributed]. Object no. 85/1285-1128.

The Kerry Studio had success with the sale of photographs through the distribution of contact sheets, and several of the images—possibly the bestsellers—were made into postcards. Charles Kerry was an early adopter of postcards: in 1903, within a year of the launch of postcards in Australia, his studio had 50,000 in stock.[21] Among these were a handful or so of Wild Australia Show images (although, again, they were not captioned as such), and it is these postcards that remain the most accessible of all the Wild Australia Show images today.

In Melbourne, the Wild Australia Show performers sat for well-known photographer J. W. Lindt (see Chapter 9). Although Lindt closed his photographic studio in 1894 (the year after he created the Wild Australia Show pictures), he continued working into the early twentieth century as a photographer and an exhibitor of his own works.[22] In Melbourne society circles, he was a favourite portrait photographer and, like Kerry, he had exhibited at the Colonial and Indian Exhibition in 1886. In cultural collections today, the best represented of his photographic output are a series of Aboriginal portraits taken in Grafton, northern New South Wales, during 1873 and 1874, and published as *Album of Australian Aborigines*, as well as a series of photographs taken in New Guinea in 1885 when he was the official photographer to Sir Peter Scratchely's expedition to explore the annexation of New Guinea.[23]

Lindt's Wild Australia Show photographs were reproduced in significantly smaller quantities than Kerry's, but at a higher print quality. Large format, mounted carbon prints can be found in collections in Melbourne, Canberra and Vienna, and in an album given by Lindt to Brabazon Purcell that is now in the British Museum. It includes portraits of all the Wild Australia Show members and, unlike Kerry's, each photograph is annotated with the name or names of each sitter. This album, beautifully presented and carefully documented, has been the most important source for identifying each individual in the troupe. Used in tandem with the photograph of the entire group taken in Brisbane before the tour proper commenced (described earlier), it has been possible to restore personal names to the performers and

---

21   J. Annear, *The Photograph and Australia* (Sydney: Art Gallery of NSW, 2015), 230.
22   K. Gahan and K. Orchard, *Photographs Are Never Still: The J. W. Lindt Collection* (Grafton: Grafton Regional Gallery), 2017.
23   See: J. W. Lindt, *Picturesque New Guinea. With an Historical Introduction and Supplementary Chapters on the Manners and Customs of the Papuans* (Longman, Green, and Co., 1887); A. Lubcke, 'Narrative and J. W. Lindt's "Picturesque New Guinea" Series, 1885', in *Shifting Focus: Colonial Australian Photography 1850-1920*, ed. A. Maxwell and J. Croci (Melbourne: Australian Scholarly Publishing, 2015).

thus commence the process of bringing their histories and biographies to life. However, before the 'rediscovery' of Purcell's copy of the Lindt album, the process of biographical erasure through recaptioning, re-cataloguing and repurposing had proceeded apace.

When the troupe returned to Sydney (Chapter 10), they were again photographed, this time by Henry King, both in a studio as well as outside, but in a bush rather than a beach setting (see Figure 10.1). King had a photographic studio in George Street, Sydney, just a few doors up from Kerry's. Very likely, he was familiar with Kerry's photographs of the troupe taken a few months earlier, and these inspired him to make his own series.

While both Kerry and King used plain studio backdrops for portraits and photographed men and women from the waist up, in King's photographs, they were usually unadorned, whereas Kerry had many decorate themselves in body paint and with traditional ornaments.

By the middle of 1893, the troupe members had become quite seasoned sitters for professional photographers, and a collection of over 150 photographs of them had been created by three major studios and an itinerant photographer.[24]

Reproductions: Postcards, paintings and publications

Neither the entrepreneurs who put the Wild Australia Show together nor the performers made any money from the Show. Some of the photographic studios that created images of the Show and its performers did make money, but not by peddling the Show itself. Their photographs of troupe members, whether of individuals or groups, sitting stock still or performing some action, retained a certain currency within changing contexts and consumption patterns, both in Australia and internationally, from the early 1890s up to the present. Visually striking, the photographs did not rely on the continued existence of the Wild Australia Show to be desired, valued and consumed. They could speak to myriad other contexts and interests, and appeal to professional collectors, creative artists and ordinary consumers alike.

---

24 Aird and Memmott, 'Photographic Identification of the Troupe Members of the Wild Australia Show', 13.

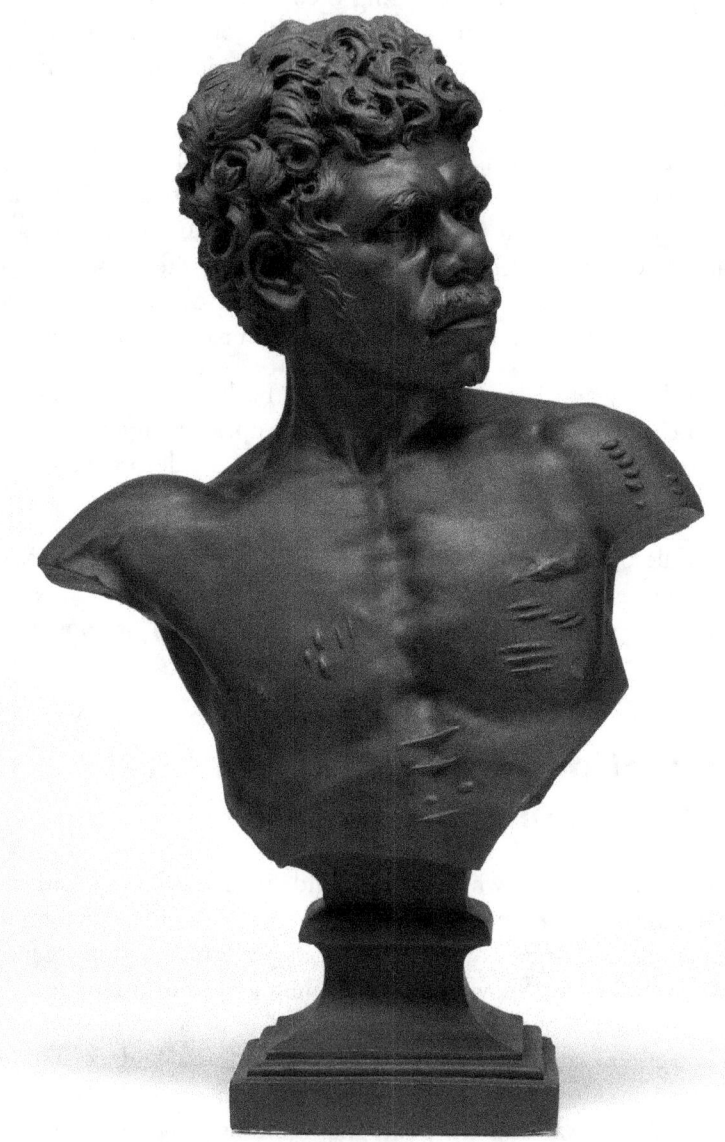

Figure 11.3: Bust by James White (Australia 1862–1918), *Kunkardi*, 1897

Notes: Plaster 89.5 x 56 x 33 cm. The bust is based on an 1893 photograph by Henry King.

Source: Art Gallery of New South Wales. Gift of Mr A. Dattilo-Rubbo 1924.
Image: Art Gallery of New South Wales, 1253.

In the immediate aftermath of their creation, the original photographs were transformed into both singular pieces of fine art and multiples of cheap and ubiquitous postcards. The earliest example of a Wild Australia Show photograph being used as artistic inspiration occurred within a few years of the Show's demise. In 1897, the King Studio's photographic portrait of Kungkardi, a young man of the Kutjar people of the Gilbert River, was the model used by sculptor James White for a plaster bust (see Figure 11.3). He called the work *Conamdatta, Northern Queensland Aboriginal*. The piece is now in the collections of the Art Gallery of New South Wales, having been gifted in 1924 by Mr A. Dattilo-Rubbo, an artist and teacher, originally from Italy, who was active in Australia from 1897, the same year the sculpture was made.

According to the gallery's online catalogue entry for the piece (where, on the cultural advice of Michael Aird, Conamdatta is now referred to as 'Kunkardi'):

> Little is known about the English-trained sculptor James White. He produced public sculptures for Sydney and Melbourne, but of his extant works 'Kunkardi' is the most inspired. The subject is modelled in a neo-classical, ennobling style, but the expressive facial features and striking scarification registers an individual and cultural identity that transcends symbolic guise.[25]

Here, the suggestion is that the sculpture returns to the 'subject' a humanity and identity that photographic reproductions risked minimising or flattening. Certainly, it is an elegant sculpture that provides a life-sized and sympathetic representation of the young man in *ronde-bosse*. The only known sculpture of a Wild Australia Show performer, the piece contrasts with the life casts made of many other Indigenous performers, particular in Europe, which were popular acquisitions of museums in the nineteenth and early twentieth centuries.[26]

25 See: Art Gallery NSW, 'Kunkardi', www.artgallery.nsw.gov.au/collection/works/1253/#about.
26 M. Bouquet, *Bringing It All Back Home: … to the Oslo University Ethnographic Museum* (Oslo: Scandinavian University Press, 1996), 18–19.

White's bust of Kungkardi has been included in at least two public exhibitions: in 1987 in *Australian Sculpture 1890–1919* at the Art Gallery of New South Wales and in 2003 in *Presence and Absence: Portrait Sculpture in Australia* at the National Portrait Gallery, Canberra. As part of these exhibitions, the photograph on which the sculpture is based was reprinted in catalogues, providing yet another occasion for its reproduction and context for its circulation.[27] A photograph of the bust is also in circulation, archived online in the 'Image of the Black in Western Art Research Project and Photo Archive' at Harvard University, where it has become part of an art historical discussion that pays close attention to race and formerly excluded identities.

Similarly, a Kerry Studio photograph of Narimbu ('Narimboo, Chief of the Workii Tribe') is the basis of a painting by artist Oscar Friström, completed in 1909 and titled *Nahmbo* (Figure 11.4).[28] Kerry had used this photographic portrait for postcards as well as for enlargements, and had also incorporated it into the letterhead for his business. It was clearly an image that appealed. Copying from a photograph was Friström's preferred method for painting portraits, although we also know that he made a portrait of Werdbura while meeting the troupe at its rehearsal camp at St Lucia in late 1892 (see Figure 7.5).[29] A decade later, the painted portrait was reproduced on the cover of *Bland Stenåldersmänniskor! Queensland Vildmarker* (Among stone age man in the Queensland wilderness), a book written by the Swedish zoologist and ethnographer Eric Mjöberg and published in 1918.[30] The painting is now held in the collections of the Ipswich Art Gallery outside Brisbane along with some other Friström paintings.[31]

27 See: Art Gallery NSW, 'Kunkardi'.

28 W. R. Johnston, 'Reviving Oscar Friström: His Aboriginal Paintings', *Queensland History Journal* 22, no. 4 (2014): 271–86.

29 Several original prints used by Friström while painting portraits are held in the Queensland Museum collection. Pencil-drawn perspective lines can be seen on some of these drawings. A photo taken by Charles Kerry was used by Friström to paint a portrait of Kudajarnd, and both the photo and the oil painting are held at the State Library of Queensland. See: T. Schafer, 'Oscar Fristrom Collection', State Library of Queensland, 7 February 2022, www.slq.qld.gov.au/blog/oscar-fristrom-collection.

30 E. Mjöberg, *Bland Stenåldersmänniskor! Queensland Vildmarker* (Stockholm: Albert Bonniers, 1918).

31 O. Friström, *Nahmbo*, 1909, Ipswich Art Gallery Collection.

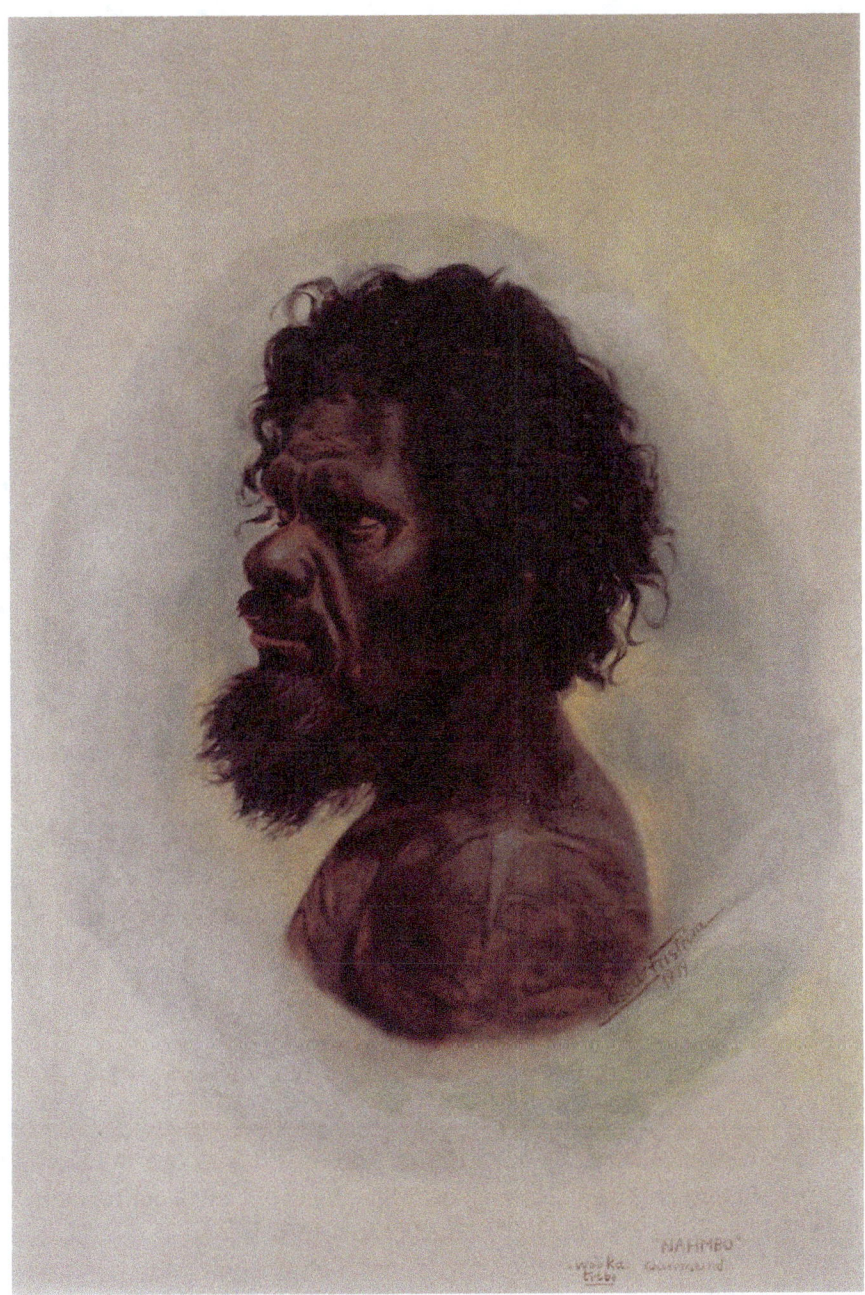

Figure 11.4: Nahmbo, portrait by Oscar Friström, 1909

Notes: Oil on board, 46 x 30 cm.

Source: Ipswich Art Gallery collection. Acquired through the Ipswich Arts Foundation, 2010.

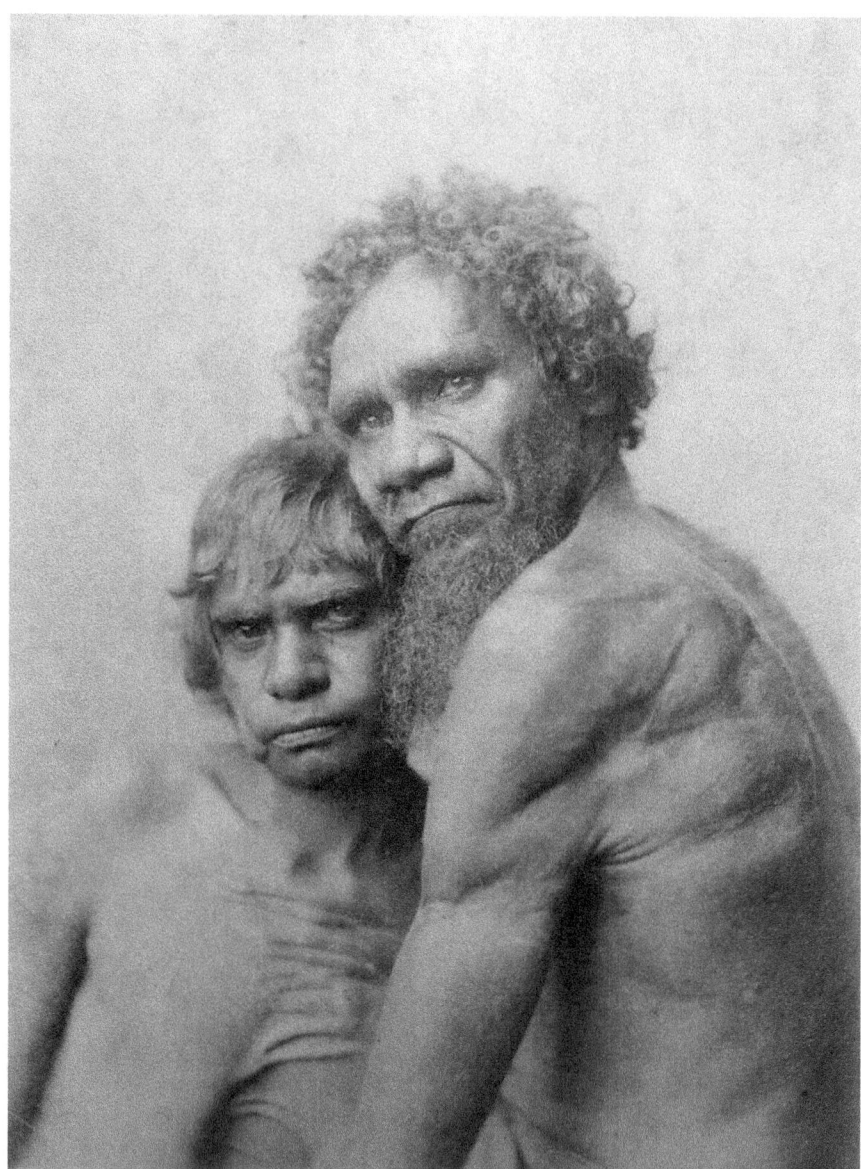

Figure 11.5: Kudajarnd and Langinkab (originally captioned Coontajandra and Langingubble) by J. W. Lindt in Melbourne, early 1893

Notes: The image was later used on the cover of *Blackfellows of Australia* (see Figure 11.6).

Source: The Trustees of the British Museum. Shared under a Creative Commons Attribution-NonCommercial-ShareAlike 4.0 International (CC BY-NC-SA 4.0) licence.

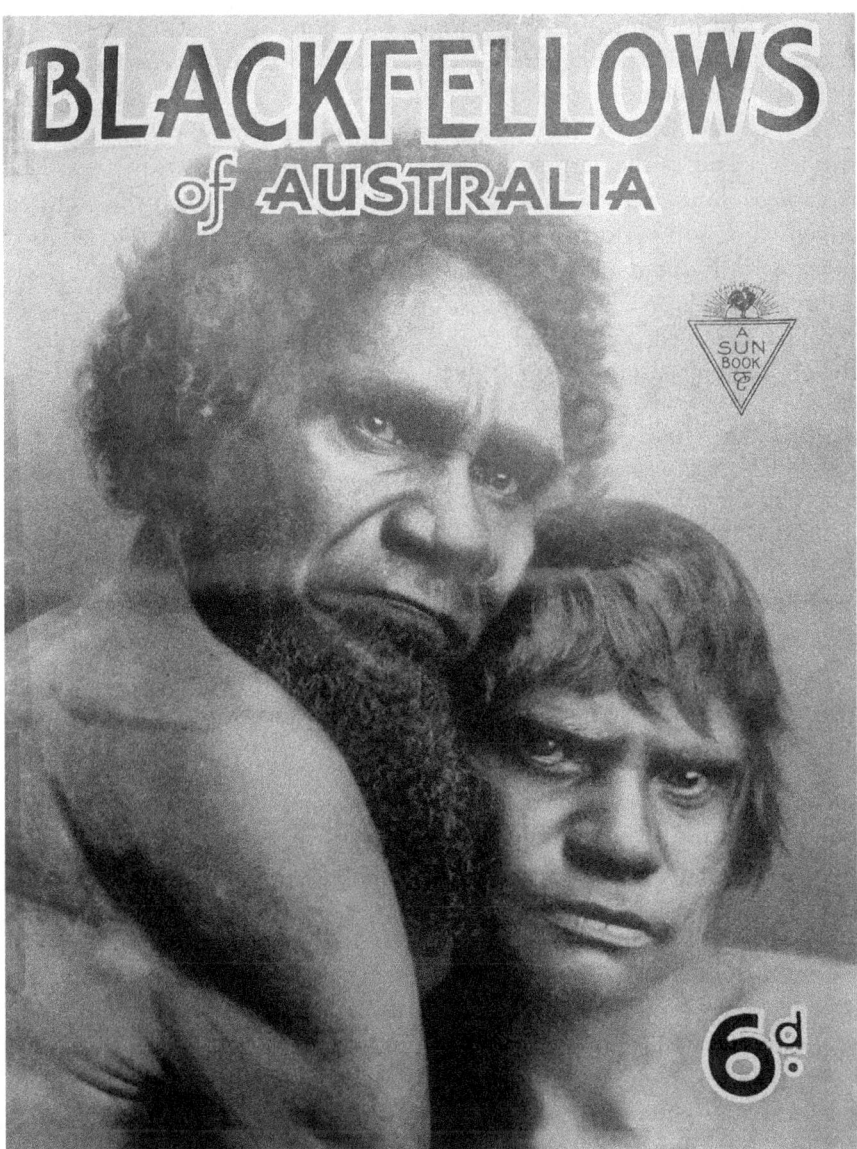

Figure 11.6: Cover of *Blackfellows of Australia* by Charles Barrett and A. S. Kenyon (Melbourne, [1936])

Source: The Royal Anthropological Institute (RAI).

J. W. Lindt's sympathetic photographic portrait of Kudajarnd and Langinkab has had a long afterlife (Figure 11.5). It was first reproduced as a (pencil?) drawing in an undated (but possibly c. 1900) *Cirque Robinson et ses peuplades sauvages* (Robinson's circus and the savage peoples), which was advertised as the 'largest exhibition of the century'.[32] In this way, the reworked photograph was used to promote a circus in which the pictured couple did not perform. The conversion from photograph to stylised drawing introduced notable, if subtle, changes, including extending the frame to reveal more of Langinkab's breast and accentuating the absence of clothing to project a racialised trope of 'savage' people. A few decades later, the photograph surfaced again, this time used on the front cover of Charles Barrett and A. S. Kenyon's *Blackfellows of Australia* (c. 1936), where it was used in a more documentary, less sensationalist, style (see Figure 11.6).[33]

The photographs of the Wild Australia Show that were most reproduced circulated as postcards, and the majority of these were produced by the Kerry Studio between 1903 and 1928.[34] Many are still in circulation as 'vintage postcards' or 'collectables' and can be bought on eBay or through antiquarian auctions. Of the thousands of postcards Kerry created, sold and circulated, several used Wild Australia Show images, although none were identified as such. The choice of image for a postcard would have been informed by earlier print sales—and then a title, often fanciful, added.

At least eight of Kerry's Wild Australia Show photographs were made into postcards across three series, including 'Series 4 Aboriginal Life', 'Series 5 Aboriginal Warriors and Gins' and 'Series 97 [no title]'.[35] Among the photographs chosen for postcards is the staged narrative tableau (described in Chapters 7 and 8) that brought settlers and Indigenous people together in a violent confrontation. The postcard image displays an act of violent retribution by a native policeman for an unseen act of Indigenous violence against white settlers. In the image, three 'aggressors' are being fired upon by a uniformed native policeman, and a fourth man lies prone, either already dead or injured (Figure 11.7). The postcard was captioned 'Australian Aboriginals and Black Tracker'. The use of the more generic and neutral term 'black tracker' as

---

32   See: Africa Musuem, 'Science, "Races" and Hierarchy', expohumanzoo.africamuseum.be/en/ exhibition/science_races. 'Peuplade' is a way of describing a group of people but placing them in a timeframe of a developing society, reinforcing the second term 'savage'.

33   C. Barrett and A. S. Kenyon, *Blackfellows of Australia* (Melbourne: Lawrence Kay for Pictorial Newspapers, c. 1936).

34   N. Peduzzi, 'Travelling Miniatures: Kerry and Co's Postcards of the Pacific, 1893–1917' (PhD thesis, University of East Anglia, 2011), 71. One of these postcards is postmarked 1928, when Kerry's studio was already closed, indicating that shops were still selling stock and the card still appealed.

35   Ibid., 138–40, 171.

opposed to 'native policeman' probably sought to address moral sensitivities about the activities of the Native Police, thereby garnering wider market appeal. This is the only postcard sourced from the Wild Australia Show that is known to have been hand-tinted and reproduced in full colour. The colour, presumably, was designed to add to the drama. The erasure in this image is of the white troopers who led the Native Police units. As historian Jonathan Richards and others have noted, they operated as a law unto themselves on Queensland's frontiers.[36] In these imagined, portable historical tableaux, only Aboriginal people are pictured in the roles of both giving and receiving violence. The effect is to detach the violence and responsibility for it from white settlers, even as the situation is entirely driven by settler colonialism and theft of land. The postcards (and the stage show from which they originated) functioned, then, as a form of denial of settler culpability.

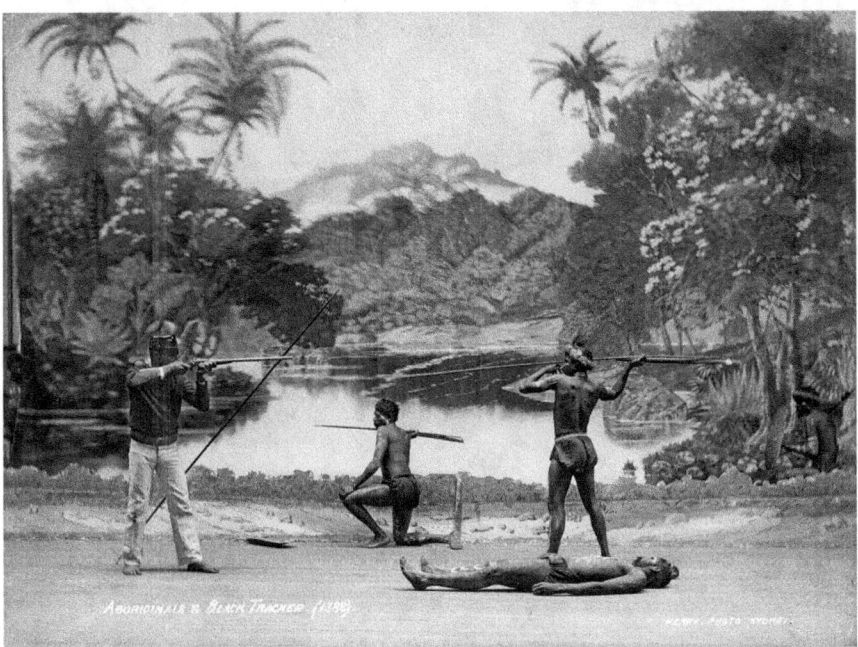

Figure 11.7: Four members of Wild Australia Show troupe performing historical tableau of Native Police shooting on stage in Sydney in either December 1892 or January 1893

Source: Powerhouse Museum. Gift of Australian Consolidated Press under the Taxation Incentives of the Arts Scheme, 1985. Photographer: Kerry and Co., Sydney. Object no. 85/1284-659.

---

36 J. Richards, *The Secret War: A True History of Queensland's Native Police* (St Lucia: University of Queensland Press, 2008).

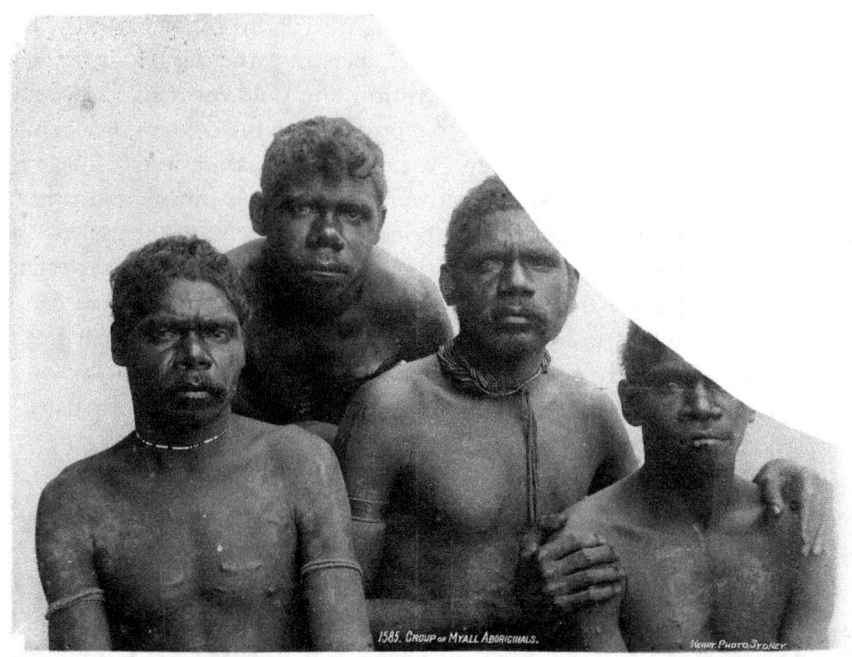

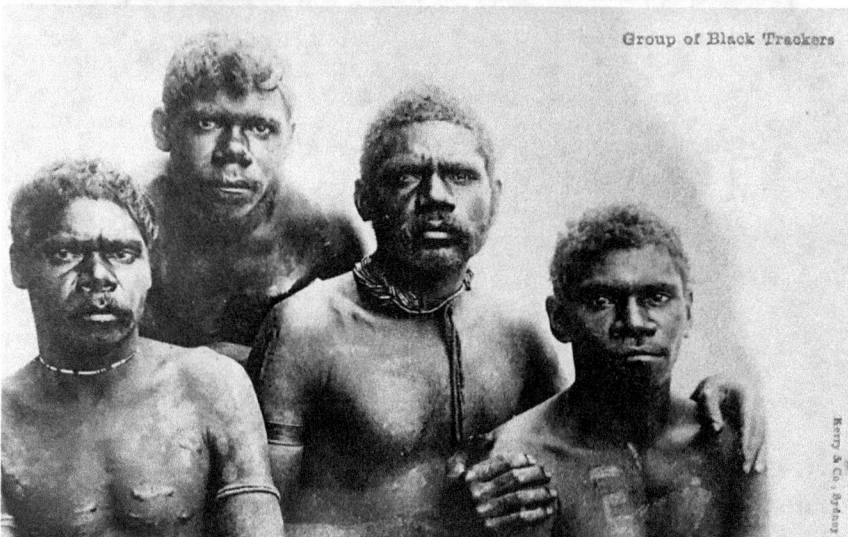

Figure 11.8: Four members of the Wild Australia Show troupe photographed in the Kerry Studio in Sydney in 1893

Notes: From left to right: Kuthanta, Kungkardi, Najindin, Nerrthu. The image was later used on a postcard that carried various captions, including 'Group of Black Trackers'.

Source: Powerhouse Museum. Gift of Australian Consolidated Press under the Taxation Incentives of the Arts Scheme, 1985. Photographer: Kerry and Co., Sydney. Object no. 85/1284-761.

In a similar vein, another postcard showing a group of four men of the Wild Australia Show is captioned 'Group of Black Trackers' (see Figure 11.8). Although it is possible that the four men had served as black trackers before joining the troupe, that was not their primary occupation when the photograph was taken. A more accurate caption of the image would have been: 'Group of Professional Performers' or 'Group of Travelling Actors' or 'Four Members of the Wild Australia Show Troupe'. According to Peduzzi's analysis of Kerry Studio postcards of Aboriginal people, the glass plate from which this image came was captioned 'Group of Myall Aboriginals', and the albumen print as 'Group [of] Men from Interior of Queensland'. Although seemingly insignificant, these shifts in captioning are, in fact, quite loaded. 'Myall' represents them as living in a traditional way, exoticising them as 'authentic' and 'primitive', akin to Meston's intent in his use of the word 'wild' in the Wild Australia Show's title. The descriptor 'black trackers' presents them as skilled in traditional knowledge but 'tamed' or 'recruited' in service to settler society. This is a more acceptable role than that of professional touring performers, who could be seen as 'inauthentic' and 'out of place'. Never do the captions declare the place where the images were taken—the metropolis of Sydney. Any number of descriptions were possible, depending on time, place and audience appetite, but 'black trackers' was deemed the most marketable as a postcard.[37] Similarly, when a postcard was made from the photograph of Kaurareg dancer Dugum wearing an elaborate mask, it was redescribed. The fairly neutral 'Prince of Wales Island Man with Mask' became 'Aboriginal with Devil's Mask' for the postcard version,[38] again to trade in ideas of exoticism, savagery and sorcery.

The reframing of original photographs with altered captions in a cheap, readily accessible format was shaped by, and embedded in, settler constructions of Aboriginality. Taken by white photographers for white-owned and operated studios, and with white settlers and travellers as the target market, the choice of image and caption recruited representations of the original Wild Australia Show performers for new and other forms of exhibition. No matter how much agency the men and women of the Wild Australia Show might have been able to express when the original

37   Peduzzi, 'Travelling Miniatures', 178.
38   Ibid., 150. See also: C. Knowles, 'Unmasking the Torres Strait: Objects and Relationships, in *Ancestors, Artefacts, Empire: Indigenous Australia in British and Irish Museums*, ed. G. Sculthorpe, M. Nugent and H. Morphy (London: British Museum, 2021), 203.

photographs were created, that evaporated through subsequent framing and captioning as the troupe members were trapped in an imposed, largely negative narrative.

Among the photographs of individual performers created by the King Studio, the portrait of Dangakura, a Wakaya man, who had significant scarification across his chest and arms, proved particularly popular. In addition to being chosen as a postcard image, it was also used as a smaller vignette, simply captioned 'An Aboriginal', on the addressee side of several other studio postcards featuring scenic views. It is quite easy to see why this portrait might have been chosen as a postcard image, if the purpose of postcards is to attract a buyer and compel a sale. Dangkura holds the photographer's gaze; his face is relaxed and open, assertive and appealing.

Perhaps this is why this particular photograph was chosen to feature prominently in a recent publication. On a stylistically stripped-back front cover of *MUSE*, the magazine of the University of Sydney Macleay Museum (now part of Chau Chak Wing Museum), Dangakura looks out at the reader with the same compelling gaze. However, in this twenty-first-century publication, it is Dangakura's biography *as a performer* that is foregrounded. The accompanying caption reads: 'Dangakura, a member of the performance troupe *Wild Australia* Studio portrait, Sydney, June 1893. [Photo: Henry King; Macleay Museum HP99.1.1]'.[39] No longer anonymous nor generic, he has had his status as an accomplished performer restored, and the context and conditions of the photograph's creation are likewise made clear—neither erased nor obscured.

The prompt to publish the image in this way on the magazine's cover was directly attributable to the Wild Australia Show exhibition at the University of Queensland that same year, for which photographs in the Macleay Museum's collections had been requested for loan. Seeing that exhibition provoked Macleay Museum curator Rebecca Conway to reconsider the ways in which Wild Australia Show images in the University of Sydney's collections were documented, interpreted and displayed. As she notes:

> One of the most exciting outcomes for the Macleay is applying the [University of Queensland's] project's research to our holding. Since viewing the exhibition and its catalogue I have been able to locate an additional 26 images of the troupe within our collections, and have

39   [Cover image], *MUSE*, University of Sydney, no. 11 (2015): 2.

identified 13 people by name. Many images were previously titled simply 'Queensland Aboriginal', and we can now provide more respectful and meaningful captions and narratives.[40]

Thus, by publishing the photograph of Dangakura on the cover and discussing the implications of Aird's and Memmott's work on the Wild Australia Show, Macleay Museum engaged in and contributed to the same processes of historical reclamation—of replacing absence with presence and generic type with named individual.

While these are examples of the ways in which captions can be, and are being, rewritten to reflect new knowledge and understanding, it is regrettably still the case that misleading or erroneous captions attached to Wild Australia Show photographs remain, in some cases, difficult to dislodge. Where captions form part of documentary and archival records, disentangling truth from fiction is an ongoing challenge. For instance, one of the two Brisbane photographs taken at Chelmer Reach on the Brisbane River in late 1892 was, a hundred years later (in the mid-1990s), reproduced on the back of a Woodford Folk Festival program. The Woodford Folk Festival is held in Maleny, Queensland, and this image, closely cropped along the top, bottom and left edge, was captioned:

> This historic photograph was taken at Bridge Creek, Maleny in the late 1800's /It is believed to be one of the last gatherings of tribal groups visiting the Maleny area for the great Bunya Festival which were held regularly and were attended by thousands of Aboriginal people.

The mistake was not the festival organisers' alone. The photograph was sourced by them from the State Library of Queensland, where it had been mistakenly catalogued as relating to the Noosa district.[41] Once published, such misattribution has ongoing repercussions. The photograph continues to circulate in local history publications and in native title research and reports as an illustration of the 'last Bunya gathering'. While the performers themselves ensured that their cultural knowledge and affiliations were

---

40   R. Conway, 'Wild Adventures', *MUSE: Art, Culture, Antiquities, Natural History*, no. 11 (2015): 3, www.sydney.edu.au/content/dam/corporate/documents/chau-chak-wing/our-research/muse/muse-issue11-jul-2015.pdf.
41   'Aborigines-Noosa District, 1880s', probably Bridge Creek area near Tytherleigh's Falls in 1880s, neg. number 57373, State Library of Queensland.

recognised and respected, a century later they became unwittingly tangled up in other people's histories, ending up in places far from their own Country. Such are the long and complex afterlives of images.

Remembering: Reclaiming history

As the expansive archive of Wild Australia Show photographs has become more widely known, it has served as a catalyst for creative and artistic engagements with the Wild Australia Show and other hidden histories of Aboriginal performance. After seeing the *Wild Australia Show* exhibition at the University of Queensland in 2015, Rhoda Roberts, then head of First Nations programming at the Sydney Opera House, arranged for a selection of the photographic portraits to be displayed on digital screens lining the walkway, Bennelong Passage, at the Opera House during the Homeground Festival that year (see Figure 11.9).

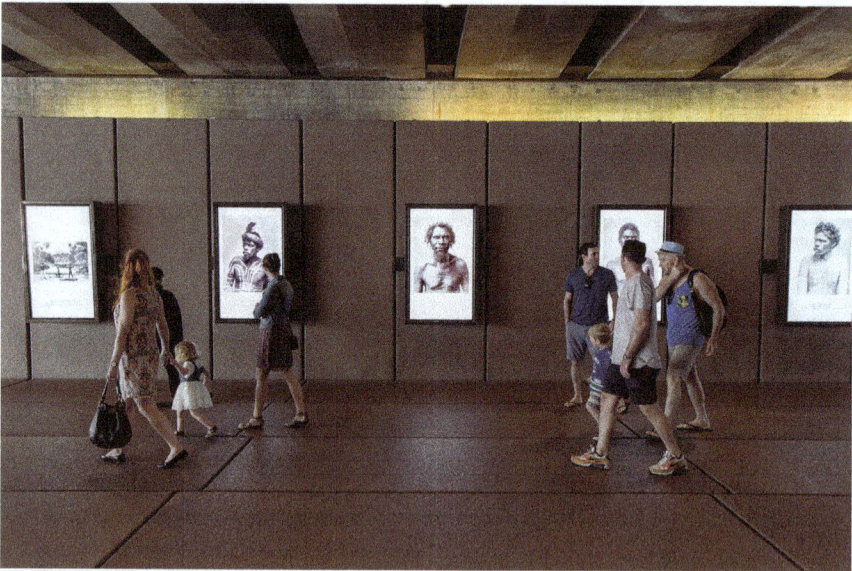

Figure 11.9: Bennelong Passage leading to Sydney Opera House lined with enlarged photographs of Wild Australia Show performers installed as part of the Homeground Festival, 2015

Photographer: Daniel Boud.

Subsequently, the Wild Australia Show was among the historical performance troupes that inspired her show *Natives Go Wild!*, which played at the Opera House for a few nights in October 2019. An ensemble of circus and burlesque performances, presented in familiar entertainment styles of the late nineteenth and early twentieth centuries, including circus, sideshows and 'human zoos', *Natives Go Wild!* also revealed and celebrated hidden histories of Aboriginal and Islander performers. Scripted by Roberts and performed by contemporary Aboriginal and Pacific Islander artists, it showcased the little-known stories of men and women who joined the circus or followed the fairground routes, sometimes suppressing their Aboriginal and Islander identities and assuming stage personas as Spanish, Indian or other.[42]

Similarly, performance artist Jackie Sheppard was also inspired by the increased visibility of the Wild Australia Show to create a performance piece, *Wild Australia Tour*. First staged as part of Barring Yanabul, a Yirramboi First Nations Festival held in 2017, the dance work roved through Melbourne streets from the Arts Centre to the State Library.[43] Sheppard devised the work in response to their ancestral ties to the Country of some of the Wild Australia Show performers and, in doing so, emphasised the exploitation of the troupe members. For instance, the work showed the performers being removed from Country in chains—an accusation levelled at Purcell after the Show had ended. It also evoked their later abandonment by Meston in Melbourne, which forced them to earn a living as street performers. Posing for photographs and performing violent acts were also referenced in the work. In a discussion of the piece, Sheppard noted:

> At each stop, the men were forced to pose for colonial propaganda photos depicting native police massacring their 'savage' countrymen—the message being, 'Hey, we're not perpetrating this genocide; the savages are killing each other!'[44]

---

42   See, for instance: M. V. St Leon, 'Celebrated at First, Then Implied and Finally Denied: The Erosion of Aboriginal Identity in Circus, 1851–1960, *Aboriginal History* 32 (2011): 63–81, doi.org/10.22459/AH.32.2011.04; M. V. St Leon, *The Wizard of the Wire: The Story of Con Colleano* (Canberra: Aboriginal Studies Press, 1993).
43   T. Yunkaporta, 'Wild Australia: Reliving the Shocking Story of Indigenous Slave-Performers', *Guardian*, 6 May 2017, www.theguardian.com/artanddesign/2017/may/06/wild-australia-reliving-the-shocking-story-of-indigenous-slave-performers.
44   Ibid.

Sheppard's piece highlighted Meston's role in exhibiting and exploiting Aboriginal people and culture for his own gain and glory, something he would continue to do for two decades after the Wild Australia Show ended. Between 1894 and 1915, Meston organised about 30 performances involving Aboriginal people (mainly men, but also some women), including many for settler ceremonial events and historical commemorations.[45] In 1898, he had been appointed southern protector of Aborigines in Queensland, and he leveraged that position to exhibit Aboriginal people and arrange Aboriginal performances, some of which toured to Sydney and other parts of New South Wales. For instance, in 1901, he organised a group of Aboriginal men from Queensland to participate in a re-enactment of Captain Cook's landing at Botany Bay as part of the week-long Federation celebrations in Sydney.[46] A few months later, he organised 'seventy men and nine women, coming from all parts of the State [of Queensland], and including also a number of men from the other Australian States' to perform before the Duke and Duchess of York at Government House.[47]

Meston held the post of southern protector for five years before being dismissed in 1904, but that did not stop him from exhibiting Aboriginal people. Along with writing and publishing newspaper articles, staging Aboriginal performances was essential to his self-promotion as the foremost expert on all things Aboriginal in Queensland.[48] In 1905, in a bid to secure another government-sponsored position, he wrote of himself:

> No man knows Queensland better, or probably as well, or can speak so authoritatively on the attractions and resources. I am equally at home in press or on the platform. I have a splendid series of Queensland pictures for the lantern, taken specially for me and could soon increase it to a complete collection.[49]

---

45   J. Richards, unpublished summary of Meston's post–Wild Australia Show performances, in possession of author.

46   M. Nugent, '"An Echo of That Other Cry": Re-enacting Captain Cook's First Landing as Conciliation Event', in *Conciliation on Colonial Frontiers: Conflict, Performance, and Commemoration in Australia and the Pacific Rim*, ed. K. Darian-Smith and P. Edmonds (New York: Routledge, 2015).

47   'The Aboriginal [Corroboree]', *Brisbane Courier*, 22 May 1901, 5.

48   See: C. Taylor, 'Constructing Aboriginality: Archibald Meston's Literary Journalism, 1870–1924', *Journal of the Association for the Study of Australian Literature* 2 (2003): 121–39.

49   A. Meston to chief secretary, March 1905, Unofficial Correspondence of the Premier and Chief Secretary's Department, QSA ITM89295 [no letter number].

Meston's offer of his services to the Queensland Government went unheeded.

Undeterred, he continued touring Aboriginal people locally, such as four men from Deebing Creek Mission (Albert Collins, Billy Mitchell, Harold McDonald and Jack Morgan) who were in Ipswich in March 1905 to perform corroborees and mock combat with nullahs and shields while Meston lectured.[50] Ten years later, in July 1915, he gave what we believe was his last public performance when he supervised 10 Aboriginal men from Queensland to perform a corroboree and two exhibitions of boomerang and spear throwing at an Australia Day event for wounded soldiers at the Sydney Show Grounds.[51] A decade later, Meston was dead.

Meston's frenetic exhibiting—pursued as much for his own self-promotion and economic survival as for the benefit of Aboriginal people or edification of settler audiences—represents another kind of afterlife of the Wild Australia Show, not least because it rehashed the demonstrations of skill, cultural dances and historical tableaux that made up its repertoire. The Aboriginal performances Meston promoted, along with his extensive journalistic output on Aboriginal topics, is integral, too, to his reputation as a leading figure in the repressive treatment of Aboriginal people in Queensland. Intimately associated with the drafting of the *Aboriginals Protection and Restriction of the Sale of Opium Act 1897* and responsible during his time as southern protector for carrying out, with noticeable enthusiasm, the forced removals of Aboriginal people across Queensland that it legislated, Meston is a much-maligned man in Aboriginal collective memory today.

Jackie Sheppard's performance piece engages with these legacies as well, casting Meston not merely as a showman but also a monster who is held responsible for the deep physical and psychological wounds caused when families are forcibly separated and when people are removed from their ancestral Country. These wounds have not fully healed, but contemporary creative and performance arts provide a salve for them as they revisit, re-story and reclaim the horrible histories that caused them.

---

50   'Picturesque Queensland', *Queensland Times*, 18 March 1905, 12.
51   A. Meston to home secretary, 27 July 1915, Home Secretary's Office, Inwards Correspondence, QSA ITM847776, 1915/6844.

In other ways, Sheppard is less concerned with spotlighting Meston as with showing, and celebrating, how the individual troupe members were as one in their desire to hold the travelling group together, support each other along the way and, ultimately, make their way home. Their work, like ours, seeks to privilege Aboriginal people's agency, highlighting the performers' resilience, creative control and mutual support. While it deals with Meston's mistreatment of the troupe, the performance re-stages the performers' stories and imagines *their* feelings, *their* losses and *their* strength. As it brings these histories back into view, it also reminds audiences that these histories were almost lost and remain little known. In engaging with the Wild Australia Show's story in an embodied performance, Sheppard has created a thought-provoking and confronting work, using present performance to engage with stories of performances past.

In August 2018, a video of Sheppard's *Wild Australia Tour* was shown during Jacob Boehme's keynote address at the Australian Performing Arts Market in Brisbane. The address, published online by Blakdance in August 2019,[52] included this description:

> [Jackie] and co-performers Suri Bin Saad and Benjamin Creek walked the length of Swanston Street in Melbourne's CBD, starting from the forecourt at Arts Centre Melbourne and finishing on the steps of the State Library. The piece was developed in response to archives [Jackie] had unearthed whilst researching the stories of [their] ancestors, and [their] family.[53]

Boehme used Sheppard's performance art to challenge his audience. He continued:

> I raise the examples of the Wild Australia Tour and a nation's history in the international export of blakfulla arts and culture, within the context of an arts market that seeks to question its conventions and its future, because I have to ask—has much really changed?[54]

Here, Boehme suggests, past and present are continuous, and so it makes little sense to confine the Wild Australia Show to history and posterity. It still speaks to the present and the future.

---

52   J. Boehme, 'Keynote Address at Australian Performing Arts Market 2018', Blakdance, www.blak dance.org.au/media-releases/jacob-boehme-keynote-address-at-australian-performing-arts-market-2018.
53   Ibid.
54   Ibid.

For *Natives Go Wild!* and *Wild Australia Tour*, Rhoda Roberts and Jackie Sheppard, respectively, were inspired by the example the original Wild Australia Show represented, both in terms of the lived experiences of the troupe members during the Show's tour and their fates afterwards, including the ensuing anonymisation, forgetting and elision of their stories and identities. Roberts's and Sheppard's creative reclamations and re-engagements with the archives and images of the Wild Australia Show work to interrupt their usual uses and effects when consumed by, and circulated within, settler society. Critically and creatively engaging with the images and other records allows new emphases and perspectives to emerge. When combined with the proper naming of individuals and the reconstruction of their biographies, alternative interpretations are asserted, new cultural spaces created, and afterlives extended and enriched.

Memories: Connecting with family and community

As part of our project, we were interested to see what memories remained about the Wild Australia Show in the places from which the troupe members came. In pursuit of this, during 2017 and early 2018, Paul Memmott, Michael Aird and a small team created a 12-banner exhibition, using a highly adaptable and cost-effective method, designed to tour regional centres.[55] The lightweight banners could adapt to any type of venue, and were put on display in civic buildings, libraries, cultural hubs and information centres. The first banner exhibition opened in Mount Isa in May 2018 before travelling to Tennant Creek, Thursday Island, Normanton, Karumba and Croydon (see Figure 11.10). In November 2018, the exhibition was opened at Gab Titui Cultural Centre on Waiben Thursday Island by the Peters family, descendants of 'King Gida', one of the three male Kaurareg performers (see Chapter 5).

---

55   The 12 banners were: 1. 'Introduction, Meston's Wild Australia Show 1892–1893'; 2. 'Who Was Archibald Meston?', 'Background on the Different Performers'; 3. 'Where Did the Troupe Come from?', 'Where Did They Go?'; 4. 'The Performers from the Wakaya Desert'; 5. 'The Performers from the Northern River Camps'; 6. 'The Performers from the Croydon River Town Camps'; 7. 'The Kaurareg Performers from the Torres Strait'; 8. 'The Kabi-Kabi Performer from the Mary River', 'The Places Where the Troupe Performed'; 9. 'The Troupe in Brisbane'; 10. 'The Troupe in Sydney'; 11. 'The Troupe in Melbourne'; 12. 'What Happened after the Show?'.

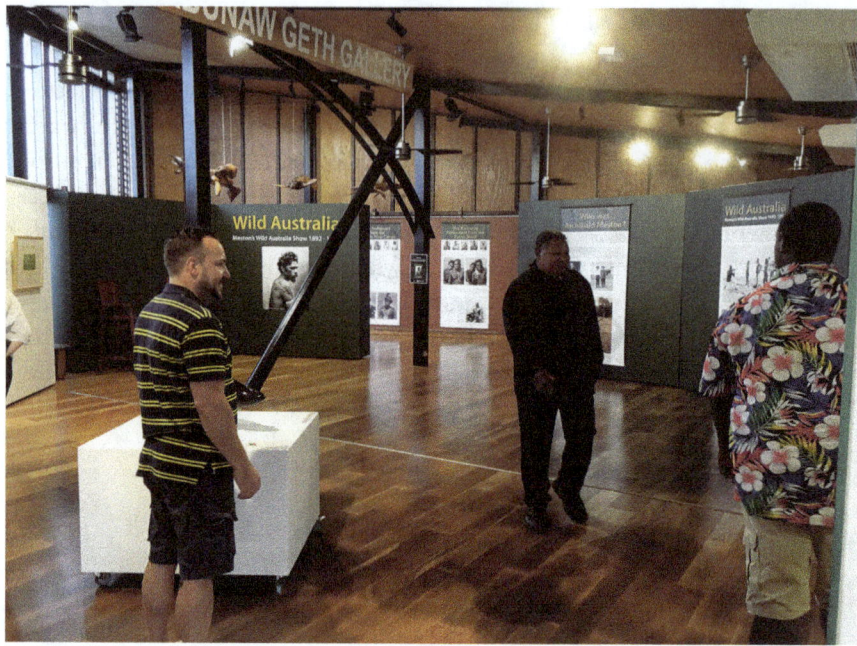

Figure 11.10: Banner exhibition installed at Gab Titui Cultural Centre, Thursday Island, 2018

Photographer: Paul Memmott.

In all of these places, the banner exhibition was proposed as an opportunity for local people and communities to view the photographs of the Wild Australia Show troupe, to learn about its story, and to trace its timeline of recruitment, performance and eventual return home. Rather than a definitive or complete account, the banner exhibition was designed as an open-ended and collaborative tool to generate further information and knowledge. It was designed as a means of dialogue with local audiences who may have had some personal, familial and ancestral connections to the people in the photographs. Visitors were invited to comment on, add to, or correct content.

Each community that viewed the banner exhibition responded to and connected with it differently. On Thursday Island, for instance, the opening was followed by an emotionally charged forum that aired the traumatic Kaurareg history and highlighted the need for healing. At the opening, Milton Savage, chairman of the Kaurareg Native Title Corporation, said: 'The truth can set you on fire. This *Wild Australia Show* tells us about intergenerational trauma. It has an effect on Kaurareg people today.'[56] In other places, some people were puzzled that they had not heard about the Wild Australia Show before. We, too, were surprised that there was not a deeper vein of memory about the Show in the places from which the performers hailed. While the dearth of documentation on post-Show lives was expected, we had not quite understood the extent to which family and community connections with the men and women who made up the troupe were broken. Even in the case of Gida, a man who *is* remembered today by his Countrymen and women, it was news to some that he had been a member of the Wild Australia Show troupe. This chapter in his life story was, until then, unknown—but it quickly became a new detail to add with pride to his extensive curriculum vitae.[57]

Nevertheless, the banner exhibition—as yet another means by which the story of the Wild Australia Show has become publicly known—provided a space for community reconnection and reclamation that could potentially lead to the creation of new productions, interpretations or artworks inspired by the troupe's story. The banner exhibition aimed to empower communities to connect with the men, women and children who performed in the Wild Australia Show, and who had since been lost to their descendants, communities and Country. And in this, and other ways, the Wild Australia Show lives on.

---

56   Kaurareg Elder Milton Savage, 29 November 2018, quoted in P. Memmott, J. Richards and J. Kane, 'A Man of the "Wild" Queensland Frontier: King Gida of the Kaurareg', *Memoirs of the Queensland Museum—Culture* 12 (2021): 64, doi.org/10.17082/j.2205-3239.12.1.2021.2021-03.
57   Ibid., 63–5.

Author biographies

Michael Aird is the director of the University of Queensland Anthropology Museum and an Australian Research Council (ARC) research fellow. He has worked in Aboriginal arts and cultural heritage since 1985, maintaining an interest in documenting aspects of urban Aboriginal history and culture. He has curated over 30 exhibitions, including *Portraits of Our Elders* (1993), a Queensland Museum travelling exhibition; *Transforming Tindale* (2012) at the State Library of Queensland; and *Captured: Early Brisbane Photographers and Their Aboriginal Subjects* (2014) at the Museum of Brisbane. In 1996, he established Keeaira Press, an independent publishing house, which has produced over 35 books. Other publications he has contributed to include *Photography's Other Histories* (2003), edited by Christopher Pinney and Nicolas Peterson; *Calling the Shots: Aboriginal Photographies* (2014), edited by Jane Lydon; the Art Gallery of New South Wales exhibition catalogue, *The Photograph and Australia* (2015), edited by Judy Annear; and *Ancestors, Artefacts, Empire: Indigenous Australia in British and Irish Museums*, edited by Gaye Sculthorpe, Maria Nugent and Howard Morphy.

Michael was a researcher on the ARC Linkage Project 'Wild Australia Show', providing expertise on the photographic archive of the Wild Australia Show performers. His interest in the Wild Australia Show spans three decades. It came about through photographs he kept finding of the same people, which he eventually connected to the performance troupe that Archibald Meston assembled and toured. When he and Paul Memmott discovered a mutual interest in the Wild Australia Show, they joined with Mandana Mapar to develop an exhibition at the Anthropology Museum at the University of Queensland in 2015. Michael's extensive knowledge about the photographic archive, and his insights into its creation and circulation, contributed to various chapters in the book where photographs are described, and, most substantially, to the large section in Chapter 11 that follows the lives of certain images reproduced in new forms after the Show ended.

Lindy Allen is an independent scholar and curator, and a material culture and cultural heritage specialist. With over 40 years of experience in the museum sector, including as senior curator of Northern Australian Collections at Museums Victoria, Melbourne, from 1989 to 2018, she has worked extensively and developed collaborative cross-cultural research projects with many Indigenous communities across Australia. Lindy co-edited the seminal volume *The Makers and Making of Indigenous Australian Museum Collections* (2008). She has curated over 35 major exhibitions, including the acclaimed Museums Victoria and University of Melbourne touring exhibition *Ancestral Power and the Aesthetic: Arnhem Land Paintings and Objects from the Donald Thomson Collection* (2009). Lindy has been a chief investigator on an ARC e-Research Project and partner investigator on five ARC Linkage Projects. She has researched the history of artefacts and photographic collections from Arnhem Land and Cape York, and the agency of Indigenous people in the creation of these collections, as well as linking contemporary custodians with their cultural patrimony in museums and establishing its relevance today. She organised the groundbreaking Milingimbi Makarrata Forum in 2016 that brought together directors and curators of national and international museums with Yolŋu leaders at Milingimbi as part of the ARC Linkage Project *The Legacy of Collecting at Milingimbi Mission*.

Lindy was a partner investigator on the ARC Linkage Project 'Wild Australia Show'. She focused on two key themes: the history of the ethnographic collections assembled by Meston and Brabazon Purcell, and the troupe's time in Melbourne. On the collections, she joined forces with Chantal Knowles and Sophie Price from the Queensland Museum to trace Meston's and Purcell's donations and sales of items to that institution, and they published their findings in Price, Allen and Knowles, 'The (Not-So) Sacred Ibis: Archibald Meston, the Colonial Collector, and the Queensland Museum', in *Memoirs of the Queensland Museum—Culture* (2021). Lindy also undertook research on a message stick in the Pitt Rivers Museum, Oxford, that was possibly collected by Purcell; at the Australian Museum, Sydney, on items that had been bought from or donated by Meston; at the Linden Museum, Stuttgart, on items that were commissioned from Meston; and in the Meston-Stokes collection at the South Australian Museum, Adelaide. Except for the message stick, none of the items she researched could be directly connected to the Wild Australia Show enterprise. While it was known that the troupe had performed at the Royal Exhibition

Building, Melbourne, Lindy's research uncovered many of their subsequent appearances in that city, as detailed in Chapter 9, the chapter she wrote for the book.

Chantal Knowles is a museum professional who has worked in the United Kingdom, Australia and Aotearoa New Zealand, and has developed permanent galleries at National Museums Scotland and the Queensland Museum. She is head of Human History at Tāmaki Paenga Hira Auckland War Memorial Museum. Her research focuses on the role of objects and collections in creating and sustaining historical narratives. Chantal is a PhD student at Monash University and the ARC Centre of Excellence for Australian Biodiversity and Heritage. She has recently been an ARC partner investigator for a University of Sydney–led research project that reviewed the official collection made by First Resident Lieutenant-Governor Sir William MacGregor in colonial British New Guinea. She is co-director of Te Aho Mutunga Kore, a textile and fibre centre at Auckland Museum launched in January 2023, which prioritises Māori and Pacific access to collections in order to decentre the museum and enable projects led by and for communities, knowledge holders and makers.

Chantal was a partner investigator on the ARC Linkage Project 'Wild Australia Show'. For the project, she focused on two key themes: Meston's collections in the Queensland Museum, and the creation and circulation of Wild Australia Show photographs. On the first, she collaborated with Sophie Price and Lindy Allen, producing the first detailed account of Meston's collections, which is published as Price, Allen and Knowles, 'The (Not-So) Sacred Ibis: Archibald Meston, the Colonial Collector, and the Queensland Museum', in *Memoirs of the Queensland Museum—Culture* (2021). On the second, she worked closely with Michael Aird to understand the creation of the original photographs of the Wild Australia Show taken during the tour, and their subsequent circulation and reproduction after the Show was over. Chantal's analysis of the Wild Australia Show photographic archive and its many surrogates is presented in Chapter 11.

Paul Memmott is a trans-disciplinary researcher (architect/anthropologist) and director of the Aboriginal Environments Research Collaborative and the Indigenous Design Place at the University of Queensland. Paul's field of research encompasses the cross-cultural study of the people–environment relations of Indigenous peoples with their natural and built environments, including Aboriginal housing and settlement design,

Aboriginal access to institutional architecture, Indigenous constructs of place and cultural landscapes, vernacular architecture, native title, social planning in Indigenous communities, homelessness and family violence. His book *Gunyah, Goondie + Wurley: Aboriginal Architecture of Australia* (2007) won three national awards in 2008, including the prestigious Bates Smart Award of the Institute of Architects and the Stanner Award of the Australian Institute of Aboriginal and Torres Strait Islander Studies. His books on Aboriginal housing include *Take 2: Housing Design in Indigenous Australia* (2003) and *Humpy House and Tin Shed: Aboriginal Settlement on the Darling River* (1991). In 2021, Paul received the Order of Australia for distinguished service to ethno-architecture and anthropology, to Indigenous housing and cultural heritage, and to tertiary education. His career has spanned over 50 years.

Paul initiated the ARC Linkage Project 'Wild Australia Show' and was a chief investigator. He has been assembling a manuscript on the Wild Australia Show for many years, and he drew on it for his contributions to this book. He wrote the four chapters that constitute 'Act I: Recruiting', in which he locates all of the performers within their ancestral Country. Providing relevant historical and cultural context, these chapters are designed to allow readers to appreciate what might have motivated the various performers to become involved. In pursuit of this aim, Paul developed a creative method to imagine what various individuals might have been thinking and feeling at the point of recruitment, drawing on a diverse range of sources, including settler memoirs and newspaper reports, anthropological literature, linguistic evidence, photographic analysis and historical studies. Jonathan Richards and Jessica Kane provided valuable research assistance. Paul also wrote Chapter 7 on the troupe's time in Brisbane before embarking south, and co-wrote Chapter 10 on the troupe's return to Brisbane and then home. He led the research project and team from 2016 to 2022.

Maria Nugent is a historian associated with the Australian Centre for Indigenous History in the School of History at The Australian National University. Her work straddles colonial history and post-colonial memory. She is the author of *Botany Bay: Where Histories Meet* (2005) and *Captain Cook Was Here* (2009); co-author of *Mapping Attachment: A Spatial Approach to Aboriginal Post-Contact Heritage* (2004) and *Indigenous Australia: Enduring Civilisation* (2015); and co-editor of *Indigenous Intermediaries: New Perspectives on Exploration Archives* (2015), *Brokers and Boundaries: Colonial Exploration in Indigenous Territory* (2016), *Mistress of Everything:*

Queen Victoria in Indigenous Worlds (2016) and *Ancestors, Artefacts, Empire: Indigenous Australia in British and Irish Museums* (2021). She has held various ARC fellowships and grants, including both a postdoctoral and a future fellowship. She was a visiting professor in Australian studies at the University of Tokyo in 2015–16, and is a former editor of *Aboriginal History* and chair of its board.

Maria was a chief investigator on the ARC Linkage Project 'Wild Australia Show'. She was invited to join as a historian of nineteenth-century Aboriginal people, performance and policy. Her main contributions concerned how to situate the Wild Australia Show within broader histories of Aboriginal performance and how to address methodological challenges of doing a performer-centred analysis in the absence of performer-authored texts, especially when relying on accounts about performers that were almost always produced by others. She discusses these and other issues in Chapter 1. Building on her knowledge of the post-invasion history of Aboriginal people in Sydney, she also researched and wrote about the troupe's time in Sydney in Chapters 8 and 10. These build on a chapter she published entitled '"Protection Talk" and Popular Performance: The Wild Australia Show on Tour, 1892–1893', in *Aboriginal Protection and its Intermediaries in Britain's Antipodean Colonies*, edited by Sam Furphy and Amanda Nettelbeck (2020). Maria also took responsibility for the editorial work on the multi-authored manuscript.

Jonathan Richards is a professional historian who mostly works in the Queensland State Archives (QSA) at Runcorn, undertaking research for academics, community groups, and government and Indigenous people throughout the state, especially northern Queensland. He is a specialist researcher in records about death, frontier violence and the experiences of Indigenous people under Queensland's criminal justice system. He is the author of *The Secret War: A True History of Queensland's Native Police* (2008), which is the first comprehensive scholarly investigation of this notorious force's complete operational history. Other notable publications include, with M. Finnane, '"You'll Get Nothing Out of It"? The Inquest, Police and Aboriginal Deaths in Colonial Queensland', *Australian Historical Studies* (2004); and '"Many Were Killed from Falling Over Cliffs": The Naming of Mount Wheeler, Central Queensland', in *Indigenous and Minority Placenames: Australian and International Perspectives*, edited by I. D. Clark, L. Hercus and L. Kostanski (2014).

Jonathan was employed as a research associate on the ARC Linkage Project 'Wild Australia Show'. Given his extensive knowledge of the QSA, he was able to identify a wide range of sources pertinent to the project. Jonathan has a particular interest in Archibald Meston and is currently working on a biography of him, some of which is presented in Chapter 2, which Jonathan wrote, complemented with biographical detail of Meston's business partner Purcell. Jonathan has traced Meston's ongoing involvement in Aboriginal performance and exhibition after the Wild Australia Show ended, and some of this can be found in Chapter 11. With his extensive knowledge of Queensland history, the history of the Native Police and Meston, he contributed research to most chapters in the book.

www.ingramcontent.com/pod-product-compliance
Lightning Source LLC
Chambersburg PA
CBHW070215190526
45161CB00002B/87